WADSWORTH COLLEGE
READING SERIES

**3rd
EDITION**

Wadsworth College
Reading Series

BOOK
1

Edith Alderson, Editor

WADSWORTH
CENGAGE Learning·

Australia · Brazil · Japan · Korea · Mexico · Singapore · Spain · United Kingdom · United States

WADSWORTH
CENGAGE Learning·

Wadsworth College Reading Series, Book 1, Third Edition
Edith Alderson, Editor

Publisher: Lyn Uhl

Director of Developmental Studies: Annie Todd

Development Editor: Laurie K. Dobson

Assistant Editor: Elizabeth Rice

Editorial Assistant: Matthew Conte

Media Editor: Amy Gibbons

Marketing Manager: Elinor Gregory

Marketing Assistant: Brittany Blais

Marketing Communications Manager: Linda Yip

Design and Production Services: PreMediaGlobal

Manufacturing Planner: Betsy Donaghey

Rights Acquisition Specialist: Timothy Sisler

Cover Designer: Walter Kopec

Cover Image: Thinkstock/Getty Images

Compositor: PreMediaGlobal

For product information and technology assistance, contact us at
Cengage Learning Customer & Sales Support, 1-800-354-9706

For permission to use material from this text or product, submit all requests online at **cengage.com/permissions**
Further permissions questions can be emailed to
permissionrequest@cengage.com

Library of Congress Control Number: 2011944740

Student Edition

ISBN-13: 978-1-111-83940-6

ISBN-10: 1-111-83940-9

Wadsworth
20 Channel Center Street
Boston, MA 02210
USA

Cengage Learning is a leading provider of customized learning solutions with office locations around the globe, including Singapore, the United Kingdom, Australia, Mexico, Brazil and Japan. Locate your local office at **international.cengage.com/region**

Cengage Learning products are represented in Canada by Nelson Education, Ltd.

For your course and learning solutions, visit **www.cengage.com**

Purchase any of our products at your local college store or at our preferred online store **www.cengagebrain.com**

Instructors: Please visit **login.cengage.com** and log in to access instructor-specific resources.

Printed in the United States of America
2 3 4 5 6 7 21 20 19 18 17 16

CONTENTS

PREFACE

The *Wadsworth College Reading Series,* Third Edition, is a three-level series that uses a progressive, unified approach to improving students' reading comprehension and critical thinking skills—and all at an affordable price! Praised in the second edition by users across the country, the third edition of this innovative series contains additional features and support materials that will enhance students' abilities to become effective readers.

Hallmark Features of the Text

The *Wadsworth College Reading Series,* Third Edition, includes the following features:

- **Integration of Skills and Strategies:** Along with presenting the major reading skills—identifying the main idea, supporting details, implied main idea, transitions, patterns of organization, and others—the book introduces students to a world of reading strategies that will enable them to practice good habits while reading. Strategies such as SQ3R, annotating, and note taking will help students improve their comprehension of what they read and will enable them to learn different strategies that will help them comprehend and analyze what they read.

- **Consistent Chapter Structure:** Each chapter covers skills and strategies in a consistent and clear manner.

- **Coverage of Visuals:** A different type of visual, such as diagrams, maps, and graphs, is covered at the end of each chapter. Students who do not need the instruction might skip this part of the chapter.

- **Critical Thinking:** In addition to a multitude of skills exercises designed to help students build comprehension, the text features questions at the end of the reading selections that build on important critical thinking skills. Many practice exercises, too, require the application of critical thinking.

- **Vocabulary Strategy Building:** Every chapter covers a particular vocabulary strategy and relates that strategy to reading selections from the chapters.

- **Focus on Academic Achievement:** Tips and selected readings about studying and succeeding in school are integrated throughout the text.

What's New in the Third Edition

Based on user and reviewer response, several new features have been added to the new edition of Book 1 to help students learn key concepts and strengthen their vocabulary and reading skills:

- **Reorganized Chapter Materials:** The reading strategy has been moved ahead of the reading selections. Students are encouraged to practice the chapter reading strategy on their choice of reading selections. Because there are multiple reading selections, students could possibly practice the strategy several times. The chapter review has been moved to the end of the chapter. Although most questions follow the cloze procedure format, questions in later chapters in the text require more thoroughly written answers.

- **More Longer Reading Selections:** Students and instructors now have a choice of three longer reading selections in Chapters 2 through 8. These choices allow students more practice reading longer pieces as well as a greater diversity of material to read.

- **Longer Reading Selections from Career Area Textbooks:** At least one longer reading selection in Chapters 2 through 8 has been selected from career area textbooks such as fire science, law enforcement, computer technology, and sports medicine. Many students taking developmental reading courses will pursue degrees in the career areas. These readings allow them to experience the actual textbook material from a career they may be considering. For students who are undecided in their career choice, these readings may inspire them to investigate a particular career.

- **Longer Biographical Reading Selections:** At least one longer reading selection in Chapters 2 through 8 is of biographical content. These biographies are selected to represent the great diversity that students will experience their lives. These biographies are of people they may very well read about in their career classes or in their general studies courses.

- **Updated Practice Materials:** New, updated practice materials have been largely selected from career area textbooks. Students have authentic college text materials on which to practice their reading skills. These high-interest materials have been carefully chosen to be at students' instructional reading level.

- **Streamlined Skill Explanations:** Skill explanations have been streamlined for greater ease of comprehension.

- **Chapter Tests Are Now in a Separate Document:** Chapter tests have been removed from the textbook. This allows for greater security and validity for administering chapter assessments. The Combined Skills Tests for comprehensive assessment at the end of the textbook have also been removed for security and validity of results. All chapter tests are now available in both an Instructor's Manual and online format.

■ **Web Links:** Web links have been added to allow students additional instruction and the interactive links will provide them with the opportunity for additional practice.

Chapter Organization

In addition, each chapter in each level of The *Wadsworth College Reading Series,* Third Edition, contains the following elements:

■ **Goals:** A list of goals at the beginning of each chapter tells students what they will learn when they have completed the chapter.

■ **Pretests:** These pretests, which appear in Chapters 2 through 8, assess the student's knowledge of the skill to be introduced. This assessment helps both instructors and students target specific areas for improvement.

■ **Explanation:** Each chapter is broken up into sections, with each section devoted to explanation and practice of a particular concept. Material is divided into manageable sections of information that are followed by practice of a specific skill.

■ **Exercises:** An ample number and variety of exercises is included in every chapter. Most of the exercises contain paragraphs from textbooks, magazines, newspapers, and journals so that students can read various types of selections and learn new information about a variety of different subjects. Exercises are arranged using a step-by-step progression to build concepts and skills gradually.

■ **Reading Strategy:** Every chapter includes an important reading strategy that students can use to help them comprehend and remember what they've read. Students are encouraged to practice the strategy on the longer reading selections at the end of each chapter.

■ **Chapter Review:** A closing exercise tests students' knowledge of the concepts presented in each chapter.

■ **Longer Reading Selections:** Longer reading selections follow the explanatory material in Chapters 1 through 8 and are included to give students practice in identifying different skills in context. Readings are chosen for their high interest, diverse topics, and cultural relevance for today's students. In addition, each reading is selected with the level of student in mind as well as students' ethnic, cultural, and educational experiences. New to this edition is the "Practicing the Active Reading Strategy," which asks students to apply active reading techniques to longer selections before and after they read.

■ **Questions for Discussion and Writing:** These questions ask students to think about their own experiences, as well as what they have read in the longer reading selections. The main points, topics, and theses of the longer readings are used as springboards to encourage student reflection on personal experiences and as stimuli for strengthening academic skills such as research, argument, and summary. These questions give students the opportunity to develop their writing skills by responding to a professional reading selection.

■ **Vocabulary:** Vocabulary is integrated in several different ways throughout each chapter. First, definitions of words or phrases that may be new to beginning students now appear as footnotes. In addition, words that may be unfamiliar are taken from the longer reading selection that appears later in Chapters 1 through 8 and used in a vocabulary exercise that follows the selection. Students are given the opportunity to glean the meanings of certain words from context and expand their overall vocabulary. Lastly, each chapter includes instruction in a specific vocabulary strategy, such as context clues, that will help students improve their reading comprehension. The instruction is followed by one or more exercises that draw examples from readings in the text to give students practice with that particular strategy.

■ **Chapter Review:** A closing exercise tests students' knowledge of the concepts presented at the end of each chapter.

Ancillaries

The *Wadsworth College Reading Series*, Third Edition, is supported by an innovative teaching and learning package.

■ **Aplia™**—Aplia is an online, auto-graded homework system that improves learning by increasing student effort and engagement—without requiring more work from the instructor.

■ **Annotated Instructor's Edition**—The annotated Instructor's Edition includes solutions to exercises in the student edition.

■ **Instructor's Manual and Test Bank**—Streamline and maximize the effectiveness of your course preparation. This time-saving resource, which includes a helpful chapter-by-chapter Q & A format, also includes a Test Bank.

■ **ExamView®**—Create, deliver, and customize tests and study guides (both print and online) in minutes with this easy-to-use assessment and tutorial system. ExamView offers both a Quick Test Wizard and an Online Test Wizard that guide you step by step through the process of creating tests, while its "what you see is what you get" interface allows you to see the test you are creating on the screen exactly as it will print or display online.

■ *The Wadsworth Guide to Reading Textbooks*—This guide has five full textbook chapters and an accompanying study guide section from a variety of disciplines. Following each textbook chapter are two sections of instruction and exercises for the students. The first section, "Textbook Features," explains methods for improving reading skills.

Acknowledgments

I would like to express my very deepest gratitude to my extraordinary assistants, Tanya Bahn and Michelle Lowry. Without the exceptional work of these two marvelous reading professionals, the task of revising this text would have been almost impossible.

I am greatly indebted to Laurie Dobson, my Development Editor, for her constant patience and unflagging good humor while leading me through the forest of textbook revision.

I am especially appreciative of Annie Todd, Director of Developmental Studies, for thinking that I had the knowledge and experience to bring something new and different to these books.

For their fine work on this project, I would like thank the terrific folks at Cengage Learning and PreMedia Global including: Elizabeth Rice, Assistant Editor; Matt Conte, Editorial Assistant; Beth Kluckhohn, Project Manager; Nicole Zuckerman, Program Manager; Shawn De Jong, Permissions Project Manager; and Sara Golden, Photo Researcher.

I am also indebted to the wonderful students in my reading classes over the past decades for showing me what perseverance really looks like.

I would like to thank the many incredible adjunct reading instructors that I have had the great pleasure of knowing and working with over the course of my career. You all amaze me with your dedication to our students.

A huge thank you goes to Kathleen Perryman, my colleague, co-teacher, and friend, who inspired and motivated me to be a better teacher.

My gratitude also goes to my family and friends for their constant faith and support, especially my fantastic husband and sons—Daryl, David, and Michael.

I would also like to thank the following reviewers for their time and effort:

Christine Barrilleaux, Tallahassee Community College
Barbara Cox, Redlands Community College
Eric Hibbison, J. Sargeant Reynolds Community College
Miriam Kinnard, Trident Technical College
Laura Meyers, Hawkeye Community College
Darlene Pabis, Westmoreland County Community College

Hattie Pinckney, Florence-Darlington Technical College
Nancy Rice, New England Institute of Technology
Jerolynn Roberson, Miami Dade College
Deborah Spradlin, Tyler Junior College

Edy Alderson

WADSWORTH COLLEGE READING SERIES

Dmitry Shironosov/Shutterstock.com

Improving Reading and Thinking

Goals for Chapter 1

- ■ Explain why effective reading is critical to academic, professional, and personal success.

- ■ Explain how reading improves thinking skills.

- ■ Describe four techniques for improving reading skills.

- ■ List the different goals of reading for information.

- ■ Explain the four types of mental skills required for reading.

- ■ Describe the organization and features of this book.

- ■ Explain and apply the steps of active reading.

Do you enjoy reading? If your answer is no, why not? Like many people, you may have several reasons for disliking the printed word. You might think reading is too passive, requiring you to sit still for too much time. You may not like it because it takes too long. You may say that most of the things you read just don't interest you or seem relevant to your life. You may object to reading because it seems too hard—you don't like having to struggle to understand information. These are the most common reasons people give to explain their dislike of reading.

What people don't realize is that most of these reasons arise from a lack of experience and effort. When you first decided you didn't like to read, you probably began to avoid reading as much as possible. This avoidance led to a lack of practice, which set up a vicious cycle: lack of practice led to undeveloped skills. This lack of skills meant more difficult and unrewarding experiences when you did read. As a result, you probably read less and less, and you gave yourself few opportunities to practice your reading skills. Thus, the cycle began again.

You can break this cycle, though, and make your reading experiences more enjoyable. The first step is to realize how much you already know about the reading process.

Reading and Academic Success

Solid reading skills will be critical to your success in college. Most college courses require a great deal of reading. Your professors will ask you to read textbooks, articles, books, stories, and handouts. You'll be responsible for re-membering much of this information and revealing your knowledge of it on tests. You'll have to read the instructor's notes, and you'll have to read your own notes on lecture material to prepare for your tests. In addition, you'll be asked to conduct research, which requires reading all types of sources, including websites on the Internet. Various assignments will ask you to read not only your own writing but also that of your classmates.

Not only will you have to simply read and remember information, you also will be asked to evaluate it, judge it, agree or disagree with it, interpret it, compare it with something else, summarize it, and synthesize it with other things you've read. You can accomplish all of these tasks only if you can first attain a solid grasp of the ideas and information in the source.

Exercise **1.1**

In the following list, place a check mark beside every reading-related activity you've already done at least once. Then, respond to the questions that follow by writing your answers on the blanks provided.

_____ Read a textbook

_____ Read a magazine or journal article assigned by a teacher

1

_____ Read information on a website for a class assignment

_____ Read a novel or another book assigned by a teacher

_____ Researched a topic in the library by reading several sources about it

_____ Read a memo at work

_____ Read a letter from a friend

_____ Read an e-mail message from a friend, teacher, or colleague

_____ Read a blog about an interesting topic

_____ Read subtitles[1] while watching a foreign film

_____ Read a newspaper

_____ Read a story to a child

_____ Read aloud in class

_____ Read a prepared speech to an audience

1. If you could choose anything to read, what would it be? Why?

   _____

   _____

   _____

2. What types of reading situations do you find the most difficult?

   _____

   _____

   _____

3. What do you think you need to do to become a better reader?

   _____

   _____

   _____

4. What would you like to learn in this textbook that you think would help you become a better reader?

   _____

   _____

   _____

1. **subtitles:** translations of the dialogue

Reading and Professional Success

When you enter the workforce, you may be surprised by how much reading you'll need to do. Many jobs will require you to read e-mail messages, letters, memorandums, policy and procedure manuals, instructions, reports, logs and records, summaries of meetings, newsletters, and many other types of documents.

Often, a lot is at stake concerning your comprehension of these materials. Your personal safety may depend on your understanding of the information in manuals or other instructions. Your efficient and effective job performance may rest on your ability to comprehend written information sent to you by your supervisors and co-workers. Even your promotions and raises may depend, in part, on your ability to read and understand materials such as reports about trends, new research, or other innovations in your field.

Exercise **1.2**

Read the following memo and then write your answers to the questions on the blanks provided.

> **To:**   All Employees of Ace Storage Facilities
>
> **From:** Dan Denton, President
>
> **Date:** January 2, 20xx
>
> **Re:**   New Bonus for Your Money-Saving Idea

To all employees:

On behalf of the executive team at Ace Storage Facilities, I'd like to thank each and every one of you for your hard work and commitment to this corporation. As you know, we value your input about making our company more efficient and effective. Therefore, we have created a new policy to encourage you to share more of your ideas with your management team.

Effective immediately, you may be able to earn a $500 bonus for an idea that saves our company money. To be eligible for this bonus, you must complete a new form that is now available in all break rooms. The information required on this form must be typed, and all sections of the form must be filled out. In the section about your suggestion, you must describe your idea and your estimate of its cost savings in two hundred words or fewer. Completed forms should be placed in the box beside the time clock. You may submit as many ideas as you like, but each of them should be described on a separate form.

All ideas will be reviewed by the senior management team. If your idea is selected for implementation,[1] you will receive a $500 bonus in your next month's paycheck. So please share with us your thoughts about making our company more cost-effective, and contact Betty in the human resources office if you have any questions about this new policy.

1. Are all ideas submitted by employees rewarded with a $500 bonus?

2. Does President Dan Denton want you to call his office if you have questions about his new policy? _____

3. Can you write the information by hand on the form you fill out?

4. How long can the description of your idea be? _____

5. What should you do if you have more than one money-saving idea?

6. Where can you get one of the forms you need to fill out? _____

Reading and Personal Success

You will need to read well during many occasions in your personal life. For example, you may want to learn more about a hobby or subject area that interests you. If so, you'll need to read books, articles, and web pages to increase your knowledge. You may want to find out how to improve your personal finances by learning how to save or invest your money. You may need to assemble something you purchased—such as a child's toy or a barbecue grill—by following the directions. You or one of your loved ones may become sick with a particular disease or disorder, causing you to want more information about treatment options. You may even want to read for entertainment, picking up a pop culture magazine or a mystery novel just for the fun of it.

1. **implementation:** use

1

You'll also have to read personal correspondence such as letters and e-mail messages, legal documents such as contracts, and reports from your children's teachers, among other things. You'll read all of these documents more capably and confidently when you improve your reading skills.

Exercise **1.3**

Read the following selection. Then, write your answers to the questions on the blanks provided.

We've Got the Dirt on Guy Brains

I like to think that I am a modest person. (I also like to think that I look like Brad Pitt naked, but that is not the issue here.)

There comes a time, however, when a person must toot his own personal horn, and for me, that time is now. A new book has confirmed a theory that I first proposed in 1987, in a column explaining why men are physically unqualified to do housework. The problem, I argued, is that men—because of a tragic genetic flaw—cannot see dirt until there is enough of it to support agriculture. This puts men at a huge disadvantage against women, who can detect a single dirt molecule 20 feet away.

This is why a man and a woman can both be looking at the same bathroom commode,[1] and the man—hindered by Male Genetic Dirt Blindness (MGDB)—will perceive the commode surface as being clean enough for heart surgery or even meat slicing; whereas the woman can't even *see* the commode, only a teeming, commode-shaped swarm of bacteria. A woman can spend two hours cleaning a toothbrush holder and still not be totally satisfied; whereas if you ask a man to clean the entire New York City subway system, he'll go down there with a bottle of Windex and a single paper towel, then emerge 25 minutes later, weary but satisfied with a job well done.

When I wrote about Male Genetic Dirt Blindness, many irate[2] readers complained that I was engaging in sexist[3] stereotyping, as well as making lame excuses for the fact that men are lazy pigs. All of these irate readers belonged to a gender that I will not identify here, other than to say: Guess what, ladies? There is now scientific proof that I was right.

This proof appears in a new book titled *What Could He Be Thinking? How a Man's Mind Really Works*. I have not personally read this book, because, as a journalist, I am too busy writing about it. But according to an article by Reuters[4],

---

1. **commode:** toilet

2. **irate:** angry

3. **sexist:** unfairly generalizing about the other gender

4. **Reuters:** an international news agency

the book states that a man's brain "takes in less sensory[1] detail than a woman's, so he doesn't see or even feel the dust and household mess in the same way." Get that? We can't see or feel the mess! We're like: "What snow tires in the dining room? Oh, those snow tires in the dining room."

And this is only one of the differences between men's and women's brains. Another difference involves a brain part called the "cingulate gyrus," which is the sector where emotions are located. The Reuters' article does not describe the cingulate gyrus, but presumably in women it is a structure the size of a mature cantaloupe, containing a vast quantity of complex, endlessly recalibrated emotional data involving hundreds, perhaps thousands of human relationships; whereas in men it is basically a cashew filled with NFL highlights.

In any event, it turns out that women's brains secrete more of the chemicals "oxytocin" and "serotonin," which, according to biologists, cause humans to feel they have an inadequate supply of shoes. No, seriously, these chemicals cause humans to want to bond with other humans, which is why women like to share their feelings. We men, on the other hand, are reluctant to share our feelings, in large part because we often don't have any. Really. Ask any guy: A lot of the time, when we look like we're thinking, we just have this low-level humming sound in our brains. That's why, in male-female conversations, the male part often consists entirely of him going "hmmmm." This frustrates the woman, who wants to know what he's really thinking. In fact, what he's thinking is, literally, "hmmmm."

So anyway, according to the Reuters' article, when a man, instead of sharing feelings with his mate, chooses to lie on the sofa, holding the remote control and monitoring 750 television programs simultaneously by changing the channel every one-half second (pausing slightly longer for programs that feature touchdowns, fighting, shooting, car crashes or bosoms), his mate should *not* come to the mistaken conclusion that he is an insensitive jerk. In fact, he is responding to scientific biological brain chemicals as detailed in the scientific book *What Could He Be Thinking? How a Man's Mind Really Works*, which I frankly cannot recommend highly enough.

In conclusion, no *way* was that pass interference.*

1. According to Dave Barry, what "flaw" makes men unable to see dirt on the bathroom commode? _____

2. How long would it take a man to clean the entire New York subway system, according to Barry? _____

3. Barry offers scientific proof that he is right about men and dirt. Why, according to the book that Barry mentions, do men not see dirt like women do? _____

---

1. **sensory:** of the senses

---

* "We've Got the Dirt on Guy Brains," 11/23/2003 *Miami Herald*. Copyright 2003 by Dave Barry. Reprinted by permission of Dave Barry.

4. What chemicals do women's brains secrete more of than men's do, causing them to "share their feelings"? _____

5. Is this essay meant to entertain readers or inform them about "Male Genetic Dirt Blindness"? How do you know? _____

_____

_____

Reading and Better Thinking

Better reading skills help you improve your chances for academic, professional, and personal success. They will also help you improve your overall thinking skills. This is because reading requires you to follow and understand the thought processes of the writer. When you can do that effectively, you get opportunities to sharpen a variety of your own mental skills:

1. You evaluate information and decide what's important.

2. You learn to see relationships among things, events, and ideas.

3. You make new connections among things, events, and ideas.

4. You practice following the logic (or seeing the lack of logic) of someone else's thoughts.

5. You add more information to your memory.

These are the very skills that will strengthen your ability to make decisions, think creatively, and think logically in every area of your life.

Exercise **1.4**

Read the following letter to the editor from a newspaper and write your answers to the questions on the blanks provided.

I think the best way to prevent most traffic accidents is to ban the use of cell phones while driving. In the past 10 years, since cell phones were introduced to the American public and became part of everyone's life, traffic accidents and deaths in cars have increased significantly. In many of these accidents, it is a fact that someone talking on a cell phone has caused the accident.

It is a proven scientific fact that people cannot do two things at once, so why do people think that they can drive and talk on the phone at the same time?

However, I don't think that cell phones are the only cause of accidents or the only thing that should be banned. I think that in addition to banning the use of cell phones in cars, people should not be allowed to eat, chew gum, change the radio station they are listening to, sing along to the song on the radio, put on makeup while they drive, talk to anyone else in the car, or look out any window besides the windshield in front of them while driving. In my opinion, banning these activities will significantly cut down on the number of traffic accidents, injuries, and deaths that occur every day.

In the last three years, my car has been hit 14 times, all by people either using cell phones, talking to someone else in their car, eating, or singing along to the radio. I have also witnessed a number of accidents and near-accidents involving drivers engaged in the activities mentioned above.

People should keep their eyes on the road at all times. Concentration is the key to being a good, safe driver, so by banning many activities that most of us associate with driving—talking on the phone, eating while driving, and singing—we will have safer roads in America.

1. What new piece of information did you learn by reading this excerpt?

   _____

   _____

2. Which sentence gave you your first clue that the author is not logical?

   _____

   _____

3. Can you think of another solution to decreasing the number of traffic accidents besides the ones the author suggests? _____

   _____

How to Improve Reading Skills

Now that you understand *why* it's so important to read well, you're probably wondering *how* you can become a better reader. The obvious answer is practice. The more you read, the more opportunities you'll have for improving your abilities. But simply reading everything in sight will not necessarily improve your skills. In general, you should commit yourself to doing four other things as well.

1. Understand the different purposes for reading

2. Be aware of the mental skills required for reading

3. Develop individual reading skills

4. Learn and use different reading strategies

Understand the Different Purposes for Reading

When you set out to read something, you should know *why* you're reading it. The two basic purposes for reading are to gain information and to be entertained. Obviously, when you read for entertainment, your primary goal is your own pleasure. When you read for information, though, you may have one or more different goals:

1. **Gain a general understanding of the ideas or points.** For example, as you're reading this section of this textbook, you're trying to comprehend the ideas being presented.

2. **Discover the facts or answer questions about the material.** When you read the paragraphs in the exercises of this book, for example, you read them to find answers to the questions you must answer.

3. **Memorize the information.** You often read a textbook chapter so that you'll recall its information when you take a test.

4. **Find information or ideas that prove a point you want to make.** When you conduct research for a paper you need to write, you read to find statements or information that back up your opinions.

5. **Make a decision based on the information.** You read brochures from businesses, for example, to decide whether to buy their particular products or services.

When you read something, you may need to accomplish just one of these goals or perhaps all five at the same time. In any case, getting the most out of everything you read means clearly identifying your purpose before you begin.

© 2012 Cengage Learning. All rights reserved. May not be scanned, copied or duplicated, or posted to a publicly accessible website, in whole or in part.

Exercise **1.5**

Read the following reading situations. Then, place a check mark on the blank next to every MAJOR purpose for reading that applies to that situation. (More than one choice may apply.)

1. You read a newspaper article to find out about a fire that burned down a house in your neighborhood.

_____ Gain a general understanding of the ideas or points

_____ Discover the facts or answer questions

_____ Memorize the information

_____ Find information or ideas that prove a point you want to make

_____ Make a decision based on the information

1

2. You read the notes you wrote down during your professor's lecture as you prepare for your history exam.

_____ Gain a general understanding of the ideas or points

_____ Discover the facts or answer questions

_____ Memorize the information

_____ Find information or ideas that prove a point you want to make

_____ Make a decision based on the information

3. You read the technical instructions that came with the bicycle you purchased and need to assemble.

_____ Gain a general understanding of the ideas or points

_____ Discover the facts or answer questions

_____ Memorize the information

_____ Find information or ideas that prove a point you want to make

_____ Make a decision based on the information

4. You read a flyer sent to you by a candidate running for office in your town or city. This flyer states the opinions of the candidate.

_____ Gain a general understanding of the ideas or points

_____ Discover the facts or answer questions

_____ Memorize the information

_____ Find information or ideas that prove a point you want to make

_____ Make a decision based on the information

5. You read a report to find out about the number of traffic accidents that occurred last year at an intersection in your neighborhood. You plan to argue that your city government needs to install a traffic light at that intersection.

_____ Gain a general understanding of the ideas or points

_____ Discover the facts or answer questions

_____ Memorize the information

_____ Find information or ideas that prove a point you want to make

_____ Make a decision based on the information

Be Aware of the Mental Skills Required for Reading

"Reading" is actually a collection of different mental skills. They include attitude, concentration, memory, and logical thought. These skills are all interrelated and connected. Some of them depend upon others. When you become aware that these different skills are at work, you can learn to improve them.

Attitude. A positive attitude is the first essential mental component for successful reading. Your attitude includes your feelings about reading, about *what* you read, and about your own abilities. If these feelings are negative, your reading experiences will be negative. If these feelings are positive, your experiences will be more enjoyable.

A positive attitude not only makes reading more pleasurable, it also creates the right mental environment for gaining new information. As a matter of fact, all of the other mental skills required for reading are useless unless you approach each reading task in the right frame of mind. If you are quick to pronounce a particular text "boring" or "worthless," you are likely to create a mental block that will prevent you from absorbing the information. Instead, approach each new reading task with intellectual curiosity. Expect to find something of value, something you'll be able to use in your life.

Also, don't let a poor attitude about your own reading abilities get in your way. If you expect to fail, if you tell yourself you just don't get it, then you virtually guarantee your failure. If you believe you can improve, however, then you'll create the necessary mental foundation for improving your skills and becoming a good reader.

Exercise **1.6**

Read the following selection and respond to the questions by writing your answers on the blanks provided.

Toward Right Livelihood

Visit Sena Plaza in downtown Santa Fe, and you will see a public garden that is a wonderland of color and texture. The person responsible for this beautiful garden is Barbara Fix, a graduate of Stanford Law School who chose gardening over a high-powered law career. She says, "I've been offered many jobs in my life. I could have been on Wall Street making six figures, but the only job I ever hustled for was this one—six dollars an hour as the gardener at Sena Plaza."

Barbara Fix is an example of someone who appears to have achieved "right livelihood." The original concept of right livelihood apparently came from

1

the teachings of Buddha.[1] In recent years, the concept has been described by Michael Phillips in his book *The Seven Laws of Money* and by Marsha Sinetar in her book *Do What You Love . . . The Money Will Follow*. Right livelihood is work consciously chosen, done with full awareness and care, and leading to enlightenment.[2] When Jason Wilson gave up a challenging business career to become a carpenter, he embraced the concept of right livelihood. He later started his own home construction business. Ronald Sheade, once a vice president at a *Fortune* 1,000 company,[3] now teaches eighth-grade science in a suburb of Chicago. He doesn't make big money anymore, but he loves teaching and now gets to spend more time with his family.*

1. When you read the title of the selection, "Toward Right Livelihood," what did you think the selection would be about? Why? _____

_____

2. Did you assume the passage would be boring or too difficult? If so, why?

_____

_____

3. As you read this passage, did you discover a fact or idea that interested you? Did you discover some information in this passage you could actually use in your life? If so, what was it? _____

_____

4. If you followed the concept of right livelihood, what kind of work would you do? _____

_____

Concentration. Once your positive attitude has prepared your mind to absorb new information, you're ready to employ the second mental skill necessary for reading: *concentration*. **Concentration** *is the ability to focus all of your*

---

1. **Buddha:** Siddhartha Gautama, Indian spiritual leader

2. **enlightenment:** full and complete understanding

3. ***Fortune* 1,000 company:** a company that has achieved success and earned recognition as one of the most successful companies in the United States

---

* Adapted from Barry L. Reece and Rhonda Brandt, *Effective Human Relations in Organizations*, 7th ed. (Boston: Houghton Mifflin Co., 1999), 458–59. Copyright © 1999 by Houghton Mifflin Company. Reprinted with permission.

attention on one thing while ignoring all distractions. You cannot understand or remember information unless you read with concentration.

Many people, however, find concentration difficult to achieve, especially when they read more challenging material. Too often, they allow distractions to pull their thoughts away from the sentences and paragraphs before them. But you can learn to concentrate better. How? By practicing effective techniques for combating the two types of distractions: external and internal.

External distractions *are the sights, sounds, and other sensations that tempt you away from your reading.* These distractions include ringing phones, people talking or walking nearby, the sound of a stereo, or a friend who stops by to chat. Though they are powerful, they are also the easier of the two types of distractions to eliminate.

To avoid having to deal with external distractions, you merely prevent them from happening by choosing or creating the right reading environment. Try to select a location for reading—such as an individual study area in your library or a quiet room in your house—where distractions will be minimal. Before a reading session, notify your friends and family that you'll be unavailable for conversation and socializing. If you must read in places with more activity, try wearing earplugs or sitting with your back to the action so you're not tempted to watch the comings and goings of others.

Internal distractions are often more challenging to overcome. *They are the thoughts, worries, plans, daydreams, and other types of mental "noise" inside your own head.* They will prevent you from concentrating on what you're reading and from absorbing the information you need to learn.

You can try to ignore these thoughts, but they will usually continue trying to intrude. So how do you temporarily silence them so you can devote your full attention to your reading? Try the following suggestions:

1. **Begin every reading task with a positive attitude.** A negative attitude produces a lot of grumbling mental noise like complaints and objections to the task at hand. When you choose to keep a positive attitude, you'll eliminate an entire category of noisy thoughts that interfere with your concentration.

2. **Instead of fighting internal distractions, try focusing completely on them for a short period of time.** For 5 or 10 minutes, allow yourself to sit and think about your job, your finances, your car problems, your boyfriend or girlfriend, the paper you need to write, or whatever is on your mind. Better yet, write these thoughts down. Do a free-writing exercise (a quick writing of your own thoughts on paper without censoring them or worrying about grammar and spelling) to empty your mind of these thoughts. If you can't stop thinking about all of the other things you need to do, devote 10 minutes to writing a detailed "to do" list. Giving all of your attention to distracting thoughts will often clear them from your mind so you can focus on your reading.

3. **Keep your purpose in mind as you read.** As discussed earlier, having a clear goal when you read will help you concentrate on getting what you need to know from a text.

4. **Use visualization to increase your interest and improve your retention of the information.** As you read, let the words create pictures and images in your mind. Try to "see" in your mind's eye the scenes, examples, people, and other information presented in the text.

Exercise **1.7**

Free-write for 10 minutes about what's going on inside your mind at this moment. Write your thoughts on a separate sheet of paper for this activity,

Exercise **1.8**

Read the following passage and practice the visualization techniques you read about earlier. Write your answers to each question on the blanks provided.

Do you remember a student in primary or secondary school who always insulted, teased, or threatened other students or started fights? These students are described as *bullies*. Bullying is a specific type of aggression in which (1) the behavior is intended to harm or disturb others, (2) the behavior occurs repeatedly over time, and (3) there is an imbalance of power, with a more powerful person or group attacking a less powerful one. The bully may be physically or psychologically more powerful, and the aggression may be verbal, physical, or psychological. If two adolescents of equal strength quarrel or fight, however, it is not considered bullying.*

1. Identify one specific type of aggression listed in the paragraph that describes bullying. _____

    _____

2. Visualize a specific bully from your past. Describe this person's physical appearance and personality traits. _____

    _____

3. Visualize a specific type of bullying from your past and describe it, identifying it as verbal, physical, or psychological in nature. _____

    _____

---

* Adapted from Paul S. Kaplan, *Adolescence* (Boston: Houghton Mifflin Co., 2004), 197.

Memory. **Memory,** *the ability to store and recall information, is also essential to the reading process.* When reading you use your memory constantly. You must remember the meanings of words. You must remember what you know about people, places, and things when you encounter references to them. You must remember all of the ideas and information presented before that point in the text. You must remember the text's overall main point while you read the subpoints or details. You must remember your own experiences that either support or contradict the text's message. You may also need to remember other texts you've read that either agree or disagree with the new information you're reading.

You can use many techniques to improve your memory. A few of the most common are:

1. **Improve your concentration.** The more intensely you focus on something, the better the chance you'll remember it.

2. **Repeat and review.** Most of the time, the more you expose yourself to new information, the more easily you'll recall it.

3. **Recite.** Saying information aloud helps strengthen your memory of it.

4. **Associate new information with what you already know.** Making connections between your present knowledge and what you need to learn helps you to store new information in your mind more effectively.

Exercise **1.9**

Read the following passage through once. Then cover it so you can't see it and test your memory of the information by writing, on the blanks provided, your answers to the questions.

On the evening of March 5, 1770, an angry crowd of poor and working-class Bostonians gathered in front of the guard post outside the Boston customs house. The crowd was protesting a British soldier's abusive treatment a few hours earlier of a Boston apprentice[1] who was trying to collect a debt from a British officer. Suddenly, shots rang out. When the smoke cleared, four Bostonians lay dead, and seven more were wounded, one mortally. Among those in the crowd was an impoverished[2] 28-year-old shoemaker named George Robert Twelve Hewes. Hewes had already witnessed, and once experienced, abuses by British troops, but the appalling[3] violence of the "Boston Massacre,"

1. **apprentice:** one who is learning a trade
2. **impoverished:** poor
3. **appalling:** frightful

as the shooting became known, led Hewes to political activism.[1] Four of the five who died were personal friends, and he himself received a serious blow to the shoulder from a soldier's rifle butt. Over the next several days, Hewes attended meetings and signed petitions denouncing[2] British conduct in the shooting, and he later testified against the soldiers. Thereafter, he participated prominently[3] in such anti-British actions as the Boston Tea Party.*

1. In what year did the Boston Massacre take place? _____

2. What was the crowd protesting? _____

   _____

3. What was George Hewes's profession? _____

4. What kind of injury did Hewes sustain in the massacre? _____

5. What other anti-British action did Hewes take part in? _____

Logical thought. Another mental skill required for effective reading is logical thinking. Logical thought is composed of many different mental tasks, including those in the following list:

Sequencing and ordering: seeing the order of things and understanding cause/effect relationships

Matching: noticing similarities

Organizing: grouping things into categories

Analysis: understanding how to examine the different parts of something

Reasoning from the general to the particular and from the particular to the general: drawing conclusions and making generalizations

Abstract thought: understanding ideas and concepts

Synthesis: putting things together in new combinations

If you want to improve your ability to think logically, try one or more of the following suggestions:

1. **Practice active reading.** Using outlining, in particular, forces you to work harder to detect relationships in information.

1. **activism:** action as a means of achieving a goal
2. **denouncing:** openly condemning or criticizing
3. **prominently:** noticeably or openly

* Adapted from Paul Boyer et al., *The Enduring Vision* (Boston: Houghton Mifflin Co., 2004), 123.

2. **Play with games and puzzles.** Card games, computer games, and board games such as chess, checkers, and backgammon will give you opportunities to sharpen your analytical skills.

3. **Solve problems.** Work math problems. Read mysteries (or watch them on television) and try to figure out who committed the crime before the detective does. Try to think of ways to solve everyday problems, both big and small. For example, come up with a solution for America's overflowing landfills or figure out how to alter backpacks so they don't strain your back.

4. **Practice your argument and debating skills.** Discuss controversial issues with people who hold the opposing viewpoint.

5. **Write more.** Writing requires a great deal of logical thought, so write letters to your newspaper editor or congressional representatives about issues that are important to you.

Exercise **1.10**

Read this passage from a newspaper. Then, on the blanks provided, write your answers to the questions that follow.

Hard to Be a Boy in a Girls' World

A *BusinessWeek* cover piece titled "The New Gender Gap" details the lamentable[1] state of boydom. One of the reasons, some experts say, is female schoolteachers who don't have the foggiest[2] notion of what it is like to be a boy.

The experts do not blame female teachers entirely for what has happened to boys. Some of them simply assert that girls are different, wired by nature to have nimbler fingers that produce beautiful handwriting and are endowed[3] with the innate[4] ability to remain in their seats. A boy, on the other hand, requires frequent recesses lest he go stark raving mad.

Whatever the reason, it's clear that something very bad is happening to boys. They are 30 percent more likely to drop out of school, something like four to six times as likely to kill themselves and 85 percent more likely to commit murder than girls. When they get older, they don't go to college or graduate school in the numbers women do and don't bother to vote, either.

1. **lamentable:** sad

2. **foggiest:** vaguest

3. **endowed:** supplied

4. **innate:** inborn

1

If they weren't (real) men, they would demand some sort of preferential[1] treatment. You go, guy.

What's happening? Probably several things. Not only do boys continue to be taught by women who think they are just unruly[2] girls, but girls are now purposely favored. It was girls, remember, who supposedly were overlooked in school and whose self-esteem suffered accordingly. This has become conventional wisdom, even though it hardly conformed to my own school experience and seemed, moreover, to be counterintuitive.[3] Why would female teachers ignore girls? Boys nowadays also have all the wrong role models: rap singers and inarticulate[4] athletes, for instance. Much of the entertainment industry panders[5] to the worst in boys.

My gut also tells me that the incredible overemphasis on sports is bad for boys. In the minds of too many of them, it has gone from being a recreational activity to a supposed career path. Why study to make a modest income when you can play to make really big bucks?

Alas for the home team, none of the possible answers fully satisfies. It seems, instead, that girls are doing better than boys because girls are really better than boys. In a society that no longer needs brawn[6] or values aggression—that is, in some respects, more feminine—girls are better endowed by nature to succeed. A socialist[7] (if there are any left) might even suggest that the entire women's liberation movement[8] was capitalism's[9] response to the need for more and better workers—people with better motor skills, the astounding ability to empathize and express feelings and the patience to sit still.

Because this is about boys and men—and supposedly this is a man's world—the tendency is to dismiss this problem. But never mind the cost to society of countless male dropouts. Think instead of individual boys and men—angry, confused, depressed. The statistics on suicide alone tell a sad story. Boys will be boys, all right, but some of them don't make it to be men.

---

1. **preferential:** partial to; in this context, better treatment

2. **unruly:** undisciplined, out of control

3. **counterintuitive:** against intuition or instinct

4. **inarticulate:** not well spoken

5. **panders:** caters

6. **brawn:** strong muscles

7. **socialist:** someone who believes that power and wealth should be distributed equally within a specific community

8. **women's liberation movement:** a 1960s effort by U.S. women to end discrimination and gain equal rights and pay

9. **capitalism:** economic system in which private individuals and companies control production of goods

So boys, depressed and beaten down, fall further and further behind—zonked on Ritalin,[1] diagnosed as learning-disabled and prepared by evolution for roles that are no longer valued.

Much has changed since Henry Higgins[2] bellowed, "Why can't a woman be more like a man?" The answer, Mr. Higgins, is now plain: It simply doesn't pay.*

1. The author gives several possible reasons for boys' struggles. What is one reason? _____

   _____

   _____

   _____

   _____

2. Think of another possible reason, not mentioned by the author.

   _____

3. Predict two possible effects of having a society that contains too many "depressed and beaten down" men.

   Effect #1: _____

   Effect #2: _____

4. Do your own experiences support or refute the author's opinion about boys? Explain your answer. _____

5. Argue *against* the author's main point about boys. Give facts and/or examples in support of your opinion. _____

Develop Individual Reading Skills

Another way to improve your reading comprehension is to develop the isolated skills you must use to read well. For example, you can learn techniques for recognizing the main idea of a paragraph or for detecting patterns used to organize information. The rest of this book is designed to help you develop and practice these skills.

1. **Ritalin:** drug prescribed for hyperactive children

2. **Henry Higgins:** a character in the play *My Fair Lady*

---

* "Endangered Boyhood" by Richard Cohen. From The Washington Post, Copyright © 2003 The Washington Post. All rights reserved. Used by permission and protected by the Copyright Laws of the United States. The printing, copying, redistribution, or retransmission of the Material without express written permission is prohibited.

Exercise **1.11**

Check off in the following list the skills you believe you need to improve. Next to each item that you check, write on the blank provided the number of the chapter in this book that focuses on helping you strengthen that skill.

_____ Recognizing the overall point (the main idea) of a reading selection

_____

_____ Understanding how details support the main idea of a reading selection

_____

_____ Figuring out how a reading selection is organized _____

_____ Understanding visuals—maps, charts, graphs—in reading selections

_____

_____ Figuring out implied main ideas, points that are not stated directly in a reading selection _____

_____ Recognizing transitions, words that link sentences and paragraphs together _____

_____ "Reading between the lines" (making inferences) by drawing conclusions from the information in a reading selection _____

Learn and Use Different Reading Strategies

Reading strategies are techniques you use when you read. Some of them—such as active reading—are designed to improve your comprehension and retention of information. Others—such as skimming and scanning—provide you with tools you can use to find what you need in certain circumstances.

This book explains a different reading strategy in each chapter. Make sure you understand each of them so that you can begin using them to read better right away.

How This Book Will Help You Improve

Goals of This Book

The *Wadsworth College Reading Series* is one of three books in a series designed to help you improve your reading skills. This text—the first in the sequence—focuses on the basic skills necessary to effective reading. Each chapter concentrates on one essential skill you can immediately use to strengthen your reading comprehension.

This book, along with the other two in the series, is based on the belief that you can indeed become a better reader. Even if you have struggled in the past, you can learn and practice the skills you need to get more out of anything you read.

Organization and Features

Each of the eight chapters in this textbook includes several helpful features.

Test Yourself. At the beginning of each chapter, except Chapter 1, a section called "Pretest" will help you identify what you already know about the skill covered in that chapter. It will also help you pinpoint specific areas you need to target for improvement.

Exercises. Throughout each chapter, you'll have numerous opportunities to check your understanding with practice activities. As you complete each exercise and receive feedback on your answers, you will progress toward better reading comprehension.

Reading strategy. Each chapter includes an explanation of a different reading strategy. Strategies are techniques you can use to get more out of what you read. Using these techniques, you can begin to improve your reading comprehension right away.

Interesting readings. The readings within practices, along with the longer reading selection in each chapter, are drawn from a variety of interesting sources. These readings have been carefully chosen as enjoyable and/or useful. They have also been selected to clearly demonstrate a particular skill or concept. Furthermore, they'll give you practice reading different kinds of sources, including textbooks, magazine articles, newspaper articles, and essays.

The longer reading selections in each chapter are followed by questions designed to check your reading skills and increase your vocabulary. Also included are discussion questions that will encourage you to sharpen your thinking skills and find ways to apply the information to your own life.

Vocabulary strategy. Each chapter presents a different vocabulary strategy. In this section, you will learn techniques for discovering the meanings of unfamiliar words. You will also learn about different types of specialized vocabulary in order to improve your overall reading comprehension. A practice activity draws from the readings in the chapter to give you an opportunity to check your understanding.

Chapter review. Filling in the blanks in a brief summary of the major points and concepts in the chapter will help you reinforce them in your mind.

Exercise **1.12**

Preview this textbook. Write your answers, on the blanks provided, to the following questions about its features and organization.

1. How many chapters does this book contain? _____

2. In which chapter is the topic of main ideas covered? _____

3. In which chapter will you learn the different patterns of organization that writers use? _____

4. In which chapter will you find the most "visual" material—that is, charts, graphs, maps, and photos—and find out how to read them? _____

5. In which chapter will you learn how to determine what is the implied main idea in a paragraph? _____

6. In which chapter will you review how to use dictionaries? _____

7. Look at Chapter 7 and define the term *inference.* _____

_____

8. How many biographical reading selections are there? Which one would you most like to read? _____

_____

9. Look at the table of contents and count the number of reading selections contained in this text. _____

10. How many different reading strategies are presented in this text? _____

Reading Strategy: Active Reading

Many people don't get everything they can out of reading simply because they are *passive* readers. **Passive readers** *are people who try to read by just running their eyes over the words in a passage.* They expect their brains to magically absorb the information after just one quick reading. If they don't, they blame the author and pronounce the work "dull" or "too difficult." They don't write anything down. If they come to a word they don't know, they just skip it and keep reading. If they get bored, they let their attention wander. They "read" long sections and then realize they have no memory or understanding of the information or ideas.

Continued

To read more effectively, you must become an *active reader*. **Active readers** *know they have to do more than just sit with a book in front of them.* They know they have to participate by interacting with the text and by thinking as they read. They read with a pen or pencil in their hand, marking key words or ideas or jotting notes in the margins. They reread the text if necessary. Also, they consciously try to connect the text's information to their own experiences and beliefs.

Active reading is essential to understanding and remembering ideas and information, especially those in more difficult reading selections. It includes any or all of the following tasks:

■ Identifying and writing down the point and purpose of the reading

■ Underlining, highlighting, or circling important words or phrases

■ Determining the meanings of unfamiliar words

■ Outlining a passage to understand the relationships in the information

■ Writing down questions when you're confused

■ Completing activities—such as reading comprehension questions—that follow a chapter or passage

■ Jotting down notes in the margins

■ Thinking about how you can use the information or how the information reinforces or contradicts your ideas or experiences

■ Predicting possible test questions on the material

■ Rereading and reviewing

■ Studying visual aids such as graphs, charts, and diagrams until you understand them

Remember: The purpose of all these activities is to comprehend and retain more of what you read. So for challenging reading, such as textbook chapters or journal articles, active reading is a must. Also, you should perform these tasks for any reading that you're expected to remember for a test.

However, you should still get in the habit of reading actively when you read for information. Even if you're just reading for your own pleasure, you'll remember more by using active reading techniques.

To read actively, follow these steps:

1. When you sit down to read a book, get pens, pencils, and/or highlighter markers ready, too.

2. As you read each paragraph, mark points or terms that seem important. You may choose to underline them, highlight them, or enclose them in boxes or circles—this includes any words or key information phrases that are in bold print because the author wishes to call attention to them. Consider jotting down an outline or notes in the margins as you read. If you're reading a textbook, write in the margins the questions you want to remember to ask your instructor.

3. As you read, continually ask yourself these questions: How can this information help me? How can I use this information? What will my instructor want me to remember? How does this reading support or contradict my own ideas or beliefs and experiences?

4. After you have read the entire selection, complete any activities that follow.

The following passage has been actively read.

It's Better to Be Looked Over Than Overlooked

The first [stage] is the "attention getting" phase. Young men and women do this somewhat differently. As soon as they enter the bar, both males and females typically ① establish a territory—a seat, a place to lean, a position near the jukebox or dance floor. Once settled, they ② begin to attract attention to themselves.

Tactics vary. Men tend to pitch and roll their shoulders, stretch, stand tall, and shift from foot to foot in a swaying motion. They also exaggerate their body movements. Instead of simply using the wrist to stir a drink, men often employ the entire arm, as if stirring mud. The normally smooth motion necessary to light a cigarette becomes a whole-body gesture, ending with an elaborate shaking from the elbow to extinguish the match. And the whole body is employed in hearty laughter—made loud enough to attract a crowd. Thus simple gestures are embellished, overdone.

Then there is the swagger with which young men often move to and fro. Male baboons on the grasslands of East Africa also swagger when they foresee a potential sexual encounter. A male gorilla walks back and forth stiffly as he watches a female out of the corner of his eye. This parading gait is known to primatologists as bird-dogging. Males of many species also preen. Human males pat their hair, adjust their clothes, tug their chins, or perform other self-clasping or grooming movements that diffuse nervous energy and keep the body moving.

Continued

Margin notes:

Main point: Men and women use body language to attract attention and signal availability.

This is true!

Men: simple gestures are exaggerated.

embellished = add more details Men swagger (bird-dog) and preen, too.

Author compares men to gorillas.

gait = way of moving

Older men often use different props, advertising their availability with expensive jewelry, clothing, and other accoutrements that spell success. But all of these signals can be reduced to one basic, three-part message: "I am here; I am important; I am harmless." What a difficult mixture of signals to give out simultaneously—importance and approachability. Yet men succeed; women regularly court men.

"It is better to be looked over than overlooked," Mae West once said. And women know it. Young women begin the attention-getting phase with many of the same maneuvers that men use—smiling, gazing, shifting, swaying, preening, stretching, moving in their territory to draw attention to themselves. Often they incorporate a battery of feminine moves as well. They twist their curls, tilt their heads, look up coyly, giggle, raise their brows, flick their tongues, lick their upper lips, blush, and hide their faces in order to signal, "I am here."

Some women also have a characteristic walk when courting; they arch their backs, thrust out their bosoms, sway their hips, and strut. No wonder many women wear high-heeled shoes. This bizarre Western custom, invented by Catherine de Medici in the 1500s, unnaturally arches the back, tilts the buttocks, and thrusts the chest out into a female come-hither pose. The clomping noise of their spiky heels helps draw attention, too. With this high-heeled gait, puckered lips, batting eyes, dancing brows, upturned palms, pigeoned toes, rocking bodies, swaying skirts, and gleaming teeth, women signal approachability to men.*

Now, try applying the active reading strategy yourself. As you read the longer selections at the end of each chapter you will be directed to follow the steps described above. By practicing the active reading strategy throughout this book you will become a more successful reader.

Margin notes:

Older men display their wealth and success.

accoutrements = accessories

Women use same tactics as men use.

Women also use feminine moves.

coyly = shyly

Women have a distinctive walk that signals availability.

Men's walk is natural, but women's walk is not?

Reading Selection

Practicing the Active Reading Strategy

■ Before and While You Read

You can use active reading strategies before, while, and after you read a selection. The following are some suggestions for active reading strategies that you can employ before you read and as you are reading.

---

* "It's Better to Be Looked Over Than Overlooked" from *Anatomy of Love: The Natural History of Monogamy, Adultery, and Divorce* by Helen E. Fisher. Copyright © 1992 by Helen E. Fisher. Used by permission of W. W. Norton & Company, Inc.

1

1. Skim the selection for any unfamiliar words. Circle or highlight any words you do not know.

2. As you read, underline, highlight, or circle important words or phrases.

3. Write down any questions about the selection if you are confused by the information presented.

4. Jot notes in the margin to help you understand the material.

WEBSITE READING: COLLEGE SUCCESS
Learning Styles and Maximizing Your Success in School

What do you know about how you learn? This passage will help you to think carefully about your learning styles and how they affect your ability to succeed in school. Each section of the passage is followed by a brief question to help you think about how the information you just read applies to you.

1   College is different from high school. Entering any new environment brings new challenges and distractions. Also, each step of the learning process usually brings more and harder work. You obviously learned to succeed at your last educational stop. However, you may need to readjust now. This is especially true for adult returning students and students beginning a new field of study. By expanding on your current learning skills, you will better meet the challenges ahead. We hope that the following will provide useful information and tools to make this next educational step a success.

Learning Styles

2   **What are they? How do they match with teaching styles?** There are many types of learning styles. Often, these types match our personality style. Each of us has a different style or combination of styles. The majority of us can use most styles.

However, we tend to rely on or prefer certain styles. Hopefully, these are the styles that have brought us success in the past. If this is not the case, it may be helpful to look again at one's approach. We all learn differently, but we can all learn effectively. It is important to understand your own learning style and use it to your best advantage in the classroom.

3   There are also many teaching styles. We do best when our learning styles match with an instructor's teaching style. Below is some information about learning styles, teaching styles, and how to bridge the two.

Eyes or Ears

4   **Do you remember best what is said to you or what you read? Do you prefer television or newspapers as your source of news?** Some people learn best by reading. They need to see something to remember it. Others learn best by listening. Information sticks once they hear it.

5   If you have a visual style, you may have difficulty with an instructor who believes telling people what to learn and know is enough. Instructors who rely heavily on class discussion will also cause you some anxiety. Handouts, reading assignments, and written information on the blackboard are most helpful to you.

6   On the other hand, if you have an auditory style, you may be in trouble with an instructor who writes a lot and assigns reading that is not discussed in class. Class discussions and study groups are a better way for you to learn.

Do you think you are a visual or auditory learner or both? Why?

_____

_____

_____

Movement

7   **Does it help you to rewrite your notes or take notes as you read?** Some people's learning is improved by movement. In other words, they learn as they write notes in class. Or when they are reading an assignment, they remember the content best if they take notes as they read. Sometimes the act of highlighting important information while reading works in the same way.

Do you learn best when you are moving? Give an example.

_____

_____

_____

Group or Solitary

8   **Do you find you remember more when you study in a group or alone?** Some people draw their energy from the outside world. They like to interact with other people, activities, or things. This is often called _extroversion_. Others prefer to gain their energy from their own internal ideas, emotions, or impressions. Some people call this _introversion_.

9   If you tend to be more extroverted, you communicate freely and like to have other people around. Thus, working in groups and talking material over with others helps you understand and process new ideas better. You may be impatient and distracted working on your own. A class that is less varied and not as action-oriented may be a particular challenge. You like instructors who are active, energetic, and enthusiastic. You also prefer a more friendly and personal approach. In addition, you probably find larger classes exciting.

10   If you are more introverted, you probably work happily alone. You don't mind working on one project for a long time without interruption. You may be quiet in the classroom and dislike classes with a lot of oral presentations and group interaction and work. Sometimes having to communicate with others is hard. You work best if you read lessons over or write them out before discussion, think before participating, and ask questions before completing tasks or exercises. You like classes that require being thoughtful and introspective. You may dislike a professor with a more personal style

of attention and closeness. A quiet and tactful style works best for you. Smaller classes are your preference.

Do you prefer to work with a group or alone? Does your choice depend upon the people you have to work with or the subject matter you need to learn?

_____

_____

_____

Practical or Innovative

11   **Do you like to follow an established way of doing things? Or would you rather follow your inspirations?** Some people prefer to take information in through their five senses, taking note of what is actually there. They want, remember, and trust facts. They are sometimes called _practical types_. Others prefer to take information in through a "sixth sense," focusing on what might be. These people like to daydream and think about what might be in the future. One could call them _innovative_.

12   If you are a practical type, you probably like an established, routine way of doing things. You prefer using skills you already know rather than new ones. Taking note of details, memorizing facts, and reaching a conclusion step-by-step is your ideal. You learn best if you have clear directions to follow. Films, audiovisuals, hands-on exercises, and practical examples are most helpful. You learn best when instructors are factual and thorough, working out details in advance and showing you why things make sense.

13   If you are more innovative, you probably like to solve new problems. You may dislike doing the same thing repeatedly and may be impatient with routine details. You may also find yourself daydreaming during factual lectures. You work best when you can see the big picture, have independence and freedom, and use new approaches in your work. You like enthusiastic instructors who point out challenges and future benefits and then let you figure out your own way.

Do you like to follow rules that are already set or do you prefer to be creative with your work? Explain.

_____

_____

_____

Thinking or Feeling

14   **Do you respond more to people's thoughts or feelings?** Some people prefer to organize information in a logical way. They respond more easily to people's thoughts and are more analytical. If you are such a person, emotions play less of a part in your life, decisions, and interactions with others. You work best if you can organize and outline a subject, know your objectives and goals, get to the task, and receive rapid feedback. You are most motivated when you can see logical reasons for studying certain material or working on a particular project. You probably prefer teachers who are task-focused, logical, well-organized, less emotional, and generous with feedback.

15   Other people prefer to organize and structure information in a personal, value-oriented way. If this sounds familiar, you are likely to be very aware of other people and their feelings. You prefer harmony. You probably learn best if you can identify with what you are doing and have an emotional connection to it. You like an environment with little competition and with opportunity to respond more personally. You probably prefer teachers who are friendly and easy to work with. You also like a teaching style that is positive, tells you why what you are doing is valuable, and supports your personal goals.

Do you respond more to people's thoughts or feelings? Explain your answer.

_____

_____

_____

Open-Ended or Closure-Driven

16   **Do you like to get things settled and finished? Or would you rather leave things open for alterations?** Some people prefer to live a planned and organized life. They go on vacation and plan out all of their activities before they go. Other people like to be more open-ended, living more spontaneously and flexibly.

17   If you need closure, you probably work best when you can plan your work and follow that plan. You like to get things finished and do not like to be interrupted. In an effort to complete a task, however, you may make decisions too quickly. You learn best if you can stick to a routine and follow a specific time frame and precise guidelines. You probably prefer instructors who are structured, timely, precise, and organized. You also like specific performance guidelines.

18   For those who are more open-ended, you probably like change and undertaking many projects at once. You may have trouble making decisions and may postpone unpleasant jobs. You probably learn best if you can be original, physically active, and spontaneous. You like instructors who are more open, creative, spontaneous, and informal. You dislike deadlines and too much direction, wanting to follow your own path.

Do you learn better when there is structure in your assignments or do you work better with open-ended assignments? Give an example.

_____

_____

_____

Solutions

19   **What if your learning style and a teaching style are mismatched?** It is tempting to respond to this problem by thinking, "If people would only change their approach, my life would be much easier." However, this doesn't get anyone very far, and there are better solutions.

■ Try to get as much as you can out of every course.

■ Try to "translate" the material into a form you understand.

■ Practice approaching the class in another way. Be open to a new way of learning. Adapt to the instructor's style and see what you can learn. You may be surprised. If you are successful, you will add new skills without giving up what you already do well.

■ Ask questions. Talk to the instructor. Ask for what you need (i.e., more structure, more freedom, additional readings, more explanation of course goals). A clear, direct, respectful, and responsible communication is best. Also remember that communication is both verbal and nonverbal.*

■ Vocabulary

Read the following questions about some of the vocabulary words that appear in the previous selection. Use the context of the selection to circle the letter of the correct answer.

1. If your learning style is *auditory*, what does that mean? (paragraph 6)

   a. You learn best when you hear something.

   b. You learn best by doing something.

   c. You learn best by holding something in your hand.

   d. You learn best by seeing something repeatedly.

2. If you are *extroverted* (paragraph 9), you are

   a. shy   c. depressed

   b. reserved   d. outgoing

3. However, if you are *introverted* (paragraph 10), you are

   a. easily distracted   c. unhappy

   b. easily motivated   d. shy

4. A synonym (a word that means the same thing that another word does) for *introspective* (paragraph 10) is

   a. shy   c. delighted

   b. thoughtful   d. manipulative

5. "One could call them *innovative*." In paragraph 11, *innovative* means

   a. inventive   c. neurotic

   b. old-fashioned   d. mean-spirited

---

* Developed by Dr. Lauren Slater, Staff Psychologist, Pace University Counseling Center, Westchester campuses, NY, www.pace.edu

Practicing the Active Reading Strategy

■ After You Read

Now that you have read the selection, answer the following questions, using the active reading strategies that you have learned in this chapter.

1. Identify and write down the point and purpose of this reading selection.

2. Besides the vocabulary words included in the exercise, are there any other vocabulary words that are unfamiliar to you? If so, write a list of them. Can you figure out the meaning of these words from the context of the reading selection? If not, then look up each word in a dictionary and write the definition that best describes the word as it is used in the selection.

3. Predict any possible questions that may be used on a test about the content of this selection.

■ Questions for Discussion and Writing

Answer the following questions based on your reading of the selection.

1. What did you learn from this article about your learning style?

   _____

   _____

2. How will understanding your learning style help you become a better student? _____

   _____

3. If you had to think about your academic career up to this point, do you think you would have done better in school if you had identified your learning style earlier? Why or why not? _____

   _____

www.vark-learn.com

By taking the very brief questionnaire on the website, you will discover more about how you learn. The help-sheets for each of the learning styles will offer suggestions about how to use your learning style to become a better student.

Vocabulary Strategy: Using the Dictionary

To increase your vocabulary and to ensure your comprehension of readings, you'll want to use a dictionary. The best hard-copy dictionaries for college-level reading are those that include the word *college* or *collegiate* in their title and are not older than five years. For example, *The American Heritage College Dictionary* would be a good reference to have. You may also want to get in the habit of carrying a paperback dictionary with you to class.

However, today's students often prefer to use online dictionaries. These dictionaries allow you to simply search for a word. Online dictionaries frequently have audio so you can hear the pronunciation of a word. Although some dictionary sites seem to be cluttered, others are easier to use. Because not all of the dictionary sites have the same information, you may want to bookmark several good sites for easy reference. Some good dictionary sites are **www.dictionary.com**, **www.yourdictionary.com**, **www.wordnik.com** and **visuwords.com**.

Most dictionaries, hard copy or online, contain the following information:

- The spelling and pronunciation of the word, including its syllables and capital letters
- The word's part of speech (noun, verb, adjective, etc.)
- Words made from the main word, including plurals and verb forms
- The different meanings of the word, including special uses
- Synonyms (words that mean the same thing) for the word
- The history of the word
- Labels that identify the word's subject area or level of usage (for example, *slang* or *informal*)

The entry for a word may also contain a sentence that demonstrates the correct usage of the word. In addition, an entry may include antonyms, or words with the opposite meaning.

To use a hard-copy dictionary effectively, you must understand how to locate a word and how to read the entry for that word once you find it.

Guide Words

All hard-copy dictionaries list words in alphabetical order, which helps you find a word quickly. Another feature that helps you locate a particular word is the two **guide words** at the top of the page. The first guide

Continued

word identifies the first word listed on that page. The second guide word tells you the last word on the page. Refer to Figure 1.1 to see an example of a dictionary page with guide words. If you want to find the word *"vol-cano,"* for example, you'd know to look for it on the page labeled with the guide words *vol-au-vent* and *volumeter* because the first *four* letters, *volc,* come between *vol-a* and *volu.*

But what do you do if you're not sure how to spell a word you need to find? In that case, you'll have to try different possibilities based on the sound of the word. For example, let's say you were looking for the word *quay,* which means "a wharf or dock." This is a tough one because the word sounds like *kay* and its letter *u* is silent. The beginning sound could be a *k, c,* or *q.* The long *a* sound could be spelled *a, ay, ey, uay,* or *eigh.* So you would try different combinations of these sounds until you found the right spelling. You could also try typing your best guess into a word processing program. Many of them include spell checkers that suggest other alternatives when you misspell a word.

Understanding a Dictionary Entry

Every hard-copy dictionary includes a guide at the front of the book that explains how to read the entries. This guide explains the abbreviations, symbols, and organization of meanings, so you may need to consult it to know how to decipher the information. Various dictionaries differ in these details. However, they all usually contain certain types of standard information, as follows.

Main entry. Each word in a dictionary appears in bold print with dots dividing its syllables. This word is correctly spelled, of course, and any alternative spellings for the word follow.

Pronunciation key. Usually in parentheses following the main entry, the word's pronunciation is represented with symbols, letters, and other marks. The guide may be at the front of the dictionary or at the bottom of the page and will provide a list of the corresponding sounds for each letter or symbol. The accent mark shows you which syllable to stress when you say the word.

Part of speech. The next part of the entry is an abbreviation that identifies the word's part of speech. *N.* means noun, *v.* means verb, *adj.* stands for adjective, and so on. Refer to the list of abbreviations in the guide at the front of the dictionary to find out what other abbreviations mean.

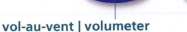

Guide Words

Pronunciation Key

Part of Speech

vol-au-vent | volumeter

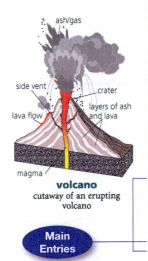

ash/gas

side vent — crater

lava flow — layers of ash and lava

magma

volcano
cutaway of an erupting volcano

Main Entries

vol-au-vent (vô′lō-vän′) *n.* A light pastry shell filled with a ragout of meat or fish. [French : *vol*, flight + *au*, with the + *vent*, wind.]

vol•can•ic (vŏl-kăn′ĭk, vôl-) *adj.* **1.** Of, resembling, or caused by a volcano or volcanoes: *a volcanic peak; volcanic islands.* **2.** Produced by or discharged from a volcano: *volcanic ash.* **3.** Characterized by the presence of volcanoes. **4.** Powerfully explosive: *a volcanic temper.* —**vol•can′i•cal•ly** *adv.*

volcanic arc *n.* A usually arc-shaped chain of volcanoes located on the margin of the overriding plate at a convergent plate boundary.

volcanic glass *n.* Natural glass produced by the cooling of molten lava too quickly to permit crystallization.

vol•ca•nism (vŏl′kə-nĭz′əm) also **vul•ca•nism** (vŭl′-) *n.* **1.** Volcanic force or activity. **2.** The phenomena associated with volcanic activity.

vol•ca•nize (vŏl′kə-nīz′) *tr.v.* **-nized, -niz•ing, -niz•es** To subject to or change by the effects of volcanic heat. —**vol′ca•ni•za′tion** (-nĭ-zā′shən) *n.*

vol•ca•no (vŏl-kā′nō) *n., pl.* **-noes** or **-nos 1a.** An opening in the earth's crust through which molten lava, ash, and gases are ejected. **b.** A similar opening on the surface of another planet. **2.** A mountain formed by the materials ejected from a volcano. [Italian, from Spanish *volcán* or Portuguese *volcão*, both probably from Latin *volcānus, vulcānus,* fire, flames, from *Volcānus,* Vulcan.]

vol•ca•no•gen•ic (vŏl′kə-nə-jĕn′ĭk, vôl′-) *adj.* Of volcanic origin.

Vol•ca•no Islands (vŏl-kā′nō) A group of Japanese islands in the northwest Pacific Ocean north of the Mariana Islands. Annexed by Japan in the late 19th century, the islands were administered by the United States from 1945 until 1968.

Meaning

History of Word

1

Figure 1.1 **Dictionary Page**

Source: Copyright © 2009 by Houghton Mifflin Harcourt Publishing Company. Adapted and reproduced by permission from The American Heritage Dictionary of the English Language, Fourth Edition.

Meanings of the word. The different meanings of a word are divided first according to their part of speech. All of the meanings related to a particular part of speech are grouped together. For example, the word *contact* can function as both a noun and a verb. All of its noun meanings appear first, followed by all of its verb meanings. Dictionaries order each set of meanings in different ways, usually from most common to least common or from oldest to newest. Different senses, or shades of meaning, are numbered. Following the list of meanings, the dictionary may provide synonyms and/or antonyms for the word.

History of the word. Some dictionaries provide information about the origin of a word. This history, called an *etymology,* usually includes the word's language of origin, along with its various evolutions.

Vocabulary Exercise 1

To complete the exercise that follows, choose two dictionaries—one hard-copy dictionary and one online dictionary. Write down your choices here.

Hard copy: _____

Online: _____

Answer each of the following questions twice—once for each dictionary. If the dictionary does not contain the information, write "No answer."

Write your answers to the following questions on the blanks provided.

1. What is the plural of *shelf*? _____

_____

2. How many different parts of speech can the word *right* be? _____

_____

3. What is a synonym for the word *ridicule*? _____

_____

4. What language does the word *tattoo* come from? _____

_____

5. How many different pronunciations does your dictionary provide for the word *harass*? _____

_____

6. Does the verb *slough* rhyme with *tough* or *plow* or *flew*? _____

_____

7. How many syllables does the word *schizophrenia* contain? _____

_____

Vocabulary Exercise **2**

Use the same two dictionaries that you chose for Exercise 1 to complete the following exercise. Look up each word twice—once in each dictionary.

On the blank following each sentence, write the correct meaning for the italicized word.

1. The company president presented her with a *plaque* to recognize her 20 years of service.

   Definition: _____

2. A buildup of *plaque* within the arteries can cause a heart attack.

   Definition: _____

3. He won first prize for his science *project*, a study of bumblebees in a zero-gravity environment.

   Definition: _____

4. A ventriloquist *projects* his voice so the dummy appears to talk.

   Definition: _____

5. During her vacations at the beach, she was *content*.

   Definition: _____

6. The *content* of late-night television shows is not appropriate for young children.

   Definition: _____

Vocabulary Exercise **3**

List the differences that you found between your hard-copy dictionary and the online dictionary. Which dictionary would you prefer to use? Why?

_____

_____

_____

_____

Chapter 1 Review

Write the correct answers in the blanks in the following statements.

1. Good reading skills are important to _____, _____, and _____ success.

2. Reading helps strengthen _____ skills.

3. The two basic purposes for reading are to gain _____ and to be entertained.

4. When you read for information, you may have one or more of the following goals: gain a general _____ of the ideas or points; discover _____ or answer questions; memorize the information; find information or ideas that prove a _____ you want to make; make a _____ based on the information.

5. Reading is actually a collection of mental skills that include _____, concentration, _____, and _____ thought.

6. A positive _____ makes reading more pleasurable and more productive.

7. _____ is the ability to focus all of your attention on one thing while ignoring distractions.

8. The two types of distractions are _____ and _____.

9. _____ is the ability to store and recall information.

10. Logical thought includes mental tasks such as sequencing and ordering, _____, _____, analysis, _____ from the general to the particular and from the particular to the general, _____ thought, and synthesis.

11. Reading _____ are techniques you can use to get more out of what you read.

12. _____ reading is essential to understanding and remembering ideas and information.

13. _____, _____, and _____ are three activities that active readers engage in while reading difficult text.

14. Online dictionaries do not need to use _____ words that are found at the top of the page in hard-copy dictionaries.

15. Students who need pronunciation of a difficult word should use a(n)

_____

1

Tara Moore/Getty Images

Main Ideas

Goals for Chapter 2

- ■ Define the terms *general* and *specific*.
- ■ Order groups of sentences from most general to most specific.
- ■ Identify the topic of a paragraph.
- ■ Determine the main idea of a paragraph.
- ■ Recognize the topic sentence of a paragraph.
- ■ Recognize topic sentences in different locations in a paragraph.
- ■ Describe the characteristics of an effective reading environment.

To read successfully, you must learn to determine the main idea of a paragraph or longer selection. The **main idea** *is the overall point the author is trying to make.* The rest of the paragraph or longer selection consists of information or examples that help the reader understand the main point.

What process do you go through to help you figure out the main idea of a selection? Take this pretest to find out how much you already know about identifying and understanding main ideas.

Pretest

Read the following paragraph and respond to the questions by writing your answers on the blanks provided.

1. Motivating goals have specific deadlines. A short-term goal usually has a deadline within a few months. A long-term goal generally has a deadline as far in the future as one year, five years, even ten years. As your target deadline approaches, your motivation typically increases. This positive energy helps you finish strong. What is the main idea of this paragraph? How do you know?

   _____

   _____

2. To figure out the main idea, what part of the paragraph did you look at first?

   _____

   _____

What is the main idea of each of the following passages? Write your answers on the blanks provided.

3. Motivating goals are challenging but realistic. It's unrealistic to say you'll complete a marathon next week if your idea of a monster workout has been opening and closing the refrigerator. Still, if you're going to err, err on the side of optimism. When you set goals at the outer reaches of your present ability, stretching to reach them causes you to grow.

   Main Idea: _____

4. Motivating goals are *your* goals, not someone else's. You don't want to be lying on your deathbed some day and realize you have lived someone else's life. Trust that you know better than anyone else what *you* desire.

   Main Idea: _____

5. Motivating goals focus your energy on what you *do* want rather than on what you *don't* want. So translate negative goals into positive goals. For example, a negative goal to not fail a class becomes a positive goal to earn a grade of B or better. Likewise, focus your thoughts and actions on where you *do* want to go rather than where you *don't* want to go, and you, too, will stay on course.

Main Idea: _____

_____

6. Motivating goals state outcomes in specific, measurable terms. It's not enough to say, "My goal is to do better this semester" or "My goal is to work harder at my job." How will you know if you've achieved these goals? What specific, measurable evidence will you have? Revised, these goals become, "I will complete every college assignment this semester to the best of my ability" and "I will volunteer for all offerings of overtime at work." Being specific keeps you from fooling yourself into believing you've achieved a goal when, in fact, you haven't. It also helps you make choices that create positive results.*

Main Idea: _____

General and Specific

Before you practice finding main ideas, it's helpful to learn how to tell the difference between the terms *general* and *specific*. You must apply these concepts to figure out the relationships of sentences within a paragraph. Understanding these relationships is the first step in improving your comprehension of the author's meaning.

The word **general** means *broad* and *not limited*. When we say a word or idea is general, we mean that it includes or refers to many different things in a large category. For example, *weather* is a general word that includes many different types of conditions, including wind, rain, snow, and hail. *Coins* is another general word that refers to a large group of items, including pennies, dimes, nickels, and quarters.

The word **specific** means *definite* or *particular*. Specific things or ideas are limited or narrowed in scope, and they refer to one certain something within a larger group. In the previous paragraph, for instance, *wind, rain, snow,* and *hail* are all certain types of weather, so we say they are more specific. *Pepsi,*

---

* Downing, Skip. *On Course: Strategies for Creating Success in College and in Life,* 6th ed. Boston: Wadsworth, 2011. Print. pp. 73–74.

Coca-Cola, and *RC* are all specific colas. *Math, English,* and *science* are three specific subjects we study in school.

The terms *general* and *specific* are relative. In other words, they depend upon or are connected to the other things with which they are being compared. For example, you would say that *school subject* is a general term and that *math* is one specific subject. However, *math* becomes the more general term when you think of specific kinds of math, such as *algebra, trigonometry,* and *calculus.* Words and concepts, therefore, can change from being general or specific, depending on their relationships to other words and concepts. Look at this list:

weather

storm

hurricane

category 4 hurricanes

Hurricane Floyd

The words in this list are arranged from most general to most specific. In other words, each item on the list is more specific than the one above it. The last item, Hurricane Floyd, names one specific storm, so it is the most specific of all.

Exercise **2.1**

Put these lists of words in order from most general to most specific. Write your answers on the blanks provided.

1. Taurus   car   Ford   machine

   _____

2. strawberry   fruit   food   plant

   _____

3. subject   science   biology   microbiology

   _____

4. hip-hop singer   singer   performer   Jay-Z

   _____

5. Kobe Bryant   sports players   basketball players   Los Angeles Lakers team members

   _____

To read well, you will need to be able to recognize the most general idea within a passage. Let's practice that skill by looking at groups of related items in different ways. Can you select the most general word in the list?

    mixer   appliances   toaster   blender

Three of the words in the group are specific, and one of the words is the most general. If you chose *appliances* as most general, you are correct. The other three items are specific kinds of appliances.

    Now examine this list and decide how the items are related. Come up with a word that includes all three items in the list.

    mouse   rat   hamster

Did you say *rodent*? The three creatures are all specific types of rodents.

    Finally, see if you can think of three specific examples of this phrase:

    supernatural occurrences

Some possible answers include *ghosts, monsters,* and *UFOs.*

Exercise **2.2**

The following groups of words include one general word and three specific words. Circle the most general word in each group.

1. dance	ballet	tap	modern
2. hockey	basketball	sports	baseball
3. running	jogging	aerobics	exercise
4. Burger King	McDonald's	fast-food restaurants	Wendy's
5. oak	walnut	maple	trees

Exercise **2.3**

On the blank following each group, write a general term that includes all of the items in the list.

1. looking up words   checking spelling   reading definitions

    General Idea: _____

2. hamburgers   turkey   ice cream

    General Idea: _____

3. nurse   doctor   X-ray technician

    General Idea: _____

4. pine   redwood   weeping willow

General Idea: _____

5. attending class   using a textbook   taking notes

General Idea: _____

Exercise **2.4**

Write on the blanks provided at least three specific ideas included in the general idea.

1. **General Idea:** Doing laundry

   Specific Ideas: _____

2. **General Idea:** States in the United States

   Specific Ideas: _____

3. **General Idea:** Maintaining your car

   Specific Ideas: _____

4. **General Idea:** U.S. presidents

   Specific Ideas: _____

   _____

5. **General Idea:** Using e-mail

   Specific Ideas: _____

General and Specific Sentences

Now that you've reviewed how words can be general and specific, you'll be able to see how the sentences that express ideas are also general and specific in relation to each other. Paragraphs are composed of both general and specific sentences. A **general sentence** *is one that states the broadest idea in the paragraph.* This idea can often be explained or interpreted in a variety of different ways. The **specific sentences** in a paragraph are those that *offer explanation or details that help us understand and accept the idea in the general sentence.* Specific sentences are essential in helping readers correctly determine the meaning of the general statement.

We saw earlier how the terms *general* and *specific* are relative when applied to words. Sentences within a paragraph, too, are relatively general and specific. For example, read the following three statements:

Dessert is my favorite part of a meal.

I especially love to eat pie.

The after-dinner treat I like most to eat is a slice of warm cherry pie.

The first sentence states the most general idea; then the second sentence clarifies a specific type of dessert—pie—that the writer enjoys. The third sentence is even more specific because it identifies the particular kind of pie the writer likes most. So in this group of sentences, each statement is more specific than the one above it.

Exercise **2.5**

Put these sentences in order from most general to most specific. Number them by writing 1, 2, or 3 on the blanks to indicate the most general (1) to the most specific (3).

1. _____ Paris is her favorite destination.

   _____ Shaneesa has always loved to travel.

   _____ She loves to visit Paris landmarks such as the Eiffel Tower and the Louvre.[1]

2. _____ Fresh, homegrown vegetables are a delicious addition to family meals.

   _____ You can grow your own food in your backyard.

   _____ Gardening is a rewarding hobby.

3. _____ Many people suffer from foot pain.

   _____ Firefighters, nurses, and people in service jobs experience more foot pain than people in other professions.

   _____ People whose jobs require that they stand for long periods of time have the most foot problems.

4. _____ Courage, teamwork, and excellence are three of her father's values that she celebrates in her book.

   _____ Sharon Robinson, daughter of baseball great Jackie Robinson, wanted to honor her father and his values.

   _____ Sharon Robinson published a collection of essays and stories about nine values embraced by her father.

1.　**Louvre:** famous Paris art museum

5. _____ Many students today would rather learn about the news on the Internet than watch it on television.

_____ Students can watch videos of breaking news events from around the world.

_____ Geography students watched a recent online video showing the damage from an earthquake in central China.

Paragraphs are combinations of sentences that all work together to develop a main idea. So sorting out the general and specific relationships among related sentences is the first step toward understanding what you read. Look at the three sentences below and try to identify the one that is the most general.

Surveys show that adults typically watch four hours of TV per day.

Americans watch too much television.

The average American school child watches about twenty-eight hours of TV per week.

Did you choose the second sentence as most general? The other two sentences offer specific facts—the number of hours of TV adults and children watch—that help explain the idea of "too much television."

Now read these three specific sentences:

High school dropouts are 50 percent more likely than high school graduates to go on welfare.

Fewer than 50 percent of high school dropouts find jobs when they leave school.

When they do find jobs, high school dropouts earn 60 percent less income than high school graduates.

How could you state the general idea these three sentences explain or support? All three are examples of the negative effects of dropping out of high school, so the sentence "Dropping out of high school has several negative consequences" would be an accurate statement of the general idea they develop.

Finally, read this general sentence:

In many ways, college is tougher than high school.

What three specific sentences could you write to explain this sentence? Some possibilities include:

The course work is more difficult.

The instructors are more demanding.

The learning pace is much faster.

Exercise **2.6**

The following groups of sentences include one general sentence and three specific sentences. Label each sentence on the blank provided with either a G for *general* or an S for *specific*.

1. _____ I enjoy eating fruit.

   _____ I put strawberries in my cereal.

   _____ I eat blueberry topping on my ice cream.

   _____ I enjoy peach pancakes.

2. _____ She has a television network that millions of people watch.

   _____ Her magazine, O, is a great success.

   _____ Oprah Winfrey is a very successful businesswoman and entertainer.

   _____ She made a movie called *Beloved*, in which she starred.

3. _____ For most college graduates working in an office from 9 to 5 is hard to get used to.

   _____ Many college graduates find it difficult to conform to others' schedules.

   _____ A lot of new graduates are used to sleeping very late and staying up past midnight.

   _____ Many recent graduates do not like having to report to a boss after being on their own for four years.

4. _____ Most student drivers have a difficult time merging onto highways and into traffic.

   _____ For a new driver, changing lanes during rush hour is very hard to do.

   _____ Learning to drive can be very difficult.

   _____ Parking was the hardest part for me when I was a new driver.

5. _____ Running tones your muscles.

   _____ Running two times a week increases the number of calories burned by 10 percent.

   _____ Running is the best form of exercise.

   _____ When I run, I feel great.

2

2

Exercise 2.7

Read the three specific sentences given. Then, in the list that follows them, circle the letter of the general sentence best supported by those three specific sentences.

1. Women and minorities make up the majority of people applying to colleges.

   Prior to 1980, the majority of college applications came from white men.

   Fewer men are applying to colleges because they are going directly into the workforce.

   General Sentences:
   a. There is a change in the types of people who are applying to college.
   b. More women go to college than before.
   c. Prior to 1980, fewer women and minorities applied to college.

2. Every American uses 80 to 100 gallons of water a day.

   U.S. citizens spend more than $5 million a year on bottled water.

   Many Americans frequently visit spas for relaxing and revitalizing water treatments.*

   General Sentences: Water can heal mental and physical ailments.
   a. Americans use too much water.
   b. Water is an important part of American life.

3. Flextime[1] saves businesses money because they don't need as much office space.

   Flextime allows workers to more effectively balance their career schedules and personal lives.

   Flextime helps businesses recruit the best workers and keep them from leaving.[†]

   General Sentences:
   a. Flextime can work only with clear-cut guidelines for employees.
   b. Flextime, or flexible hours, offers several advantages.
   c. Flextime and telecommuting are becoming more widespread in American companies.

---

1. **flextime:** working hours other than a 9 A.M. to 5 P.M., 40–hour week

---

* Adapted from Marisa Fox, "Water Cures," *O Magazine*, June 2001, 171.
† Adapted from "Flextime Programs Gain Popularity," *USA Today Newsview*, April 1998, 5.

4. Composting[1] involves making use of kitchen, lawn, and garden waste that would otherwise go to a landfill.

Putting grass clippings in your compost heap cuts down on the use of plastic bags used for gardening.

As the chemicals in the materials react and start to decompose, the compost heats up and yields rich, dark earth, perfect for fertilizing a garden.*

General Sentences:
a. Composting is one of the best things you can do for your garden and for the environment.

b. Composting is best done in the summer when it is hot.

c. Composting is easy.

5. Great white sharks typically approach humans in a very undramatic manner and may take a "sample" bit out of curiosity.

Of the 108 authenticated, unprovoked great white shark attacks along the Pacific Coast in the twentieth century only 8 attacks were fatal.

Great white sharks spit people out because humans are too bony.†

General Sentences:
a. Humans are unlikely to be killed in an encounter with a great white shark.

b. Great white sharks attack humans take place all over the world.

c. Great white shark attacks are always fatal.

Exercise 2.8

Read the general sentence given and then circle the letters of the three sentences from the list that best explain or support that statement.

1. **General Sentence:** Stephen Huneck is fast becoming a folk artist of cult status in America, mostly because of his smile-provoking art involving dogs.

---

1. **composting:** adding discarded vegetable matter to a pile of organic waste

---

* Adapted from "Ask Martha," *New York Times,* June 2, 2001, 3e.
† Hile, Jennifer. *Great White Shark Attacks: Defanging the Myths.* National Geographic Channel. Web. 23 January 2004. pp. 1–3. http://news.nationalgeographic.com

Specific Sentences:

a. Stephen Huneck has many dogs.

b. One of his dogs is Sally, a black Labrador.

c. He has created woodcut prints involving dogs.

d. One of his sculptures shows dogs eating ice cream cones.

e. Huneck's dining room table is held up by four carved dogs.

f. Some of his sculptures show dogs with their heads sticking out of car windows.*

2. **General Sentence:** A growing number of researchers say it is a good idea to let families have easier access to patients during emergency treatment in hospitals.

Specific Sentences:

a. Family members can comfort patients in a way no health-care provider can.

b. When the patient is less scared and is surrounded by family members, procedures go more smoothly.

c. Health decisions are left to the physician in charge.

d. Few hospitals have formal rules on this issue.

e. This way of treating emergency room patients is most effective when the patient is a child and a parent can stay with him or her during treatment.

f. One physician thinks that this should be done on a case-by-case basis.†

3. **General Sentence:** There are numerous benefits to earning a college degree.

a. One of the most widely recognized benefits of a college degree is increased earning power.

b. Many students take over five years to earn their college degree.

c. College graduates enjoy higher savings levels, increased personal and professional mobility, and improved health and life expectancy.

d. College students who play sports may take an extra year to earn their degree.

e. Attaining a college degree can bring personal satisfaction and accomplishment.

f. Working parents may take longer to earn their college degree.‡

---

* Adapted from Craig Wilson, "Art and Religion, Gone to the Dogs," *USA Today,* June 5, 2001, Section D, Life.

† Adapted from Pat Wingert, "Family Notes," *Newsweek,* June 11, 2001, 60.

‡ Downing, Skip. *On Course: Strategies for Creating Success in College and in Life,* 6th ed. Boston: Wadsworth, 2011. Print. p. 67.

4. **General Sentence:** Stephen King, sometimes called the "master of horror," is considered the most popular fiction writer ever and is loved by his fans.

   a. He has sold more than a billion books since his first one was published.

   b. He published a book after being hit by a car and suffering terrible injuries.

   c. He is a frequent guest on popular talk shows because he is very funny.

   d. His first manuscript was rejected.

   e. Fans line up in front of bookstores in anticipation of one of his book's publication and buy all copies available on the first day.

   f. He gets bags full of fan mail every day.

5. **General Sentence:** It is important that children, especially those who can't swim, be supervised by their parents or guardians around pools and bodies of water.

   a. Many children drown every summer because they have not been supervised properly.

   b. Even if children can swim, it is important that a parent be close by in case the children experience cramping in their legs or feet.

   c. Lifeguards should not be expected to supervise everyone's children, especially at a crowded swimming facility.

   d. Some children learn to swim at a very young age.

   e. The ocean is fun to swim in.

   f. Lakes are safer than oceans because there are no waves.

Determining the Topic

Now that you've reviewed the distinction between general and specific, let's look at the most general aspect of a paragraph: its topic. To understand what you read, you must be able to identify the topic, or subject, of a reading selection. The **topic** *is the person, place, thing, event, or idea that the passage is about, and it is usually expressed in just a word or brief phrase.* For example, read this paragraph:

> The Slinky has been a popular toy for more than fifty years. The Slinky is available on every continent except Antarctica. Ninety percent of Americans know what this coiled wire toy is. Since 1946, 250 million Slinky toys have been sold. Today, both boys and girls still enjoy this inexpensive plaything.

The topic of this paragraph is the Slinky. Every sentence in the paragraph refers to or mentions the Slinky.

To find the topic of a selection, look for the person, place, thing, event, or idea that is repeated again and again.

Exercise 2.9

Read each paragraph and write the correct topic on the blank provided.

1. How you spend the hours before bedtime plays a big role in how well you'll sleep, Dr. Maas points out in his recent book, *Power Sleep* (Harper Perennial). Although a big meal is forbidden for three hours before you settle in, having a light snack, high in carbohydrates and low in protein, will help you drift off—crackers, a cookie or two, or camomile[1] tea. Milk, of course, has always been a popular recommendation because it speeds the amino acid tryptophan to the brain, where it is converted to sleep-inducing serotonin. Other tried-and-true before-bed aids: yoga, visualization, and deep breathing.[*]

   Topic: _____

2. For the very young, the very old, and people with lung disease, air pollution is not only annoying but also dangerous. Smog causes inflammation or swelling of the airway, which makes breathing more difficult. Exposure to high smog levels can trigger asthma attacks and worsen emphysema.[2] Long-term exposure can cause scarring of the lungs.[†]

   Topic: _____

3. Success in school and in life is largely a matter of cultivating effective habits. The new habit that you choose does not have to make headlines. It can be one simple, small change in behavior. All of the researchers on studying and success in school agree that forming good habits regarding your school work is essential to your success.[‡]

   Topic: _____

1. **camomile:** an herb

2. **emphysema:** a lung disease that makes breathing difficult

[*] Adapted from "Follow the Milky Way," *Victoria*, January 2001, 81.

[†] Adapted from Anita Manning, "There's No Breathing Easy With Air Pollution," *USA Today*, April 16, 2004, 8A. Copyright © 2004, USA Today. Reprinted with Permission.

[‡] Adapted from Dave Ellis, *Becoming a Master Student* (Boston: Houghton Mifflin Co., 2000), 120. Copyright © 2000 by Houghton Mifflin Company. Reprinted with permission.

4. A writing center should have a table with chairs around it, containers of writing tools, and newsprint or unlined paper in various sizes and colors. Children like to experiment with colored felt-tipped pens, crayons, pencils, and chalk for individual chalkboards. Resource materials to encourage children to write include greeting cards, note pads, books and magazines, envelopes, special words related to a unit or holiday, magnetic letters, and the alphabet in uppercase and lowercase letters. Writing centers may also contain notice or message boards for the children and teacher to use for exchanging information.*

Topic: _____

5. It is said that women gossip more than men do. However, men gossip, too, though they tend to call it "networking." What really differs is the content of their gossip. Men are much more interested in who is up and who is down, an interest that arises from their enjoyment of competitive game playing. Women tend to gossip more about social inclusion[1] and morality. They are more interested in who has merit.[†]

Topic: _____

When you are deciding on the topic of a paragraph or passage, make sure your choice is not too *broad* or too *narrow*. A topic that is too broad suggests much more than the paragraph actually offers. A topic that is too narrow does not include everything the paragraph covers. For example, look at the following paragraph:

Many popular inventions were created by accident. In 1886, a pharmacist trying to create a nerve and brain tonic[2] made a syrup that became Coca-Cola. In 1853, a chef accidentally created potato chips for a restaurant guest who complained that his French fries were too thick. In the 1920s, Yale University students who liked to toss and catch pie plates made by the Frisbie Pie Company accidentally came up with the popular toy known as the Frisbee.

Which of these is the correct topic of the paragraph?

_____ inventions

_____ the invention of Coca-Cola

_____ accidental inventions

1. **inclusion:** the act of being included or the state of being included

2. **tonic:** a drink with healthful qualities

* From Paul Burns et al., *Teaching Reading in Today's Elementary Schools,* 7th ed. (Boston: Houghton Mifflin Co., 1999), 69.

† Adapted from Nigel Nicholson, PhD, "The New Word on Gossip," *Psychology Today,* May/June 2001, 44.

If you checked accidental inventions, you're correct. The first topic, inventions, is too broad because it includes all kinds of inventions, even those that were created intentionally. The second topic, the invention of Coca-Cola, is too narrow because the paragraph also discusses potato chips and Frisbees. Accidental inventions is the right topic because the paragraph gives examples of three different products that were all discovered by accident.

Now read another example:

> How do Americans spend most of their leisure time? Watching television. According to a national survey, adult men spend about 29 hours a week watching television; women average about 34 hours per week. The more time that individuals spend in front of the TV, the greater their risk of obesity and related chronic diseases. Compared with other sedentary activities, such as reading, writing, or driving, watching TV lowers metabolic rates so people burn fewer calories. TV viewers are likely to snack as they watch, so they also take in more calories.*

Which of the topics below is the correct one?

_____ American leisure time

_____ Negative effects of TV viewing on American health

_____ Eating snacks while watching TV

The first choice, American leisure time, is too broad. This paragraph focuses on just one specific American leisure time activity—watching television. The last choice, eating snacks while watching TV is too narrow because this paragraph also discusses other negative effects of watching too much television. Therefore, negative effects of TV viewing on American health is the correct topic. This paragraph describes several negative effects on Americans of watching too much television.

Exercise 2.10

Following each paragraph are three topics. On each blank, label the topic *B* if it is too broad, *N* if it is too narrow, and *T* if it is the correct topic of the paragraph.

1. Working in the fishing industry is one of the most dangerous jobs in America. Fishermen average 71 fatalities per 100,000 workers, which is more than twenty times the fatality rate of the average U.S. worker. Fishermen must put in very long hours during short fishing seasons. They work with heavy gear and dangerous machinery. And they tend to go out even in rough, stormy seas because they have to catch a lot of fish

---

* Hales, Diane. *An Invitation to Wellness: Making Healthy Choices.* Belmont: Thomson Higher Education, 2007. Print. p. 44.

2

to make any money, and they have only a short amount of time to do it. Not surprisingly, drowning is the most common cause of death.*

The fishing industry: _____

Long hours of fishermen: _____

Dangerous jobs: _____

2. Reciting is saying each fact or idea in your notes out loud, in your own words, and from memory. Recitation is an extremely powerful aid to memory. Recitation makes you think, and thinking leaves a trace in your memory. Experiments show that students who recite retain 80 percent of the material; students who reread but do not recite retain only 20 percent when tested two weeks later. Without retention, there is no learning.[†]

Memory aids: _____

Reciting: _____

Memory experiments: _____

3. Most people engage in *linear thinking;* that is, they begin a task, finish it, and then go on to something else. Teenagers using the Internet today, however, are *multitasking;* that is, as they are online, they are also doing other things. They may be watching television or visiting two sites at the same time. Eighty-six percent of teenage girls listen to the radio while they are using the computer. Adolescents may be e-mailing a friend and looking something up at the same time.[‡]

Multitasking adolescents: _____

Teenagers: _____

Teenagers who listen to the radio while using a computer: _____

4. Goals are specific changes you'd like to make in yourself or in your environment. To help achieve your goals, state them as results you can measure. Think in detail about how things would be different if your goal were attained. List the specific changes in what you'd see, feel, touch, taste, hear, be, do, or have. Some goals that will aid you with your schoolwork include setting aside a specific time to study every day, taking good

---

* Adapted from Les Christie, "America's Most Dangerous Jobs," *CNN/Money,* October 13, 2003, http://money
.cnn.com/2003/10/13/pf/dangerousjobs.

† From Walter Pauk and John Fiore, *Succeed in College!* (Boston: Houghton Mifflin Co., 2000), 47. Copyright ©
2000 by Houghton Mifflin Company. Reprinted with permission.

‡ Adapted from Paul S. Kaplan, *Adolescence* (Boston: Houghton Mifflin Co., 2004), 266.

notes in class, and reviewing those notes from time to time to make sure you are retaining information.*

Goals: _____

Changing yourself: _____

Taking notes in class: _____

5. Hybrid car drivers are a few years older than the average car buyer. There is also strong evidence that hybrid car drivers have higher levels of income. And in the most important market factor—satisfaction with their purchase decision—hybrid owners are unique. The percentage of hybrid owners who express being "very happy" or "somewhat happy" with their hybrids has hovered near 100 percent.[†]

Hybrid cars: _____

Type of people who drive hybrid cars: _____

Education level of hybrid car drivers: _____

Determining the Main Idea

Once you've found the topic of a paragraph, you can determine its **main idea**, *the general point the writer expressed about the topic.* The main idea is what the writer wants to prove or explain. It's the point he or she wants you to know or to believe when you finish reading the paragraph. Therefore, being able to identify main ideas is a fundamental skill for successful reading.

To find the main idea, ask yourself what the writer is saying *about* the topic. For example, read this paragraph:

The Eagles' *Greatest Hits* album is the most successful album in history. It has sold 26 million copies, more than any other album. It was the first album ever to gain platinum status for sales of one million copies. *Greatest Hits* was the number one album on the Billboard Charts for five weeks, and it spent a total of 133 weeks on the charts altogether.

The topic of this paragraph is the Eagles' *Greatest Hits* album. It's the thing that is mentioned in every sentence of the paragraph. But what is the author's point about this topic? In the first sentence, she states that this album was more successful than any other. Then, all of the other sentences in the paragraph offer details to explain that idea.

---

* Adapted from Dave Ellis, *Becoming a Master Student* (Boston: Houghton Mifflin Co., 2000), 59.
[†] *Profile of Hybrid Drivers.* Hybridcars.com. March 31, 2006. Web.

As you read the next paragraph, try to identify the topic and main idea.

Single mothers face many challenges. Their greatest difficulties are usually financial. They are the primary family breadwinners, so their greatest struggles, especially for those who are younger and less educated, often involve making ends meet. To make matters worse, single moms often do not receive regular child support from their children's fathers. They also must curtail[1] their work hours due to childcare limitations, so many can't earn full-time wages.

Did you say that the topic is *single mothers' financial challenges*? That is correct. Every sentence of this paragraph mentions single mothers, single moms, or includes a pronoun (*they* or *their*) that refers to single moms. Also, each sentence refers to difficulties related to money. Now, what does the author want you to know or believe about that topic? The second sentence says that financial difficulties are their greatest hardship. Then, the remainder of the paragraph explains why the reader should accept that idea as true.

Exercise **2.11**

Read each paragraph and then circle the letter of the correct topic.

1. In any subject, learning is enhanced when we ask questions. And there are no dumb questions. To master math and science, ask whatever questions will aid your understanding. Don't worry about what other students do or don't ask. What you need to ask may not be the same as for the other people in your class.*

   Topic:

   a. learning math and science

   b. asking questions to aid understanding

   c. students in higher education

2. Most college lecturers speak about 120 words per minute. In a fifty-minute lecture, you hear up to 6,000 words expressing ideas, facts, and details. To make sure that students understand the ideas, facts, and details they are presenting, lecturers use signal words and phrases. Signal words help lecturers convey[2] important information. Some signal words and phrases

---

1. **curtail:** shorten

2. **convey:** communicate

* Adapted from Dave Ellis, *Becoming a Master Student* (Boston: Houghton Mifflin Co., 2000), 181.

include *to illustrate, before/after, furthermore, as a result,* and *more importantly.* Being able to recognize signal words and phrases will improve your reading, writing, speaking, and listening, as well as your note taking.*

Topic:

a. fifty-minute lectures

b. signal words and phrases

c. college lecturers

3. Developing the ability to concentrate is an important study skill. Keep your mind on what you're doing and try hard to ignore distractions. Remove the telephone and the television set, and try to eliminate any other interruptions. Find a quiet place where you'll be isolated from things that might disturb you. Sometimes low-level noise like instrumental music or a steady flow of traffic helps stimulate concentration. And don't try to study if you are hungry. That's a sure way to break your concentration.†

Topic:

a. developing the ability to concentrate

b. low-level noise

c. eliminating interruptions

4. As I looked back and evaluated my own college training, I saw that the training and experience I had had in public speaking had been of more practical value to me in business—and in life—than everything else I had studied in college all put together. Why? Because it had wiped out my timidity[1] and lack of self-confidence and given me the courage and assurance to deal with people. It had also made clear that leadership usually gravitates[2] to the man who can get up and say what he thinks.‡

Topic:

a. college

b. public speaking

c. courage

---

1. **timidity:** shyness

2. **gravitates:** moves toward; is attracted to

---

* Adapted from Walter Pauk and John Fiore, *Succeed in College!* (Boston: Houghton Mifflin Co., 2000), 38.

† Adapted from Sharon Sherman and Alan Sherman, *Essential Concepts of Chemistry* (Boston: Houghton Mifflin Co., 1999), xxxi.

‡ Excerpted from Dale Carnegie, *How to Stop Worrying and Start Living* (New York: Pocket Books, 1984), xvi.

5. The tragedy involving thirteen-year-old Brittanie Cecil, who was hit and killed by a flying puck at a hockey game, could have been prevented. American hockey stadiums, like those in Europe, need to install protective netting. Even fans who are alertly watching the game cannot dodge a puck traveling 100 miles per hour, so nets would protect spectators from getting injured or killed. Some fans of the game argue that nets are difficult to see through or distracting. But in Europe, where nets are common, they are barely visible. So protective netting should be mandatory[1] in order to prevent any more deaths or injuries.

Topic:

a. hockey

b. protective nets for hockey stadiums

c. hockey fans

Exercise **2.12**

Now, read each paragraph again and write a check mark in the blank beside the correct main idea in the list.

1. In any subject, learning is enhanced when we ask questions. And there are no dumb questions. To master math and science, ask whatever questions will aid your understanding. Students come to higher education with varying backgrounds in these subjects. What you need to ask may not be the same as for the other people in your class.*

Main Idea:

_____ Asking questions helps students learn.

_____ Students' questions are very different.

_____ Math and science are tough subjects to master.

2. Most college lecturers speak about 120 words per minute. In a fifty-minute lecture, you hear up to 6,000 words expressing ideas, facts, and details. To make sure that students understand the ideas, facts, and details they are presenting, lecturers use signal words and phrases. Signal words help lecturers convey important information. Some signal words and phrases include *to illustrate, before/after, furthermore, as a result,* and *more importantly.* Being able to recognize signal words and phrases will

---

1. **mandatory:** required

---

* Adapted from Dave Ellis, *Becoming a Master Student* (Boston: Houghton Mifflin Co., 2000), 181.

improve your reading, writing, speaking, and listening, as well as your note taking.*

Main Idea:

_____ Most college lectures last for fifty minutes.

_____ Signal words and phrases help students better understand lectures.

_____ Most college lecturers speak too quickly.

3. Developing the ability to concentrate is an important study skill. Keep your mind on what you're doing and try hard to ignore distractions. Remove the telephone and the television set, and try to eliminate any other interruptions. Find a quiet place where you'll be isolated from things that might disturb you. Sometimes low-level noise like instrumental music or a steady flow of traffic helps stimulate concentration. And don't try to study if you are hungry. That's a sure way to break your concentration.†

Main Idea:

_____ The ability to concentrate can be developed.

_____ Interruptions are sure ways to break your concentration.

_____ Hunger inhibits effective studying.

4. As I looked back and evaluated my own college training, I saw that the training and experience I had had in public speaking had been of more practical value to me in business—and in life—than everything else I had studied in college all put together. Why? Because it had wiped out my timidity and lack of self-confidence and given me the courage and assurance to deal with people. It had also made clear that leadership usually gravitates to the man who can get up and say what he thinks.‡

Main Idea:

_____ College training is invaluable.

_____ Public speaking is a practical and valuable skill.

_____ Saying what you think is the key to effective leadership.

5. The tragedy involving thirteen-year-old Brittanie Cecil, who was hit and killed by a flying puck at a hockey game, could have been prevented. American hockey stadiums, like those in Europe, need to install protective

---

* Adapted from Walter Pauk and John Fiore, *Succeed in College!* (Boston: Houghton Mifflin Co., 2000), 38.

† Adapted from Sharon Sherman and Alan Sherman, *Essential Concepts of Chemistry* (Boston: Houghton Mifflin Co., 1999), xxi.

‡ Excerpted from Dale Carnegie, *How to Stop Worrying and Start Living* (New York: Pocket Books, 1984), xvi.

netting. Even fans who are alertly watching the game cannot dodge a puck traveling 100 miles per hour, so nets would protect spectators from getting injured or killed. Some fans of the game argue that nets are difficult to see through or distracting. But in Europe, where nets are common, they are barely visible. So protective netting should be mandatory in order to prevent any more deaths or injuries.

Main idea:

_____ Hockey is a very dangerous game.

_____ Hockey stadiums need to install nets to protect fans.

_____ Hockey fans are very safety-conscious.

The Topic Sentence

The **topic sentence** *is the single statement that presents the main point or idea of the paragraph.* Topic sentences have two parts: they state the topic, and they state what the author has to say about that topic. Writers do not have to include such a sentence. Chapter 4 of this book will discuss in more detail paragraphs that lack a topic sentence. However, writers often include a topic sentence to help readers quickly and easily see the main idea.

To find the topic sentence, look for the most general statement in the paragraph and then make sure the other sentences all offer information or details. See if you can locate the topic sentence in the following paragraph:

> The concept of fitness is evolving. Rather than focusing only on miles run or weight lifted, instructors, coaches, and consumers are pursuing a broader vision of total fitness that encompasses wellness and wholeness. A key trend in fitness is blending traditional forms of exercise with popular mind-body approaches such as yoga and Pilates.*

If you chose the first sentence, you're right. That statement expresses the paragraph's main idea and the rest of the paragraph explains that idea.

Exercise **2.13**

For each of the following paragraphs, write the correct topic on the blank provided. Write on the second blank provided the number of the sentence that expresses the main idea.

1. (1) Cheating in high school is very common. (2) Three out of every four high school students admit to breaking the rules by cheating on a test

---

* Hales, Diane. *An Invitation to Wellness: Making Healthy Choices.* Belmont: Thomson Higher Education, 2007. Print. p.42.

at least once. **(3)** Seventy-five percent of students have also confessed to handing in work that was completed by someone else. **(4)** A quarter of all students say they've been dishonest by working with others when they were instructed to work by themselves.

Topic: _____

Topic Sentence: _____

2. **(1)** Teenagers are master rationalizers.[1] **(2)** Some say that sports and other activities interfered with homework. **(3)** They also claim that they cheated because the assignment seemed meaningless or boring. **(4)** Many cited the pressure to get good grades. **(5)** Indeed, to many of these kids, high school seems like a tedious hurdle. **(6)** Once in college, though, many students appear to start taking school more seriously, at least when classes seem relevant to their goals. **(7)** They say, "I've never cheated in my major, but when it comes to general education requirements—those courses don't matter."*

Topic: _____

Topic Sentence: _____

3. **(1)** Patterns set in college influence lifelong activity levels. **(2)** In a survey of 367 alumni who graduated 2 to 10 years previously from a southern university, more than half of those who had exercised regularly in college were even more physically active. **(3)** The irregular exercisers were more likely to remain at the same or a lower level of activity. **(4)** The nonexercisers tended to become less active after graduation.†

Topic: _____

Topic Sentence: _____

Locations of Topic Sentences

Main ideas are often stated in the first sentence of the paragraph. However, they can appear in other places in a paragraph, too. Writers sometimes place the topic sentence in the middle of a paragraph or even at the end.

1. **rationalizers:** people who come up with self-satisfying but incorrect reasons for their behavior

---

* Examples 1 and 2 excerpts in Exercise 2.13 adapted from Emily Sohn, "The Young and the Virtueless," *U.S. News and World Report*, www.usnews.com/usnews/issue/010521/education/cheating.b.htm. Used by permission.

† Hales, Dianne. *An Invitation to Wellness: Making Healthy Choices.* Belmont: Thomson Higher Education, 2007. Print. p. 44.

Topic Sentence as First Sentence

It's very common for writers to announce the main idea in the first sentence of the paragraph. Then, the remainder of the paragraph explains why the reader should accept that point. In the following paragraph, for example, the topic sentence, which is in boldface type, is at the beginning.

> **Newspapers have definite advantages over other sources of information.** The wonderful thing about the newspaper is that all the work is done for you. There is nothing to turn on, nothing to search for, nothing between you and the information. Somebody else has already categorized, organized, edited, and condensed[1] the information for you in a form easily handled and assimilated.[2] Another great thing about the newspaper is it brings the family together. Different sections of the paper can be parceled[3] out to members of the family. There is something wonderful about the habit of a family reading and digesting the daily newspaper. Ideas are shared, opinions voiced, and lives and deaths verified.*

Topic Sentence as Second or Third Sentence

Sometimes, though, a writer needs to present a sentence or two of introductory information before stating the main point. This means that the topic sentence might occur in the second or third sentence of the paragraph. Take a look at this example:

> As much as 80 percent of Internet websites include inaccurate information. If you're doing research, how do you make sure the information you find is true? **You can examine certain parts of a website to evaluate its reliability.** Websites with addresses that include *.org, .gov,* or *.edu* are usually accurate. Websites that give the sources of their information, too, tend to be more trustworthy. Also, look for identification of the site's creators as well as contact information for those people.

The main idea is "You can examine certain parts of a website to evaluate its reliability" because most of the paragraph is about those parts. However, the writer includes some background information and a question at the beginning of the paragraph. Both of these sentences lead up to the topic sentence in the third statement.

1. **condensed:** shortened
2. **assimilated:** absorbed
3. **parceled:** divided

---

* Adapted from Joe Saltzman, "Too Much Information, Too Little Time," *USA Today,* September 1997, 67. Reprinted with permission from USA Today Magazine, Sept. 1997. Copyright © 1997 by the Society for the Advancement of Education, Inc. All Rights Reserved.

Topic Sentence in the Middle

A topic sentence can also appear somewhere in the middle of the paragraph. For example, read the following paragraph:

> An old saying in business claims that 80 percent of a company's profits come from 20 percent of its customers. That's why Centura Bank ranks its 650,000 customers on a scale of one to five. Those with the best ratings get better customer service. **This company and others are beginning to concentrate more on their best customers.** Continental Airlines, for instance, plans to give its agents access to each customer's history so they can give the best service to their top clients. First Union Bank codes its credit card customers. When a person calls for service, the bank's representatives know when they're talking to one of their best patrons.*

This paragraph begins with an introductory statement in the first sentence. Then, the second sentence offers the first of three examples given to explain the main idea in the fourth sentence. After the main idea is stated, the paragraph offers two more examples.

Topic Sentence as Last Sentence

A writer might choose to save the topic sentence for the end of the paragraph, offering it as the last sentence. This next paragraph is an example of one that builds up to the main point:

> People who attend religious services more than once a week live seven years longer than people who never attend religious services. Spiritual people also recover more quickly from surgery. Regular church-goers are less likely to have heart disease or high blood pressure. They have lower rates of depression and anxiety, too. **Obviously, being faithful has positive health benefits.**†

In this paragraph, the writer offers all of her explanations first. Then, she summarizes the point in a topic sentence at the paragraph's end.

Topic Sentence as First and Last Sentence

Finally, the topic sentence might occur twice: once at the beginning of the paragraph and then again, in different words, at the end. Writers often restate the topic sentence to emphasize or reinforce the main idea for the reader. Here is an example:

> **Jigsaw puzzles, created in the 1760s, are still a popular pastime.** Thirty million jigsaw puzzles were sold in 2000. Eighty percent of

---

* Adapted from Diane Brady, "Why Service Stinks," *Reader's Digest,* May 2001, 161–68.
† Adapted from Elena Serocki, "Heaven Can Wait," *Reader's Digest,* May 2001, 112.

2

American homes contain a jigsaw puzzle for adults. Eighty-three percent of American homes contain at least one child's jigsaw puzzle.
There's even a National Jigsaw Puzzle Championship every year. This
contest offers puzzle enthusiasts[1] $10,000 in prizes. **It's clear that
many people still enjoy this centuries-old hobby.***

This paragraph identifies the main point in the first sentence, offers explanation, and then makes the same point again in the final sentence.

Steps for Locating the Topic Sentence

To find the topic sentence regardless of location, look for the most general
statement in the paragraph. Then, verify that the rest of the sentences in the
paragraph offer information, details, or explanation for that general idea.
Here's a specific step-by-step procedure you can follow when you're trying to
determine the main idea and topic sentence in a paragraph:

Step 1: Read over the entire paragraph to get an idea of the subject matter included.

Step 2: Read the first sentence to see if it gives a general picture of the
entire paragraph. If it doesn't, it may provide some general background or contrasting information. Or the first sentence may pose a
question that the next few sentences go on to answer.

Step 3: If the first sentence does not state the main idea, read the last
sentence to see if it gives a general picture of the entire paragraph.
Turn the last sentence into a question, and then see if the other sentences in the paragraph answer that question. If they do, that last
sentence may be the topic sentence.

Step 4: If either the first or the last sentence gives that general overview of
the paragraph, the main idea, you have found your topic sentence.

Step 5: If neither the first nor the last sentence is identified as the topic
sentence, then you must evaluate each sentence in the middle of the
paragraph to see if one of the sentences states the general idea or the
main idea information. Test each possibility by turning it into a question and then determining if the other sentences in the paragraph
answer that question.

Step 6: Once the topic sentence is located, then you must look for the
general phrase located in the topic sentence that states the overall
main idea.

1. **enthusiasts:** fans

* Adapted from John Tierney, "Playing with the Puzzle People," *Reader's Digest,* May 2001, 118–23.

Exercise **2.14**

Below each paragraph, write on the blank provided the number of the sentence(s) that state(s) the main idea.

1. **(1)** The atmosphere in Escalante's room was much like that in the locker room at a football game. **(2)** Class began with warm-up exercises. **(3)** All the students slapped their hands against their desks and stomped their feet on the floor in rhythm while chanting an opening ritual. **(4)** When attention dropped, Escalante would begin the "wave," a cheer in which row after row of students, in succession,[1] stood, raising their hands, then sat quickly, creating a ripple across the room like a pennant[2] billowing in victory. **(5)** The intensity of drills and quizzes was relieved with jokes, demonstrations, and an occasional round of volleyball. **(6)** Just as the classroom clock never registered the correct time, the routine usually varied, keeping the team alert and focused.*

   Topic Sentence: _____

2. **(1)** Many young children and adults believe supplements[3] will make them faster and stronger. **(2)** In reality, people who take steroids[4] are jeopardizing their health. **(3)** Steroid use puts people at greater risk for heart attacks and strokes, increases aggressiveness, and stunts[5] growth for both genders. **(4)** It also can lead to a number of sexual side effects in males, including breast development, premature balding, testicular atrophy,[6] and decreased sperm count. **(5)** Many of these side effects are irreversible.†

   Topic Sentence: _____

3. **(1)** Cell phones are pulling drivers' attention from the road. **(2)** Navigation systems and e-mail are already available in vehicles. **(3)** Audio systems are becoming more complicated to operate. **(4)** Automakers are installing

---

1. **succession:** one after another

2. **pennant:** flag

3. **supplements:** products people eat or drink to become larger or stronger

4. **steroids:** supplements that some people take to improve their physical performance

5. **stunts:** decreases or stops

6. **atrophy:** wasting away or deterioration

---

* From Ann Byers, *Jaime Escalante: Sensational Teacher* (Springfield, NJ: Enslow Publishers, 1996).

† Adapted from Joe Biden, "Baseball Drug Testing Needs to Get Beyond First Base," *USA Today*, March 8, 2004, 13A. Copyright © 2004, USA Today. Reprinted with Permission.

all kinds of potential distractions in cars. (5) There are customized information services that shower drivers with news items and shopping tips. (6) There are TVs in the backseats, too.*

Topic Sentence: _____

4. (1) In the old days, kids headed off to camp with a few postcards. (2) Now a laptop might do better. (3) In today's world of camping, kids don't leave technology behind when they go off to summer camp. (4) According to Peg Smith, executive director of the American Camping Association, about 70 percent of summer camps are online and many allow e-mail. (5) Some also post daily shows of activities on websites; a few even have live webcams.

Topic Sentence: _____

5. (1) Although he is one of the highest-paid ball players in history, he always takes the time to sign autographs for kids at the ball field. (2) He has his own charity organization, to which he devotes a lot of time. (3) He talks about his great family in interviews, and how much he loves his mother, father, and younger sister. (4) And he's a great fielder and hitter. (5) That's what makes Derek Jeter one of the most popular professional athletes in America today.

Topic Sentence: _____

Exercise 2.15

Following each paragraph, write on the blank provided the number of the sentence that is the topic sentence.

1. (1) Stress is hard to define because it means different things to different people. (2) However, stress is usually a negative reaction, either mental or physical, to some demand (a force, a pressure, or a strain) placed upon an individual. (3) This negative reaction can take the form of worry, anxiety, and irritability. (4) It can disrupt concentration and interfere with good decision making. (5) The negative reaction can take the form of physical problems such as increased blood pressure, headaches, muscle tension, and insomnia.[1]

Topic Sentence: _____

1. **insomnia:** sleeplessness

---

* Adapted from Dann McCosh, "Driven to Distraction," *Popular Science*, December 2001, 86.

2. **(1)** Many people cope with stress in unhealthy ways. **(2)** Some use alcohol or drugs to escape or calm themselves down. **(3)** Some take up smoking to soothe their nerves. **(4)** Some people refuse to deal with problems through avoidance or procrastination.[1] **(5)** Others overeat. **(6)** Still others allow themselves to burn out, give up, and succumb[2] to depression. **(7)** And some people allow themselves to become angry and withdrawn.

Topic Sentence: _____

3. **(1)** Other people deal with stress by engaging in aerobic exercise, which can reduce anxiety by up to 50 percent. **(2)** They make sure they get proper nutrition, eating the right foods to improve their ability to respond to stress. **(3)** They get an adequate amount of sleep every night. **(4)** They reduce their intake of caffeine and give up smoking. **(5)** These methods are the healthy physical ways to cope with stress.

Topic Sentence: _____

4. **(1)** Another good way to counteract stress is to meditate. **(2)** Taking just 10 to 20 minutes a day for quiet reflection often brings relief from stress. **(3)** You can also use visualization, using your imagination to picture in your mind how to manage a stressful situation more successfully. **(4)** These and other mental strategies are good stress management techniques. **(5)** For example, you can decide to be more realistic about how many obligations[3] you can take on at one time, and you can give up the idea that you can reach perfection in everything you do.

Topic Sentence: _____

Reading Strategy:
Creating an Effective Reading Environment

If you're like most students, you probably read both at home and outside your home: perhaps somewhere on your college campus and maybe even at work during your breaks. Your reading environment can greatly affect your comprehension, so give some thought to how you can create or select the right reading environments. The right environment allows you to stay alert and to focus all of your concentration on the text, especially when it's a challenging one.

1. **procrastination:** put things off

2. **succumb:** give in

3. **obligations:** duties or responsibilities

When you're at home, you can usually create effective conditions for reading. You might want to designate a particular place—a desk or table, for example—where you always read. Make sure the place you choose is well lit, and sit in a chair that requires you to sit upright. Reading in a chair that's too soft and comfortable tends to make you sleepy! Keep your active reading tools (pens, highlighter markers, notebook or paper) and a dictionary close at hand.

Before you sit down for a reading session, try to minimize all potential *external distractions*. Turn off your phone, the television, and the radio. Notify your family members or roommates that you'll be unavailable for a while. If necessary, put a "Do not disturb" sign on your door! The more interruptions you must deal with while you read, the harder it will be to keep your attention on the task at hand.

Overcoming **internal distractions**, *which are the thoughts, worries, plans, daydreams, and other types of mental "noise" inside your own head, is often even more challenging for readers*. However, it's important to develop strategies for dealing with them, too. If you don't, they will inhibit you from concentrating on what you are reading. Internal distractions will also prevent you from absorbing the information you need to learn. You can try to ignore these thoughts, but they will usually continue trying to intrude. So how do you temporarily silence them so you can devote your full attention to your reading? Instead of fighting them, try focusing completely on these thoughts for a short period of time. For 5 or 10 minutes, allow yourself to sit and think about your job, your finances, your car problems, your boyfriend or girlfriend, the paper you need to write, or whatever else is on your mind. Better yet, write these thoughts down. To empty your mind onto a piece of paper, try a freewriting exercise, which involves quickly writing your thoughts on paper without censoring them or worrying about grammar and spelling. If you can't stop thinking about all of the other things you need to do, devote 10 minutes to writing a detailed "to-do" list. Giving all of your attention to distracting thoughts will often clear your mind so you can focus on your reading.

If you're reading somewhere other than at home (on your college campus, for instance), it will be more difficult to achieve ideal reading conditions. However, you can still search for places that have the right characteristics. First of all, find a location—such as the library—that is well lit and quiet. Try to sit at an individual study carrel[1] so you can block out external distractions. If no carrels are available, choose a table that's out of the flow of traffic, and sit with your back to others so you're not tempted to watch their comings and goings. If you must read in a more distracting place, like your college cafeteria or a bench on the

Continued

---

1. **study carrel:** cubicle or boxed-in area in which to study

grounds, you might want to get in the habit of carrying a pair of ear-plugs in your book bag so you can reduce external noise. Finally, don't forget to keep your active reading tools and dictionary with you so you'll have them on hand no matter where you end up reading.

Read and answer the following questions:

1. Where were you when you read this information about creating an effective reading environment? Describe your surroundings.

   _____

   _____

2. Is this the place where you do most of your reading? If not, where do you usually read?

   _____

   _____

3. What external distractions pulled your attention from the book as you read?

   _____

   _____

4. Could you have done anything to prevent these external distractions from happening?

   _____

   _____

5. Did you battle any internal distractions as you read? Briefly describe the thoughts that intruded upon your concentration.

   _____

   _____

6. Based on the information in this section, where could you create the most ideal environment for reading? What objects and/or procedures will you need to create that environment?

   _____

   _____

http://www.ucc.vt.edu/stdysk/studydis.html

This website will help you to evaluate three different places where you might want to study. After you take the quick survey, this site will choose which study environment will be the most beneficial to you.

Reading Selections

Practicing the Active Reading Strategy:

■ Before and While You Read

You can use active reading strategies before, while, and after you read a selection. The following are some suggestions for active reading strategies that you can employ before you read and as you are reading.

1. Skim the selection for any unfamiliar words. Circle or highlight any words you do not know.

2. As you read, underline, highlight, or circle important words or phrases.

3. Write down any questions about the selection if you are confused by the information presented.

4. Jot notes in the margin to help you understand the material.

NEWSPAPER READING: SOCIOLOGY

Is Gossip Beneficial or Harmful?

by Dr. Offra Gerstein

Do you like to gossip? Have you ever been hurt by gossip? The reading selection that follows explores some good and bad reasons to gossip. The author also offers some suggestions for dealing with gossip.

1   Gossip, the practice of sharing information about other people's lives, is familiar to all of us. We enjoy this form of idle talk and are often unaware of its harm.

2   The origins of gossip date to early man. Primitive societies used negative information to damage the reputation of their rivals and defeat them. In Old English, gossip evolved from "god-sibb." This word referred to a close female friend present at the birth of a child. This woman would assume the role of a godparent. She listened to the new mother and served as her confidant. Later, the term evolved to describe friends' intimate sharing of personal information. It further expanded to the current use of talk about a person not present.

3   If your mother tells you that gossiping is bad, she is right. If researchers inform you that gossip is unavoidable and beneficial, they too are right. The distinction is between "good" and "bad" gossip. As psychologist James Lynch puts it: "Human dialogue can be a great healer or a great destroyer."

2

4   According to researchers, gossip has some benefits. Exchanging information can create a healthy connection. It can build rules for acceptable and unacceptable behavior. It can improve society.

5   Similarly, gossip is useful in the business world. Gossip researcher Professor Frank McAndrew says, "If people are talking about good things others do, we want to emulate that good behavior. It is a nice way of socially controlling people." When a company faces bad times, gossip about the future of the employees can reduce fear and uncertainty. It can also create a feeling of fellowship.

6   However, bad gossip, the negative talk about other people's lives, can be destructive. Disappointingly enough, the researchers spend little time on this form of malice. People engage in negative gossip for several reasons. They may do it to bond with another person. They may do it to pass the time or to deny problems. They may gossip to build themselves up through comparisons with others, or they may want to hurt others.

7   Bonding with another individual brings pleasure, even when it is done at the expense of someone else. People who criticize someone else feel superior to the criticized person. "We think that what she did is outrageous. We would never do anything like this to anyone." This false feeling of superiority temporarily raises the level of self-esteem of the "gossipers." For those who compare themselves with others to create better self-esteem, the practice of knocking others becomes an unfortunate habit.

8   Another use of gossip for emotional connection is the revealing of confidential information. If someone told us a secret, we share it with another person to gain the listener's friendship while *betraying* the holder of the secret. Some people ask the listener to promise not to further relate the secret. And thus begins the chain of evil betrayal.

9   Gossip also serves as a nondemanding way of engaging in idle talk. It is an activity to pass the time with someone. It requires no strain on the brain. We can just pass judgments on what the neighbors are doing as a form of entertainment.

10   For some people, gossip is a way to avoid dealing with their own problems by concentrating on how poorly others solve theirs. It is a way to avoid criticism or even appreciation from others. When we focus on what others should do better, we are free from becoming accountable for ourselves.

11   Some people use gossip to harm others. This is terrible behavior. It is never justified.

12   Ancient Indian mythology considers gossip a form of mental illness. Religions hate and forbid it. Psychoanalysts report that gossip is harmful to the individual. It creates many emotional problems, such as suspicion, fear, mistrust, and depression. Gossip is poison to one's soul and destroys friendships and relationships.

13   Feeling "better than" or "less than" other people is a tragic way to

understand one's worth. Self-esteem must come from within the individual. It must be based on one's character and on actions that lead to self-respect.

14   To deal with gossip better:

- Create healthy ways of connecting with others that do not require negative talk about someone else.

- When you are told something about another person, ask for proof of the information. If you trust what is said without challenging its truth, you become a partner in spreading gossip.

- If you hear negative talk, refuse to listen and politely attempt to stop the speaker.

- Ask the "gossiper" to tell you positive things about the individual he is criticizing.

- When you are entrusted with a secret, feel honored and never repeat it to anyone. Repeating confidences is like stealing one's dignity.

- Feel free to share positive gossip with others. But make sure your facts are correct.

- It may be enjoyable to bond with someone temporarily through gossip. However, the damage to all parties is enormous. Resist the temptation and gain a wholesome sense of self-respect.*

■ Vocabulary

Read the following questions about some of the vocabulary words that appear in the previous selection. Then circle the letter of the correct answer to each question.

1. "We enjoy this form of *idle* talk and are often unaware of its harm." (paragraph 1) What does *idle* mean?

   a. important

   b. unimportant

   c. distracting

   d. sad

2. A *confidant* (paragraph 2) is

   a. someone to whom one tells private information.

   b. someone to fear.

   c. someone to avoid.

   d. someone to admire.

3. If you *emulate* behavior (paragraph 5) you

   a. imitate it.

   b. criticize it.

   c. do not notice it.

   d. destroy it.

---

* "Is Gossip Beneficial or Harmful?" by Offra Gerstein as appeared in the *Santa Cruz Sentinel,* January 18, 2004. Reprinted by permission of Offra Gerstein.

4. What is *malice* (paragraph 6)?

   a. conversation   c. bad attitude

   b. thirst for danger   d. desire to harm others

5. Information that is *confidential* (paragraph 8) is

   a. important.   c. secret.

   b. complicated.   d. dangerous.

■ Reading Skills

Respond to each of the following questions by circling the letter of the correct answer.

1. The topic of paragraph 2 is

   a. primitive man.

   b. the origins of gossip.

   c. Old English.

   d. friends' sharing of information.

2. What is the topic of paragraph 6?

   a. bad gossip

   b. gossip researchers

   c. negative talk

   d. hurting others

3. What is the main idea of paragraph 7?

   a. Some people gossip to bond with others or to feel better about themselves.

   b. People love having a false sense of superiority.

   c. People who gossip have high self-esteem.

   d. Gossip is always bad.

4. What is the topic sentence of paragraph 8?

   a. the first sentence

   b. the second sentence

   c. the third sentence

   d. the fourth sentence

5. What is the main idea of paragraph 9?

   a. Gossip is fun.

   b. Gossip is destructive.

   c. Gossip makes us feel connected.

   d. Gossip is a way to pass the time.

2

Practicing the Active Reading Strategy:

■ After You Read

Now that you have read the selection, answer the following questions, using the active reading strategies that you learned in Chapter 1.

1. Identify and write down the point and purpose of this reading selection.

2. Besides the vocabulary words included in the exercise, are there any other vocabulary words that are unfamiliar to you? Can you figure out the meaning from the context of the passage? If not, look up each word in a dictionary and find the definition that best describes the word as it is used in the selection. You may want to write the definition in the margin next to the word in the passage for future reference.

3. Predict any possible questions that may be used on a test about the content of this selection.

■ Questions for Discussion and Writing

Answer the following questions based on your reading of the selection.

1. Do you agree or disagree with the statement "Bonding with another individual brings pleasure, even when it is done at the expense of someone else"? Why? _____

   _____

2. Do you agree that some gossip can be positive? Why or why not?

   _____

   _____

3. List any new information you learned from this selection. Did you find the selection interesting? Why or why not? _____

   _____

2

Practicing the Active Reading Strategy

■ Before and While You Read

You can use active reading strategies before, while, and after you read a selection. The following are some suggestions for active reading strategies that you can employ before you read and as you are reading.

1. Skim the selection for any unfamiliar words. Circle or highlight any words you do not know.

2. As you read, underline, highlight, or circle important words or phrases.

3. Write down any questions about the selection if you are confused by the information presented.

4. Jot notes in the margin to help you understand the material.

BIOGRAPHY:
My Life

by Golda Meir

Golda Meir was born in Russia, but emigrated to Milwaukee, Wisconsin, when she was a small girl. She became a teacher and taught in the Milwaukee public schools. After her marriage, she emigrated to Palestine where she and her husband worked on a farm. She went on to become prime minister of Israel, the first woman to do so in Israel and only the third woman in the world to hold such a position.

1   I started school in a huge, fortress-like[1] building on Fourth Street near Milwaukee's famous Schlitz beer factory, and I loved it. I can't remember how long it took me to learn English (at home, of course, we spoke Yiddish,[2] and luckily, so did almost everyone else on Walnut Street), but I have no recollection of the language ever being a real problem for me, so I must have picked it up quickly. I made friends quickly, too. Two of those early first- or second-grade friends remained friends all my life, and both live in Israel now. One was Regina Hamburger (today Medzini), who lived on our street and who was to leave America when I did; the other was Sarah Feder, who became one of the leaders of Labor Zionism[3] in the United States. . . .

---

1. **fortress-like:** like a fort prepared for military action

2. **Yiddish:** language of European Jews

3. **Labor Zionism:** The Labor Zionist Party was committed to the development of a democratic-socialist political economy in Israel.

2   More than fifty years later—when I was seventy-one and a prime minister—I went back to that school for a few hours. It had not changed very much in all those years except that the vast majority of its pupils were now black, not Jewish, as in 1906. They welcomed me as though I were a queen. Standing in rows on the creaky old stage I remembered so well, freshly scrubbed and neat as pins, they serenaded me with Yiddish and Hebrew songs and raised their voices to peal out the Israeli anthem "Hatikvah" which made my eyes fill with tears. Each one of the classrooms had been beautifully decorated with posters about Israel and signs reading SHALOM[1] (one of the children thought it was my family name), and when I entered the school, two little girls wearing headbands with Stars of David on them solemnly presented me with an enormous white rose made of tissue paper and pipe cleaners, which I wore all day and carefully carried back to Israel with me.

3   Another of the gifts I got that day in 1971 from the Fourth Street School was a record of my grades for one of the years I had spent there: 95 in reading, 90 in spelling, 95 in arithmetic, 85 in music, and a mysterious 90 in something called manual arts. Which I cannot remember at all. But when the children asked me to talk to them for a few minutes, it was not about book learning that I chose to speak. I had learned a lot more than fractions or how to spell at Fourth Street, and I decided to tell those eager, attentive children—born as I myself had been, into a minority and living, as I myself had lived, without much extravagance (to put it mildly)—what the gist of that learning had been. "It isn't really important to decide when you are very young just exactly what you want to become when you grow up," I told them. "It is much more important to decide on the way you want to live. If you are going to get involved with causes which are good for others, not only for yourselves, then it seems to me that that is sufficient, and maybe what you will be is only a matter of chance." I had a feeling that they understood me.*

■ Vocabulary

Read the following questions about some of the vocabulary words that appear in the previous selection. Then circle the letter of the correct answer.

1. When something is *creaky,* what does that mean? (paragraph 2) "standing in rows on the *creaky* old stage I remembered so well . . ."

   a. new

   b. eerie

   c. old; in disrepair

   d. fantastic

---

1. **shalom:** peace; a traditional Jewish greeting or farewell

---

* Excerpt from *My Life* by Golda Meir. Reprinted by permission of Weidenfeld & Nicolson, a division of The Orion Publishing Group, as the Publisher.

2. One sentence includes these words: "they *serenaded* me with Yiddish and Hebrew songs and raised their voices" (paragraph 2). What does the word *serenade* mean?

   a. recited   c. spoke

   b. sang   d. danced

3. One sentence includes these words: "and raised their voices to *peal* out the Israeli anthem" (paragraph 2). What does the word *peal* mean in this context?

   a. ring   c. pretend

   b. say softly   d. remove

4. One sentence includes these words: "born as I myself had been, into a minority and living, as I myself had lived, without much *extravagance*" (paragraph 3). What does the word *extravagance* mean in this context?

   a. abundance or wealth   c. willfulness

   b. poverty   d. hopefulness

5. What is the *gist* of something? One sentence includes these words: "what the *gist* of that learning had been" (paragraph 3).

   a. despair   c. central idea

   b. hope   d. miscommunication

■ Reading Skills

Respond to each of the following questions by circling the letter of the correct answer.

1. What is the topic of paragraph 1?

   a. learning to speak English

   b. Regina Hamburger

   c. early years at school in Milwaukee

   d. making friends

2. What is the main idea of paragraph 2?

   a. Golda Meir visited her grade school after 50 years away.

   b. The students were happy to meet Golda Meir.

   c. Gold Meir was happy and proud to return to her grade school.

   d. There are different types of students who attend the school today.

3. What is the main idea of paragraph 3?

    a. Golda Meir received her old report card.

    b. Golda Meir spoke to the children.

    c. Gold Meir shared her lessons about life with the students.

    d. Golda Meir spoke about the importance of education.

Practicing the Active Reading Strategy

■ After You Read

Now that you have read the selection, answer the following questions using the active reading strategies that you learned in Chapter 1.

1. Identify and write down the point and purpose of this reading selection.

2. Did you circle or highlight any words that are unfamiliar to you? Can you figure out the meaning from the context of the passage? If not, look up each word in a dictionary and find the definition that best describes the word as it is used in the selection. You may want to write the definition in the margin next to the word in the passage for future reference.

3. Predict any possible questions that may be used on a test about the content of this selection.

■ Questions for Discussion and Writing

Answer the following questions based on your reading of the selection.

1. What did you know about Golda Meir before reading this selection?

    _____

    _____

2. Based on your reading of the selection, what do you know about Golda Meir's childhood? Her adult life? _____

    _____

3. Based on your reading of the selection, what else would you like to learn about Golda Meir? _____

    _____

2

Practicing the Active Reading Strategy

■ Before and While You Read

You can use active reading strategies before, while, and after you read a selection. The following are some suggestions for active reading strategies that you can employ before you read and as you are reading.

1. Skim the selection for any unfamiliar words. Circle or highlight any words you do not know.

2. As you read, underline, highlight, or circle important words or phrases.

3. Write down any questions about the selection if you are confused by the information presented.

4. Jot notes in the margin to help you understand the material.

TEXTBOOK READING: CULINARY ARTS
Foodservice at Sporting Events

What is your favorite food to eat at a football game or a baseball game? The following brief reading selection discusses the wide variety of food available today at sporting events. Students who choose careers in culinary arts or hospitality might read a passage such as this in their course work.

1 At least since the first strains of "Take Me Out to the Ball Game" were played and probably long before, certain foods have been linked to sporting events. Peanuts, popcorn, and hot dogs have been part of American sports for decades. But contemporary athletic facilities—football and baseball stadiums, basketball arenas, and even track fields—are now providing contemporary foodservice options to their customers. No longer limited to the traditional concession stands, today's sports facilities offer a wide variety of foodservice outposts, including all-you-can-eat pavilions and luxury suites. Sure, fans can still get a bratwurst or a sack of peanuts, but today they can also get almost anything else. For example, the Kansas City Royals' Kauffman Stadium offers such diverse options as malt shop banana splits, smoked Kansas City strip loin, and almost anything in between.

2 Some major participants in this type of foodservice, known as stadium contract feeding, include Levy Restaurants, Aramark, Custom Food Services, and Compass North America. These companies often provide not only general concession services to their customers, but premium catering services as well. These categories are sometimes divided between two vendors. For instance, the Cleveland Browns contract with Sportservice for general concessions

and with Levy Restaurants for premium foodservice in the stadium's luxury suites. But foodservice is not limited to game days. Many stadiums, arenas, and other facilities offer catering options to customers for weddings, birthday parties, or dances on days when no game is scheduled.

3   Although many national chains such as McDonald's, Quizno's, and Pizza Hut are frequently represented at sporting events, significant efforts are often made to involve local restaurants in concessions. Montgomery Inn Barbecue is available to fans of both the Cincinnati Reds and the Cleveland Browns, while fans of the Washington Nationals can enjoy Ben's Chili. Teams receive a percentage of foodservice profits, typically ranging between 40 to 45 percent. Some teams, like the New England Patriots, control their own concessions outright, and others are taking this concept a step further. For example, the New York Yankees and the Dallas Cowboys recently established Legends Hospitality Management, a joint venture that will not only handle all foodservice for the two teams' stadiums, but will also solicit business form other athletic facilities nationwide.*

■ Vocabulary

Read the following questions about some of the vocabulary words that appear in the previous selection. Try to use the context of the reading selection to circle the letter of the correct answer.

1. "[T]oday's sports facilities offer a wide variety of foodservice outposts, including all-you-can-eat *pavilions* and luxury suites" (paragraph 1). What does *pavilion* mean?

   a. a fast food court

   b. a large, covered area with tables

   c. a sit-down restaurant

   d. bleacher seats

2. "These categories are sometimes divided between two *vendors*" (paragraph 2). What are *vendors*?

   a. ushers   c. waiters

   b. ticket takers   d. sellers

3. What do you do when you *solicit* business? (paragraph 3)

   a. ignore   c. request

   b. help   d. discover

---

* *Foundations of Restaurant Management & Culinary Arts,* Level One. Pearson Education, Inc. 2011. Print. p.10.

2

■ Reading Skills

Respond to each of the following questions by circling the letter of the correct answer.

1. What is the topic of paragraph 1?

    a. the history of food at sporting events

    b. new options at the concession stand at sporting events

    c. what to eat at football games

    d. food at the Kansas City Royals' Kauffman Stadium

2. What is the main idea of paragraph 2?

    a. Stadiums offer both general and premium food service.

    b. Foodservice is available for non-sports events.

    c. Levy Restaurants provides foodservice for luxury suites.

    d. Fans at Cleveland Browns' game eat very well.

3. What is the topic sentence in paragraph 3?

    a. the first sentence

    b. the second sentence

    c. the third sentence

    d. the fourth sentence

Practicing the Active Reading Strategy

■ After You Read

Now that you have read the selection, answer the following questions, using the active reading strategies that you learned in Chapter 1.

1. Identify and write down the point and purpose of this reading selection.

2. Did you circle or highlight any words that are unfamiliar to you? Can you figure out the meaning from the context of the passage? If not, then look up each word in a dictionary and find the definition that best describes the word as it is used in the selection. You may want to write the definition in the margin next to the word in the passage for future reference.

3. Predict any possible test questions that may be used on a test about the content of this selection.

■ Questions for Discussion and Writing

Answer the following questions based on your reading of the selection.

1. Sports arenas are now used for events other than sports. What are some of those events that need foodservice? _____

_____

2. Why would efforts be made to include local restaurants in concessions at sports arenas? _____

_____

3. What improvements in food service could be made at your favorite sports arena? _____

_____

Vocabulary Strategy: Synonyms

Synonyms *are words that have the same, or similar, meanings.* Synonyms serve four purposes in texts. First of all, they add variety to a reading selection. Instead of writing the same word over and over again, authors will use different words with the same meanings to keep sentences lively and interesting. For example, in the paragraph about the Slinky, the author refers to the Slinky as both a *toy* and a *plaything.*

Secondly, authors use synonyms to express their thoughts as precisely as possible. For example, the paragraph about protective netting for hockey stadiums refers to "the recent *tragedy.*" The author could have used the word *situation* or *incident* or *misfortune,* but she used the more specific and emotional word *tragedy,* which clearly communicates how she feels about Brittanie Cecil's death.

A third use of synonyms is to connect ideas and sentences together and to reinforce ideas. Do you remember the paragraph about the reliability of websites? Notice how the italicized words are synonyms that keep the paragraph focused on the main idea:

As many as 80 percent of Internet websites include inaccurate information. If you're doing research, how do you make sure the information you find is *true?* You can examine certain parts of a website to evaluate its *reliability.* Websites with addresses that

2

include *.org, .gov,* or *.edu* are usually ***accurate.*** Websites that give the sources of their information, too, tend to be more ***trustworthy.*** Also, look for identification of the site's creators as well as contact information for those people.

Finally, texts include synonyms to help readers figure out what other words mean. For example, in the sentence below, the author provides a synonym to help the reader understand what the word *inflammation* means:

Smog causes inflammation, or swelling, of the airway, which makes breathing more difficult.

Swelling is another way to say *inflammation,* so it's a synonym used to define a word.

Vocabulary Exercise

The following paragraphs come from examples in this chapter. On the blanks following each paragraph, write two synonyms used in the paragraph for the italicized, boldface word or phrase.

1. ***People who attend religious services*** more than once a week live seven years longer than people who never attend religious services. Spiritual people also recover more quickly from surgery. Regular church-goers are less likely to have heart disease or high blood pressure. They have lower rates of depression and anxiety, too.

   Two synonyms for italicized phrase: _____

2. Single mothers face many ***challenges.*** Their greatest difficulties are usually financial. They are the primary family breadwinners, so their greatest struggles, especially for those who are younger and less educated, often involve making ends meet. To make matters worse, single moms often do not receive regular child support from their children's fathers. They also must curtail their work hours due to childcare limitations, so many can't earn full-time wages.

   Two synonyms for italicized word: _____

2

3. *Cheating* in high school is very common. Three out of every four high school students admit to breaking the rules by cheating on a test at least once. Seventy-five percent of students have also confessed to handing in work that was completed by someone else. A quarter of all students say they've been dishonest by working with others when they were instructed to work by themselves.

Two synonyms for italicized word: _____

4. Developing the ability to concentrate is another important study skill. Keep your mind on what you're doing and try hard to ignore distractions. Remove the telephone and the television set. Try to eliminate any other interruptions. Find a quiet place where you'll be isolated from ***things that might disturb you.*** Sometimes low-level noise like instrumental music or a steady flow of traffic helps stimulate concentration. And don't try to study if you are hungry. That's a sure way to break your concentration.

Two synonyms for the italicized phrase: _____

5. An old saying in business claims that 80 percent of a company's profits come from 20 percent of its ***customers.*** That's why Centura Bank ranks its 650,000 customers on a scale of one to five. Those with the best ratings get better customer service. This company and others are beginning to concentrate more on their best customers. Continental Airlines, for instance, plans to give its agents access to each customer's history so they can give the best service to their top clients. First Union Bank codes its credit card customers. When a person calls for service, the bank's representatives know when they're talking to their best patrons.

Two synonyms for the italicized word: _____

Chapter 2 Review

Write the correct answers on the blanks in the following statements.

1. Paragraphs are composed of _____ and _____ statements.

2. The most general sentence in the paragraph expresses its _____, the idea or point the writer wants you to know or to believe.

3. The sentence that states the writer's main idea is called the _____.

4. The topic sentence has two parts: the _____, or subject, of the paragraph and what the writer wants to say about that topic.

5. The topic sentence can occur anywhere in the _____.

6. The right study environment allows you to stay _____ and to focus all of your _____ on the text.

7. To create the ideal study environment, students must eliminate both _____ and _____ distractions.

8. Synonyms can help add _____ to a reading selection and help readers to _____ what unknown words might mean.

ColorBlind Images/Getty Images

Supporting Details, Mapping, and Outlining

Goals for Chapter 3

- Define the terms *major details* and *minor details*.
- Recognize major and minor details in paragraphs.
- Define the term *transitions*.
- Locate transitions that often identify major details and minor details.
- Recognize transitions in paragraphs.
- Use mapping to show major and minor details in a paragraph.
- Use outlining to show major and minor details in a paragraph.
- Describe the principles of effective time management.

In the previous chapter, you practiced finding the main idea of a paragraph. The main idea is the general point the writer wants you to know or to believe when you've finished reading the paragraph. Often, though, readers cannot understand or accept this point as true unless they get more information. The *supporting details* in a paragraph provide this information.

Before continuing, take this pretest to find out what you already know about supporting details.

3

Pretest

Identify the main idea and write it on the blank following each paragraph. Then, choose one sentence that offers a *major* detail to support that main idea. Write the number of that sentence in the blank below your main idea statement.

1. **(1)** The United States is home to many highly regarded universities with an African-American tradition. **(2)** From a shanty[1] and church in rural Alabama, African-American visionary Booker T. Washington built the future Tuskegee Institute, which has been around for 120 years. **(3)** Another example, Howard University, in Washington, DC, is the largest of these schools. **(4)** It has a fine reputation as an educational institution. **(5)** Nashville is the home to Fisk, which was founded in 1866. **(6)** Fisk is noted for having W. E. B. DuBois[2] among its graduates. **(7)** And finally, the state of Georgia has Morehouse University, whose graduates include Martin Luther King, Jr.,[3] and Spike Lee.[4]*

Main Idea: _____

_____

Major Supporting Detail: _____

2. **(1)** You should do certain things to keep children safe around cars in warm weather. **(2)** First, teach children not to play in, on, or around cars. **(3)** Second, never leave a child or pet unattended in a motor vehicle, even with the window slightly open. **(4)** Car temperatures can rise to 122 degrees within 20 minutes and 150 degrees within 40 minutes

1. **shanty:** old, dilapidated dwelling or home

2. **W.E.B. DuBois:** American civil rights leader

3. **Martin Luther King Jr.:** American civil rights leader

4. **Spike Lee:** American film director

* Adapted from "Don't Know Much About Historically Black Colleges," *USA Weekend*, July 6–8, 2001, 14.

on a hot day. (5) Always lock car doors and trunks—even at home—and keep keys out of children's reach. (6) And finally, watch children closely around cars, particularly when loading or unloading. (7) Check to ensure that all children leave the vehicle when you reach your destination. (8) Don't overlook sleeping infants. (9) Following all of these suggestions will ensure safety when it comes to children and automobiles in hot weather.*

Main Idea: _____

_____

Major Supporting Detail: _____

3. (1) The benefits of walking go well beyond the purely physical. (2) More than any other activity, walking is a sure way to jump-start the brain, set thoughts in motion, and calm our troubles. (3) Prompted by our modest exertions,[1] just a few minutes into a walk the body begins to produce endorphins, chemical compounds that reduce pain and stress and enhance memory and judgment as they course through the brain. (4) Walking also produces increased levels of serotonin, an important brain neurotransmitter that increases feelings of well-being. (5) For this reason, doctors recommend walking as a treatment for mild depression and anxiety.[†]

Main Idea: _____

_____

Major Supporting Detail: _____

4. (1) Sports psychology is the study of sport and exercise, and the mental (psychological) factors influencing performance. (2) Sports psychologists apply psychological principles and a number of different techniques to the field of sport and exercise, all aimed at improved performance and positive self-image. (3) The connection of mind, body, and athletic performance is a powerful one. (4) Athletes do so much physical preparation to get an edge on the competition that they often forget about the mental aspects of their sport. (5) It is often said that performance in a sport is

1. **exertions:** efforts

* Adapted from Cathy Elcik, "Summer Safety: Kids and Cars Don't Mix," *Westchester Family,* July 2001, 24.
† Adapted from Gregory McNamee, "Wandering Soles," *Modern Maturity,* September/October 2001, 76.

3

95 percent mental; however, most of the athlete's time is spent in physical preparation for competition.*

Main Idea: _____

_____

Major Supporting Detail: _____

5. **(1)** If you live with a chronic[1] snorer, take a hard look at his habits. **(2)** Some simple changes could stop a snoring problem for good. **(3)** For example, being overweight is the most common cause of snoring, so if you can get your bedmate to take off a few pounds, the snoring may become less frequent. **(4)** Also, don't allow your bedmate to drink alcohol before going to bed, as that can increase the frequency of snoring during the night. **(5)** Sleeping on the back is another cause of snoring. **(6)** And finally, encourage your bedmate to quit if he smokes cigarettes; smoking is known as a leading cause of snoring in addition to being an unhealthy habit.†

Main Idea: _____

_____

Major Supporting Detail: _____

Supporting details *are the specific facts, statistics, examples, steps, anecdotes, reasons, descriptions, or definitions that explain or prove the general main idea stated in the topic sentence.* They support, or provide a solid foundation for, this main idea.

Supporting details should answer all of the questions raised by the topic sentence. For example, read the following statement:

> Female surgeons are treated differently from male surgeons by their colleagues, nurses, and patients.

This topic sentence immediately raises the questions *how* and *why* in the reader's mind. To answer the questions, the paragraph must go on to offer the reasons and other explanations that prove this point.

As you read this next paragraph, notice how the supporting details clarify the main idea, which is in boldface, and explain why it's true.

---

1. **chronic:** happening over and over again

---

* France, Robert C., *Introduction to Sports Medicine and Athletic Training,* 2nd ed. Clifton Park: Delmar, 2011. Print. p. 173.

† Adapted from Ellie McGrath, "How to Sleep with a Snorer," *Good Housekeeping,* May 2000, 64–68.

If you want to become rich, you must follow four important rules. The first rule is to establish a reasonable income base. To reach and maintain that stable, middle-income base, you should earn a college degree, marry someone with an equal or higher education and stay married, and work as long as you are able to. The second rule for becoming rich is to avoid frivolous temptations. For example, don't drive expensive luxury cars; instead, buy medium-priced cars. Following rule #2 will allow you to save more money, which is rule #3. Average people who become rich often do so because they save more of their money, even if they must make sacrifices to do so. Finally, the fourth rule to becoming rich is take advantage of compound interest. If you invested $2,000 every year from age 22 to age 65 and that money earned 10 percent interest per year, you'd have over a million dollars when you retired.*

The topic sentence of this paragraph raises the question *What are these rules for becoming rich?* Then, the paragraph goes on to answer that question by explaining the four things you must do to increase your wealth. The reader would not be able to understand the topic sentence without reading the details in the rest of the paragraph. It's important to learn to recognize supporting details, for they determine your understanding and interpretation of what you read.

Major and Minor Details

Two kinds of supporting details include major details and minor details. The **major details** *are the main points that explain or support the idea in the topic sentence.* They offer *essential* reasons or other information that the reader must have in order to understand the main idea.

Minor details *offer more explanation of the major details.* Minor details are *not* usually critical to the reader's comprehension of the main idea, although they do offer more specific information that helps to clarify the points in the paragraph.

To see the difference between major and minor details, read the following paragraph:

Many Americans believe in the supernatural. For one thing, they believe in supernatural beings. A recent Gallup poll revealed that 69 percent of people believe in angels, half of them believe they have their own guardian angels, and 48 percent believe that there are aliens in outer space. Americans also believe in the existence of supernatural

---

* Adapted from Richard B. McKenzie and Dwight R. Lee, "Becoming Wealthy: It's Up to You," *USA Today*, September 1998, 16–19.

powers. For example, over 10 million people have called the Psychic Friends network to get advice about their present and future.*

The topic sentence of this paragraph, which is in boldface, raises the question *What kinds of supernatural things do they believe in?* The second and fourth sentences of the paragraph answer that question. They tell the reader that Americans believe in supernatural beings and supernatural powers. The other sentences in the paragraph offer minor details. In this case, the minor details offer examples of the kinds of beings and powers people believe are real. Therefore, they offer nonessential information that helps explain the main idea even more.

Remember the explanation of general and specific sentences back in Chapter 2? You learned that the topic sentence is the most general statement in a paragraph while the other sentences offer more specific information. Well, these other sentences (the supporting details) are also related to each other in general and specific ways. It might be helpful to visualize these relationships in a diagram form, as shown below.

Many Americans believe in the supernatural.	
For one thing, they believe in supernatural beings.	Americans also believe in the existence of supernatural powers.
A recent Gallup poll revealed that 69 percent of people believe in angels, half of them believe they have their own guardian angels, and 48 percent believe that there are aliens in outer space.	For example, over 10 million people have called the Psychic Friends network to get advice about their present and future.

This diagram offers a useful visual image of the general and specific relationships among sentences in paragraphs. The major details—represented in the blocks beneath the topic sentence—provide the solid foundation of support for the main idea. You could not remove any of these blocks without significantly weakening the base on which the main idea rests. The minor details in the next row of blocks make the structure even sturdier. Though the main idea would still be supported by the major details even if the minor details were removed, the minor details make the whole base even stronger.

* Adapted from Jill Neimark, "Do the Spirits Move You?" *Psychology Today,* September 19, 1996, 48.

To better understand what you read, you may want to try to visualize the sentences in a diagram like the one above. Sorting out these relationships is critical not only to comprehending a paragraph but also to deciding whether or not you can agree with the author's ideas.

Exercise **3.1**

Read the following paragraphs and then label the list of sentences that follow as MI for main idea, MAJOR for major detail, or MINOR for minor detail.

1. **(1)** Our agricultural system began before we were a country. **(2)** Most of the immigrants who first came to the New World were farmers. **(3)** The colonists made their living producing crops that could be sent back to Europe. **(4)** At the time of the American Revolution, well over 90 percent of the colonists made their living through agriculture. **(5)** In fact, most of the signers of the Declaration of Independence were farmers.*

   _____ Sentence 1

   _____ Sentence 2

   _____ Sentence 5

2. **(1)** Doctors now have several new treatments that alter the soft palate (the roof of the mouth) and help quiet nighttime snoring. **(2)** In one procedure, a form of microwave energy is used under local anesthesia to scar and shrink the soft tissue in the back of the throat so that it vibrates less. **(3)** Another new treatment involves injecting a substance into the palate to chemically scar the tissue. **(4)** If you don't want the back of your throat burned, then a third option is having three small polyester inserts placed in the soft palate to make it stiffer and less prone to vibrate.†

   _____ Sentence 1

   _____ Sentence 3

   _____ Sentence 4

3. **(1)** Learning to ride a motorcycle can be a very difficult thing to do. **(2)** First, balancing yourself on two wheels can be frightening, especially since if you fall, a thousand-pound machine can land on top of you! **(3)** It is also hard to manage the coordination between the gear shift and the gas pedal, although Harley Davidson makes a motorcycle that is easier

---

* Herren, Ray V., *Exploring Agriscience,* 4th ed. (Clifton Park: Delmar, 2011), Print. p. 26.

† Adapted from Daniel K. Hoh, "Sound (Free) Sleep," ABCNEWS.com, April 8, 2004, www.abcnews.go.com/sections/Living/GoodMorningAmerica/snoring_treatments_040408.htm.

3

to handle than most. **(4)** It can be a little intimidating, too, to ride a motorcycle on a major highway with cars going past you at 60 miles an hour. **(5)** It is fun, however, to feel the wind whipping through your hair as you ride.

_____ Sentence 1

_____ Sentence 2

_____ Sentence 3

4. **(1)** You can become a good writer if you put your mind to it. **(2)** The best thing to do if you want to learn to write well is to write every day. **(3)** Writing every day increases confidence in your skills, so you should set aside time in your schedule every day to write for fun, for school, or just for practice. **(4)** You should also make sure that you have a good, quiet place to write as that can increase your concentration.

_____ Sentence 1

_____ Sentence 2

_____ Sentence 3

5. **(1)** Working with a personal trainer is a good way to begin an exercise program. **(2)** Personal trainers will make sure that you are in good enough health to start exercising and will tailor a program to fit your fitness level, your body type, and your schedule. **(3)** Furthermore, you will see results faster if you work with a trainer. **(4)** A trainer will encourage you to stick with your program and make it harder for you to quit.

_____ Sentence 1

_____ Sentence 3

_____ Sentence 4

Exercise **3.2**

Read each paragraph and write an abbreviated form of each sentence in the boxes that follow to indicate their general and specific relationships.

1. Since she discovered tennis at the age of 10, Zina Garrison has encountered extraordinary, inspiring people at tennis camps and in early matches. Althea Gibson, the first great African-American tennis player, taught her about the physical and mental requirements for becoming a professional.

Arthur Ashe[1] taught her about a slice backhand and dedication to the sport. Once she had made the choice to be dedicated, Motown's Berry Gordy taught her about grace under pressure. "No matter what," he said, "win like a champion, lose like a champion."*

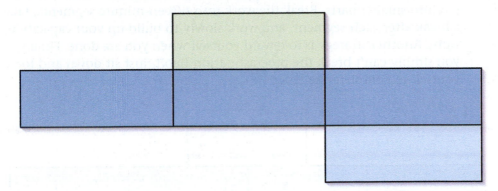

3

2. The American view of the political system has at least five important elements. The first is liberty. Americans believe they should be free to do pretty much as they please, with some exceptions, as long as they don't hurt other people. The second element is equality. Americans believe everybody should have an equal vote and an equal chance to participate and succeed. Democracy is the third element. Americans think government officials should be accountable to the people. Fourth is civic duty. Americans generally feel people ought to take community affairs seriously and help out when they can. Finally, Americans believe in individual responsibility. A characteristically American view is that, barring some disability, individuals are responsible for their own actions and well-being.[†]

---

1. **Arthur Ashe:** another great African-American tennis player

---

* Adapted from Elizabeth Kaye, "After Youth, Then What?" *O Magazine*, June 2001, 160.

† Adapted from James Q. Wilson and John J. DiIulio Jr., *American Government: The Essentials*, 9th ed. (Boston: Houghton Mifflin Co., 2004), 78–79.

3. If you find that procrastination, or putting things off, hurts your progress, here are some ways to break the habit. First, look at the benefits of doing the work at hand. Will you feel a sense of accomplishment when the job is done, and will you feel less stressed and more relieved? Next, break the job into smaller parts. Break the work into fifteen-minute segments, take a break after each segment, and work slowly to build up your capacity to work. Another strategy is to reward yourself when you are done. Finally, if you simply can't break the procrastination habit, just sit down and force yourself to complete the task.*

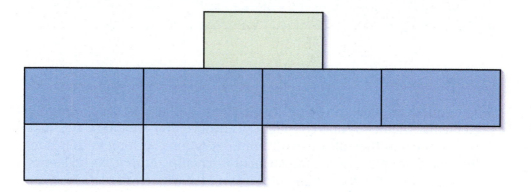

4. Several publications and materials are the means by which the people at your college express their interest in you, your needs, and your success as a student. Your *college newspaper* contains information of interest to the college community along with articles that report on local and world events from a student's point of view. Your college may also provide a *student bulletin* or other weekly publication that keeps you informed of campus activities and events and contains additional items of general interest. A *student handbook* condenses[1] and summarizes information contained in the catalog concerning the college's policies and regulations,[2] but it is usually written in a style that is more appealing to students. Throughout your campus you will find various *informational flyers* about services and events that are printed by people or departments sponsoring the events. These flyers will contain only the essentials about the service or event: the time, the place, and whether it costs anything.[†]

---

1. **condenses:** shortens

2. **regulations:** rules

---

* Adapted from Sharon Sherman and Alan Sherman, "Getting Yourself to Study," *Essential Concepts of Chemistry* (Boston: Houghton Mifflin Co., 1999), xxxi–xxxii.

† Adapted from Carol Kanar, *The Confident Student*, 5th ed. (Boston: Houghton Mifflin Co., 2004), 23.

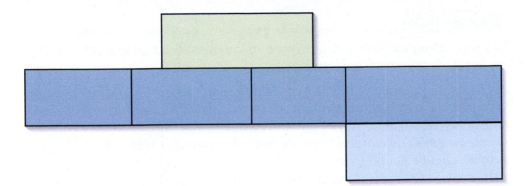

5. Americans tend to believe several long-standing myths about families past and present. The first myth concerns the roles of family members. Many people think that the 1950s, an era of breadwinning dads and stay-at-home moms, was the last decade in a long era of stable families, but 1950s families actually reversed a 100-year trend of rising divorce rates. A second myth concerns the best family structure. People assume that a return to roles common within a 1950s family would decrease the number of broken homes, but today, sole breadwinning males are often less competent fathers, and stay-at-home women often feel isolated and depressed. Another myth relates to the number and severity of family problems. Though people believe that modern families face worse problems, the truth is that families in all eras of history have dealt with difficulties like drug and alcohol addiction and abuse.*

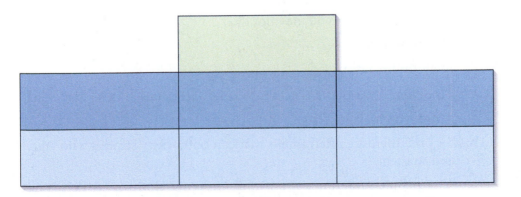

---

* Adapted from "Unrealistic Family Myths," *USA Today Newsview,* December 1997, 1–2.

3

Exercise **3.3**

Read the paragraph below and respond to the questions that follow by circling the letters of the correct answers.

(1) Are you interested in the idea of vacationing at a farm? **(2)** Before booking your trip, there are a few important things to consider, according to guidebook author Jay Golan, who stayed on farms while researching *Frommer's Philadelphia & the Amish Country,* his book about farm vacations. **(3)** First, he says, some people could be put off by rural America's old-fashioned ways. **(4)** For the most part, men do the farm work, and women do the household chores. **(5)** If you don't want your children to experience that lifestyle, you may not want to visit. **(6)** Second, there are often smells that can bother city slickers who aren't used to them. **(7)** On farms that have cattle and chickens, there can be overpowering smells in the air that people who live in and around the city find hard to take. **(8)** Third, you may get dirty. **(9)** City people sometimes show up in designer clothing, which is not the thing to wear on the farm. **(10)** You have to expect that you will pick up dirt or manure on your shoes or boots if you are going to be on a farm. **(11)** Indeed, at one farm, the owner's one rule is that people visiting the chicken house must scrub their shoes before returning to the farmhouse. Chicken droppings, it turns out, are surprisingly sticky!*

1. The main idea is expressed in sentence

   a. 1.   c. 3.

   b. 2.   d. 4.

2. The supporting details of this paragraph relate to

   a. farms.

   b. things about a farm you may not like.

   c. cows and cattle.

   d. smells on the farm.

3. Which of the following sentences is NOT a *major* detail in this paragraph?

   a. "Third, you may get dirty."

   b. "Second, there are often smells that can bother city slickers who aren't used to them."

   c. "City people sometimes show up in designer clothing, which is not the thing to wear on the farm."

   d. "First, he says, some people could be put off by rural America's old-fashioned ways."

* Adapted from Gene Sloan, "Farmers Are Bullish on City Tourists," *USA Today,* June 29, 2001, 4d. Copyright © 2001, *USA Today.* Reprinted with permission.

a home away from home for cancer patients. Finally, the Leary Firefighters Foundation raises money to help firefighters get new and improved equipment that could help save their lives during a fire.*

5. Learning doesn't occur in a tidy, step-by-step fashion. At any moment while learning, you may need to jump to a different component in the CORE system. For example, while *Rehearsing*, you might realize that some information doesn't make sense to you, so you *Organize* it in a different way. At times you may engage two or more components simultaneously. For instance, when *Rehearsing* study materials, you're probably *Evaluating* your mastery of that knowledge at the same time. Thus, you can expect to use the four components of the CORE Learning System in any order and in any combination.†

Mapping and Outlining

Earlier in this chapter, you saw how you can visualize the relationships among sentences in a paragraph by inserting each one into a block. The main idea went into the block at the top, the major supporting details went into the row of blocks just beneath the main idea, and the minor details, if any, were in the third row.

This diagram is a form of **mapping**, *a technique that involves using lines, boxes, circles, or other shapes to show how sentences in a paragraph are related.*

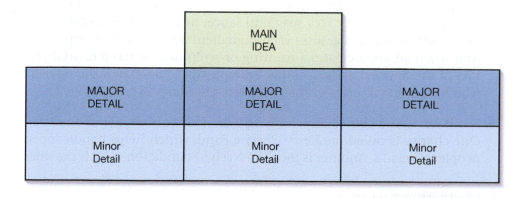

---

* Adapted from Frank DeCaro, "Denis Leary Gets Serious," *Rosie*, July, 2001, 88.

† Downing, Skip. *On Course: Strategies for Creating Success in College and in Life.* 6th ed. Boston: Wadsworth, 2011. Print. p. 17.

4. Which of the following would be considered a *minor* detail in this paragraph?

   a. "First, he says, some people could be put off by rural America's old-fashioned ways."

   b. "You have to expect that you will pick up dirt or manure on your shoes or boots if you are going to be on a farm."

   c. "Second, there are often smells that can bother city slickers who aren't used to them."

   d. "Before booking your trip, there are a few important things to consider, according to guidebook author Jay Golan, who stayed on farms while researching *Frommer's Philadelphia & the Amish Country,* his book about farm vacations."

5. People who are not used to farm life often show up with designer clothing because

   a. they are not prepared for the realities of farm life.

   b. they like to wear designer clothes all of the time.

   c. they think farmers wear designer clothes too.

   d. they are too materialistic.

Transitions

To help readers recognize the general and specific relationships among sentences in a paragraph, paragraphs usually include transitions. **Transitions** *are words that assist readers in distinguishing between major and minor details because they make connections and distinctions between the different details.* In particular, sentences that offer major details are likely to begin with words such as:

first, second, third	finally
in addition	one
and	another
also	furthermore
next	

These words signal that the sentence will offer another new point in support of the topic sentence. For an example of transitions that indicate major details, read the following paragraph. These transitions are in bold print:

Several states are considering extending daylight-saving time so that it would start earlier in the spring and end later in the fall. **One**

reason for doing so is to save energy costs. With longer daylight time, the need for electricity would be reduced, and both governments and individuals would pay less. **Another reason** for lengthening daylight-saving time is increased safety. More daylight into the evening would reduce the number of rush-hour traffic accidents and make Halloween trick-or-treating safer for children.*

The transitions in the previous list are not the only ones that identify major details. Others will be discussed later in Chapter 5. However, because they commonly introduce important supporting details, readers should be aware of their function within the paragraph.

A paragraph might also include transitions to indicate minor details. Sentences that offer minor details are sometimes introduced with words such as:

for example	to illustrate
one example	specifically
for instance	in one case

These words can indicate that the sentence is about to offer more specific information to develop the last idea further. In the next paragraph, the transitions that signal minor details are in italics, whereas those that identify major details are bolded.

> Certain traits separate the good bosses from the bad bosses. **The first characteristic** is the boss's response to his or her employees. *For example*, a bad boss orders employees around, whereas a good boss treats employees with respect by recognizing their skills and experience. **The next characteristic** is the boss's response to his employees' ideas. A bad boss, *for instance*, is close-minded and disregards others' input, but a good boss encourages workers to contribute their ideas and then listens to and seriously considers those ideas. **Finally**, a good boss and a bad boss differ in the way they handle their own egos. A bad boss cares only about his own power and prestige,[1] whereas a good boss focuses instead on providing the best, most efficient product or service[†]

It is important to note here that the transitions in the list above can also be used to introduce *major* details in a paragraph. Chapter 5 will offer more specific information about how paragraphs use transitions in different ways.

1. **prestige:** respect; high standing among others

* Adapted from "More Daylight Makes Sense," *USA Today Online*, June 18, 2001, www.usatoday.com/usatonline/20010618/3408445s.htm.

† Adapted from Paul B. Hertneky, "You and Your Boss," *Restaurant Hospitality*, August 1, 1996, 78.

Exercise **3.4**

Read each paragraph and then underline the topic sentence, circle the transitions that signal major details, and underline transitions that signal minor details.

1. You should keep in mind some basic principles of outlining when preparing an outline. First, each point in your outline should contain only one idea or piece of information. Second, your outline should accurately reflect relationships among ideas and supporting material. Third, you should use a consistent system of symbols and indentations.[1] Fourth, write out transitions and relevant portions of introductions and conclusions.*

2. Making international comparisons is often difficult because the legal definitions of crime vary from country to country. There are also differences in the way crime is measured. For example, in the United States, crime may be measured by counting criminal acts reported to the police or by using victim surveys, whereas in many European countries, the number of cases solved by the police is used as the measure of crime. Despite these problems, valid comparisons can still be made about crime across different countries using a number of reliable data sources. For example, the United Nations Survey of Crime Trends and Operations of Criminal Justice Systems (UNCJS) is the best-known source of information on cross-national data.[†]

3. One of the brain's primary jobs is to manufacture images so we can use them to make predictions about the world and then base our behavior on those predictions. For one thing, when a cook adds chopped onions, mushrooms, and garlic to a spaghetti sauce, he has a picture of how the sauce will taste and measures each ingredient according to that picture. And when an artist creates a painting or sculpture, he has a mental picture of the finished piece. Another example would be that of the novelist who has a mental image of the characters she wants to bring to life.[‡]

4. Denis Leary is a comedian who is also devoted to a couple of charities. One charity is called the Kerry Chesire Fund, which helps handicapped people in Ireland. Another is the Cam Neely[2] Foundation, which provides

1. **indentations:** blank spaces

2. **Cam Neely:** Neely was a professional hockey player for the Boston Bruins

* Adapted from James Andrews and Patricia Andrews, *Public Speaking* (Boston: Houghton Mifflin Co., 1999), 184–86. Copyright © 1999 by Houghton Mifflin Company. Reprinted with permission.

† Larry J. Siegel, *Criminology: The Core*, 4th ed. (Belmont: Wadsworth, 2011), 40. Print.

‡ Adapted from Dave Ellis, "Notice Your Pictures and Let Them Go," *Becoming a Master Student* (Boston: Houghton Mifflin co., 2000), 132.

4. Which of the following would be considered a *minor* detail in this paragraph?

    a. "First, he says, some people could be put off by rural America's old-fashioned ways."

    b. "You have to expect that you will pick up dirt or manure on your shoes or boots if you are going to be on a farm."

    c. "Second, there are often smells that can bother city slickers who aren't used to them."

    d. "Before booking your trip, there are a few important things to consider, according to guidebook author Jay Golan, who stayed on farms while researching *Frommer's Philadelphia & the Amish Country,* his book about farm vacations."

5. People who are not used to farm life often show up with designer clothing because

    a. they are not prepared for the realities of farm life.

    b. they like to wear designer clothes all of the time.

    c. they think farmers wear designer clothes too.

    d. they are too materialistic.

Transitions

To help readers recognize the general and specific relationships among sentences in a paragraph, paragraphs usually include transitions. **Transitions** *are words that assist readers in distinguishing between major and minor details because they make connections and distinctions between the different details.* In particular, sentences that offer major details are likely to begin with words such as:

first, second, third	finally
in addition	one
and	another
also	furthermore
next	

These words signal that the sentence will offer another new point in support of the topic sentence. For an example of transitions that indicate major details, read the following paragraph. These transitions are in bold print:

> Several states are considering extending daylight-saving time so that it would start earlier in the spring and end later in the fall. **One**

reason for doing so is to save energy costs. With longer daylight time, the need for electricity would be reduced, and both governments and individuals would pay less. **Another reason** for lengthening daylight-saving time is increased safety. More daylight into the evening would reduce the number of rush-hour traffic accidents and make Halloween trick-or-treating safer for children.*

The transitions in the previous list are not the only ones that identify major details. Others will be discussed later in Chapter 5. However, because they commonly introduce important supporting details, readers should be aware of their function within the paragraph.

A paragraph might also include transitions to indicate minor details. Sentences that offer minor details are sometimes introduced with words such as:

for example	to illustrate
one example	specifically
for instance	in one case

These words can indicate that the sentence is about to offer more specific information to develop the last idea further. In the next paragraph, the transitions that signal minor details are in italics, whereas those that identify major details are bolded.

Certain traits separate the good bosses from the bad bosses. **The first characteristic** is the boss's response to his or her employees. *For example*, a bad boss orders employees around, whereas a good boss treats employees with respect by recognizing their skills and experience. **The next characteristic** is the boss's response to his employees' ideas. A bad boss, *for instance*, is close-minded and disregards others' input, but a good boss encourages workers to contribute their ideas and then listens to and seriously considers those ideas. **Finally**, a good boss and a bad boss differ in the way they handle their own egos. A bad boss cares only about his own power and prestige,[1] whereas a good boss focuses instead on providing the best, most efficient product or service[†]

It is important to note here that the transitions in the list above can also be used to introduce *major* details in a paragraph. Chapter 5 will offer more specific information about how paragraphs use transitions in different ways.

---

1. **prestige:** respect; high standing among others

---

* Adapted from "More Daylight Makes Sense," *USA Today Online,* June 18, 2001, www.usatoday.com/usatonline/20010618/3408445s.htm.

[†] Adapted from Paul B. Hertneky, "You and Your Boss," *Restaurant Hospitality,* August 1, 1996, 78.

Exercise **3.4**

Read each paragraph and then underline the topic sentence, circle the transitions that signal major details, and underline transitions that signal minor details.

1. You should keep in mind some basic principles of outlining when preparing an outline. First, each point in your outline should contain only one idea or piece of information. Second, your outline should accurately reflect relationships among ideas and supporting material. Third, you should use a consistent system of symbols and indentations.[1] Fourth, write out transitions and relevant portions of introductions and conclusions.*

2. Making international comparisons is often difficult because the legal definitions of crime vary from country to country. There are also differences in the way crime is measured. For example, in the United States, crime may be measured by counting criminal acts reported to the police or by using victim surveys, whereas in many European countries, the number of cases solved by the police is used as the measure of crime. Despite these problems, valid comparisons can still be made about crime across different countries using a number of reliable data sources. For example, the United Nations Survey of Crime Trends and Operations of Criminal Justice Systems (UNCJS) is the best-known source of information on cross-national data.†

3. One of the brain's primary jobs is to manufacture images so we can use them to make predictions about the world and then base our behavior on those predictions. For one thing, when a cook adds chopped onions, mushrooms, and garlic to a spaghetti sauce, he has a picture of how the sauce will taste and measures each ingredient according to that picture. And when an artist creates a painting or sculpture, he has a mental picture of the finished piece. Another example would be that of the novelist who has a mental image of the characters she wants to bring to life.‡

4. Denis Leary is a comedian who is also devoted to a couple of charities. One charity is called the Kerry Chesire Fund, which helps handicapped people in Ireland. Another is the Cam Neely[2] Foundation, which provides

---

1. **indentations:** blank spaces

2. **Cam Neely:** Neely was a professional hockey player for the Boston Bruins

---

* Adapted from James Andrews and Patricia Andrews, *Public Speaking* (Boston: Houghton Mifflin Co., 1999), 184–86. Copyright © 1999 by Houghton Mifflin Company. Reprinted with permission.

† Larry J. Siegel, *Criminology: The Core,* 4th ed. (Belmont: Wadsworth, 2011), 40. Print.

‡ Adapted from Dave Ellis, "Notice Your Pictures and Let Them Go," *Becoming a Master Student* (Boston: Houghton Mifflin co., 2000), 132.

a home away from home for cancer patients. Finally, the Leary Firefighters Foundation raises money to help firefighters get new and improved equipment that could help save their lives during a fire.*

5. Learning doesn't occur in a tidy, step- by- step fashion. At any moment while learning, you may need to jump to a different component in the CORE system. For example, while *Rehearsing*, you might realize that some information doesn't make sense to you, so you *Organize* it in a different way. At times you may engage two or more components simultaneously. For instance, when *Rehearsing* study materials, you're probably *Evaluating* your mastery of that knowledge at the same time. Thus, you can expect to use the four components of the CORE Learning System in any order and in any combination.†

Mapping and Outlining

Earlier in this chapter, you saw how you can visualize the relationships among sentences in a paragraph by inserting each one into a block. The main idea went into the block at the top, the major supporting details went into the row of blocks just beneath the main idea, and the minor details, if any, were in the third row.

This diagram is a form of **mapping**, *a technique that involves using lines, boxes, circles, or other shapes to show how sentences in a paragraph are related.*

	MAIN IDEA	
MAJOR DETAIL	MAJOR DETAIL	MAJOR DETAIL
Minor Detail	Minor Detail	Minor Detail

---

* Adapted from Frank DeCaro, "Denis Leary Gets Serious," *Rosie*, July, 2001, 88.

† Downing, Skip. *On Course: Strategies for Creating Success in College and in Life.* 6th ed. Boston: Wadsworth, 2011. Print. p. 17.

In mapping, you lay out a visual to help you see the main idea, major supporting details, and minor supporting details. Here are some other, different ways to visualize these relationships:

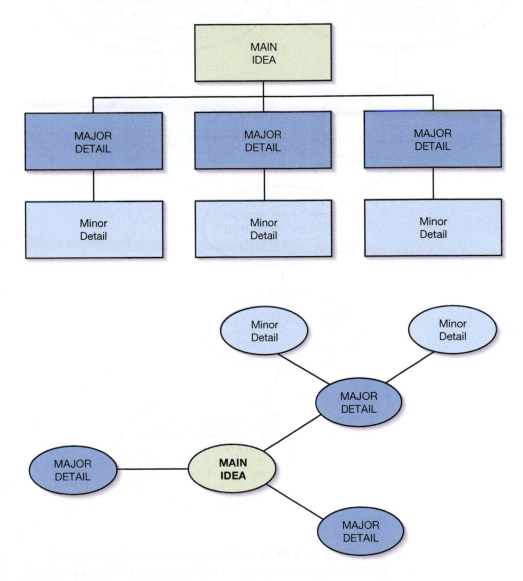

For example, using the diagram above, you might map the paragraph about good and bad bosses on page 102 like this.

3

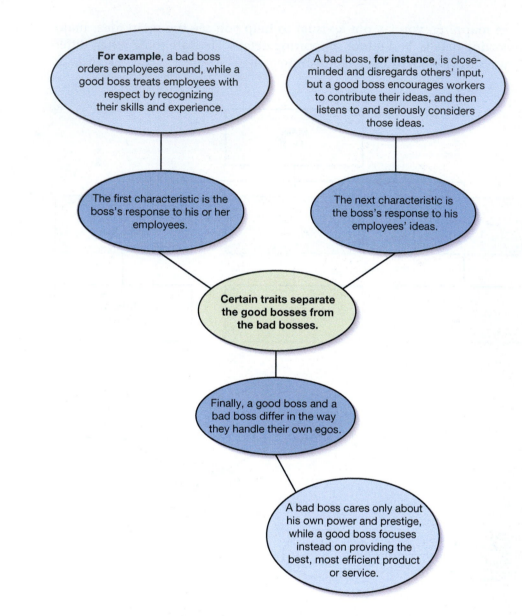

For example, a bad boss orders employees around, while a good boss treats employees with respect by recognizing their skills and experience.

A bad boss, **for instance**, is close-minded and disregards others' input, but a good boss encourages workers to contribute their ideas, and then listens to and seriously considers those ideas.

The first characteristic is the boss's response to his or her employees.

The next characteristic is the boss's response to his employees' ideas.

Certain traits separate the good bosses from the bad bosses.

Finally, a good boss and a bad boss differ in the way they handle their own egos.

A bad boss cares only about his own power and prestige, while a good boss focuses instead on providing the best, most efficient product or service.

The following interactive web links will help you to further understand how to map textbook material and will give you an opportunity to practice this important skill.

http://www.studygs.net/mapping/index.htm
http://www.studygs.net/mapping/mapflash.htm
http://www.howtostudy.org/resources_skill.php?id=14

Exercise **3.5**

Read each paragraph and then fill in the map that follows with an abbreviated form of each sentence.

1. There are two models for explaining dropping out of high school. The *frustration–self-esteem model* argues that continuous failure leads to low self-esteem and problem behaviors such as absenteeism,[1] which finally end in dropping out. The *participation-identification model* argues that lack of participation in school activities leads to poor school performance and alienation[2] from school, which lead to dropping out.*

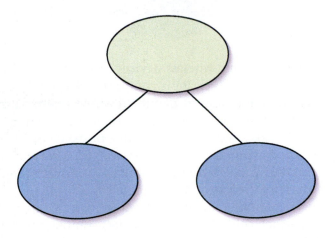

2. Adult learners are a welcome group on any campus for several important reasons. First of all, adult learners bring with them knowledge and skills that enrich the college experience for everyone. Second, most people change jobs or careers two or more times during their lives and seek additional skills or training. Moreover, learning does not end at graduation—it is a lifelong process.[†]

1. **absenteeism:** repeated failure to attend

2. **alienation:** isolation

* Adapted from Paul S. Kaplan, *Adolescence* (Boston: Houghton Mifflin Co., 2004), 248.
† Carol C. Kanar, *The Confident Student*, 7th ed. (Boston: Wadsworth, 2011), 13. Print.

3

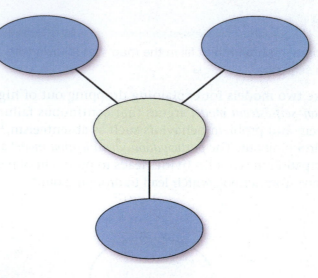

3. Some companies are using wireless devices in a variety of ways and reaping big benefits. One Illinois cleaning company called Service-Master, which scrubs Greyhound buses, uses its handheld wireless network to keep track of customer satisfaction. After each bus is cleaned, a Greyhound supervisor rates the job using an electronic form on one of the company's other computers. Another company is Office Depot, which has cut the time it spends filing and searching for delivery paperwork by 50 percent thanks to a wireless system that links trucks on 22,000 delivery routes. And police officers in Coos Bay, Oregon, no longer have to make two one-hour detours back to headquarters each shift, thanks to a wireless computer in patrol cars that allows them to submit entries to the police log through a wireless network.*

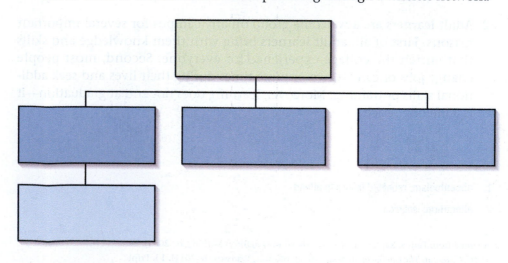

* Adapted from Michelle Kessler, "Gadgets Give Workers on the Run a Leg Up," *USA Today*, June 26, 2001, 5F.

3

4. According to the Weber Grill-Watch survey, nearly all Americans fall into one of four categories of barbecue grilling personalities. The first category is the Gallant[1] Grillers. These people, who make up 33 percent of barbecue grill owners, are adventurous and love to treat their guests to grilled food experiments. The next group is the Careful Cooks. These grillers—32 percent of grill owners—love to entertain, too, but they are more cautious and follow recipes closely. Busy Barbecuers are the third group. These people, who make up 19 percent of grill owners, like to cook only those foods that don't take much time, and they rarely try new things.

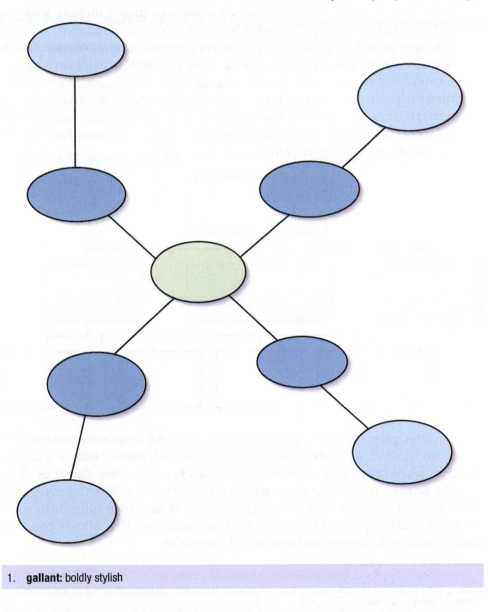

---

1. **gallant:** boldly stylish

The fourth and smallest category is the Need-It-Nows. This 12 percent of grill owners views barbecuing only as a way to produce food, not as a way to entertain or spend time with the family.*

5. The hospitality, travel, and tourism industry has recognized the advantage of putting various components together and selling them as a tour package. A tour package is a composite of related services offered at a single price. A package might include more than one form of transportation. For example, the price of a Caribbean cruise usually includes airfare to and from the point of departure. Or a package might include a day of sightseeing by chartered bus, with lunch at a popular restaurant. Another example might be an airline that offers reduced rates at certain hotels if a traveler decides to use its service. Tour packages usually save people money, and many people like having all of the arrangements made for them when they travel. A typical tour of the Rocky Mountains in the western United States would include air travel, motor coach transfers, hotel accommodations, meals, and admission fees to National Park system locations and other attractions on the itinerary.†

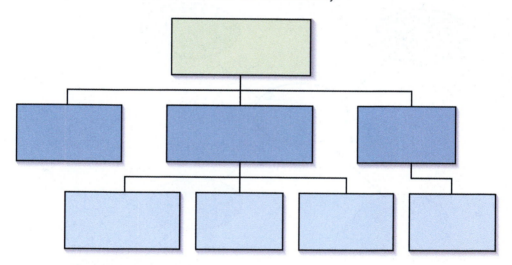

Another good way to identify the main idea and supporting details is to create an outline. An **outline** *is a list of these details labeled with a system of numbers and letters that show their relationships to one another.* Outlines often use the Roman numeral system, which effectively identifies the main idea and different topics or details. Outlines can be in sentence form or in topic form. The latter is useful for creating a brief summary that allows you, at a glance, to see the general and specific relationships.

* Adapted from "What's Your Barbecue Profile?" *USA Today*, May 1998, 10.

† Chon, Kaye (Kye-Sung), and Thomas A. Maier. *Welcome to Hospitality: An Introduction*. 3rd ed. Clifton Park: Delmar, 2010. p. 42. Print.

I. Main Idea
  A. Major detail
      1. Minor detail
      2. Minor detail

  B. Major detail
      1. Minor detail
      2. Minor detail

For example, you could outline the paragraph about daylight-saving time, on pages 101–102, as follows:

I. Reasons for extending daylight-saving time
  A. Save energy costs
      1. Reduce electricity needs
      2. Governments and individuals would pay less

  B. Increased safety
      1. Fewer rush-hour traffic accidents
      2. Halloween safer for children

MAIN IDEA

MAJOR DETAIL

Minor detail

MAJOR DETAIL

Minor detail

MAJOR DETAIL

Minor detail

To create an outline, line up the major details along one margin and label them with capital letters. Beneath each major detail, indent minor details with numbers: 1, 2, 3, etc.

If you do not like the formality of a Roman numeral outline, you can also outline a paragraph in a more visual way by using a series of indented boxes in place of the numbers and letters.

This diagram, like the Roman numeral outline, arranges major details along one margin line and indents minor details beneath each one. You could create an outline of this type for the paragraph about becoming wealthy on page 93, as follows:

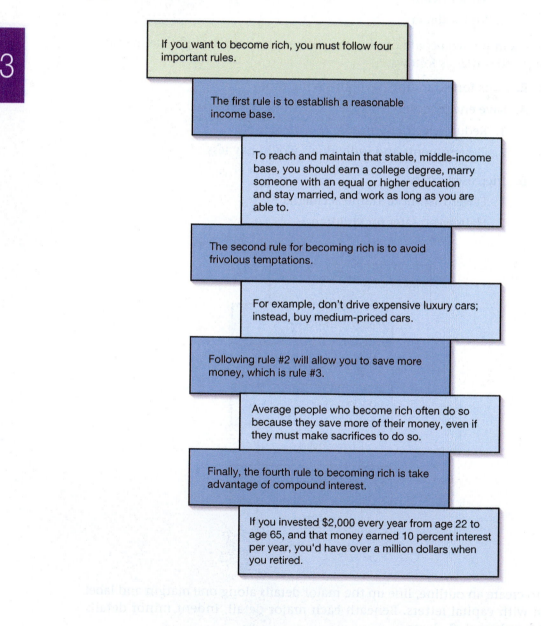

If you want to become rich, you must follow four important rules.

The first rule is to establish a reasonable income base.

To reach and maintain that stable, middle-income base, you should earn a college degree, marry someone with an equal or higher education and stay married, and work as long as you are able to.

The second rule for becoming rich is to avoid frivolous temptations.

For example, don't drive expensive luxury cars; instead, buy medium-priced cars.

Following rule #2 will allow you to save more money, which is rule #3.

Average people who become rich often do so because they save more of their money, even if they must make sacrifices to do so.

Finally, the fourth rule to becoming rich is take advantage of compound interest.

If you invested $2,000 every year from age 22 to age 65, and that money earned 10 percent interest per year, you'd have over a million dollars when you retired.

Exercise **3.6**

Complete the outline that follows each paragraph by filling in the blanks provided.

1. Celebrities, and in particular movie stars, find it very hard to have long-term relationships for a number of reasons. For one thing, celebrity couples rarely work on movies together. This means that they are often in two different locations at the same time for extended periods of time. It is also hard to have a relationship under the constant eye of tabloid[1] newspapers, television reporters, and photographers. Oftentimes, the media mistake photos taken from movies or friends seen together as romantic encounters and report on a star's unfaithfulness to his or her significant other. And finally, it is hard to stay faithful when you are surrounded by great-looking people all day long, as is the case with most movie stars. Many stars have confessed to having romantic relationships with co-stars from a movie project because of the long hours, the time away from home, and just being attracted to a costar.

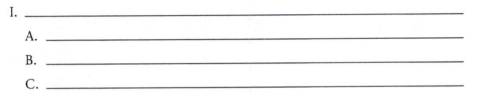

I. _____

   A. _____

   B. _____

   C. _____

2. More than one out of four teens nationwide does some type of volunteer work, and they are not only helping others but also benefiting themselves. Research confirms that teens who learn early to be social, caring, and responsible perform better in school. As a matter of fact, volunteering improves their chances of graduating at the top of their class, armed with critical leadership skills. It also makes teens feel good about themselves. For example, studies show that teens who volunteer just two hours per week have higher self-esteem and more resiliency,[2] and they are 50 percent less likely to smoke, drink, or do drugs.*

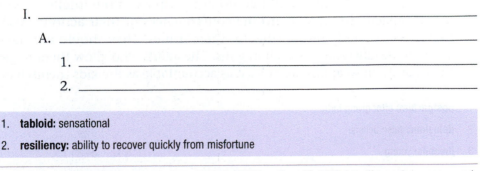

I. _____

   A. _____

      1. _____

      2. _____

1. **tabloid:** sensational

2. **resiliency:** ability to recover quickly from misfortune

* Adapted from Ann Pleshette Murphy, "Give It Up," *ABC News*, June 18, 2003, http://www.abcnews.go.com/sections/GMA/AmericanFamily/GMA030618Teen volunteers.html.

B. _____

   1. _____

   2. _____

   3. _____

3. Right after having a baby, a woman might experience one of three kinds of postpartum[1] depression. One kind of depression is called the postpartum blues. This type affects about 85 percent of new mothers and causes mood swings for up to two weeks. The second, more severe type is called postpartum depression. This condition affects about 10 percent of mothers, especially those who don't enjoy motherhood, and can produce eating or sleeping disorders for months at a time. The third and worst kind of depression is called postpartum psychosis. Fortunately, this type occurs in only one out of 1,000 mothers because it causes a woman to experience delusions[2] and believe the baby would be better off dead.*

I. _____

  A. _____

    1. _____

    2. _____

  B. _____

    1. _____

    2. _____

  C. _____

    1. _____

    2. _____

4. The U.S. justice system should not treat violent juvenile[3] offenders as adults. First of all, these children do not yet possess the intellectual or moral capacity to understand the consequences of their actions. Also, they are not totally responsible for their crimes. They should not have access to deadly weapons such as guns. The adults who allow them to get their hands on weapons are at least as accountable as the kids themselves.

1. **postpartum:** after giving birth

2. **delusions:** false beliefs

3. **juvenile:** young

* Adapted from "Most Mothers Affected by 'Blues,'" *USA Today Online*, June 22, 2001, www.usatoday.com/usatonline/20010622/3424834s.htm.

Finally, the juvenile system still gives these kids a chance to turn their lives around. Adult facilities have all but abandoned any attempt to rehabilitate[1] inmates. Juvenile facilities, on the other hand, still offer opportunities for kids to evolve into productive members of society.*

I. _____

  A. _____

  B. _____

    1. _____

    2. _____

  C. _____

    1. _____

    2. _____

5. European-American parents tend to employ one of three distinct socialization patterns, as described by Diana Baumrind. *Authoritarian parents* tend to be strict, punitive,[2] and unsympathetic. They value obedience from children and try to shape their children's behavior to meet a set standard and to curb the children's wills. They do not encourage independence. They are detached and seldom praise their youngsters. In contrast, *permissive parents* give their children complete freedom and lax[3] discipline. The third group, *authoritative parents,* falls between these two extremes. They reason with their children, encouraging give and take. They allow children increasing responsibility as they get older and better at making decisions. They are firm but understanding. They set limits but also encourage independence. Their demands are reasonable, rational, and consistent.†

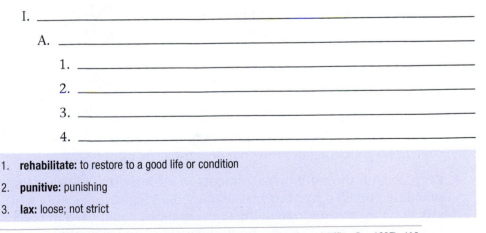

I. _____

  A. _____

    1. _____

    2. _____

    3. _____

    4. _____

---

1. **rehabilitate:** to restore to a good life or condition

2. **punitive:** punishing

3. **lax:** loose; not strict

---

* Adapted from Douglas A. Bernstein et al., *Psychology* (Boston: Houghton Mifflin Co., 1997), 410.

† Adapted from Jessica Reaves, "Should the Law Treat Kids and Adults Differently?" *Time.com,* May 21, 2001, www.time.com/time/nation/printout/0,8816,110232,00.html.

3

B. _____

    1. _____

    2. _____

C. _____

    1. _____

    2. _____

    3. _____

    4. _____

    5. _____

Reading Strategy:
Reading and Time Management

How often should you read? How long should you try to read in one sitting? How many times should you read a chapter? Is it better to read the whole chapter at once or just a section at a time?

These questions have no right or wrong answers. The most effective length, amount, and frequency of reading time will differ from student to student and from class to class. You will have to experiment to discover what works best for you, and you will probably need to make adjustments for each course you take.

However, be aware of the following general principles of effective time management:

■ Schedule time to read. Don't just try to fit reading in whenever you can; actually make an appointment to read by blocking out regular times on your calendar.

■ The best time to read is the time of day or night when you are most mentally alert. If you're a night owl, read at night. If you're a morning person, try to fit in your reading time at the beginning of your day.

■ Take frequent breaks during reading sessions. Regularly stand up and stretch, walk around, and rest your eyes for a few minutes.

■ Keep up with the reading assignments in a course by following the schedule provided by your instructor. Following the schedule will give you the basic understanding of the material you'll need in order to get the most out of class lectures, discussions, and activities.

■ Try to schedule time for multiple readings of the same chapter. Repeated exposure to information helps increase your retention of the material. If you hurriedly read large chunks of information all at once just before a test, you probably won't remember much of it. If you digest information slowly and regularly over a longer period of time, you'll remember more.

Write your answers to the following questions on the blanks provided.

1. Describe the typical length, amount, and frequency of reading time that seems to work best for you. _____

_____

2. Describe a time when you took a class that required you to alter significantly the length, amount, and/or frequency of your reading.

_____

_____

3. What time of day are you most mentally alert? Is that the time of day when you usually read? _____

_____

4. Which of the guidelines listed above do you already practice?

_____

_____

5. Which of the guidelines above do you think you should implement in order to get more out of your reading? _____

_____

 Use the following interactive websites to help you determine what is most important for you to do every day and to help you schedule your time so you can accomplish everything you need to do.

http://www.studygs.net/stressb.htm
http://www.studygs.net/schedule/index.htm
http://www.studygs.net/schedule/weekly.html

Reading Selections

Practicing the Active Reading Strategy

■ Before and While You Read

You can use active reading strategies before, while, and after you read a selection. The following are some suggestions for active reading strategies that you can employ before you read and as you are reading.

1. Skim the selection for any unfamiliar words. Circle or highlight any words you do not know.

2. As you read, underline, highlight, or circle important words or phrases.

3. Write down any questions about the selection if you are confused by the information presented.

4. Jot notes in the margin to help you understand the material.

TEXTBOOK READING: COLLEGE SUCCESS
College Lectures: Is Anybody Listening?

by Robert Holkeboer and Thomas Hoeksema

Do you have classes that are mostly lecture? How difficult is it for you to pay attention during these classes? The following reading selection discusses some of the negative aspects of lecture classes in college.

1   Today, American colleges and universities (originally modeled on German ones) are under strong attack from many quarters. Teachers, it is charged, are not doing a good job of teaching, and students are not doing a good job of learning. American businesses and industries suffer from unenterprising, uncreative executives educated not to think for themselves but to mouth outdated truisms the rest of the world has long discarded. College graduates lack both basic skills and general culture. Studies are conducted and reports are issued on the status of higher education, but any changes that result either are largely cosmetic or make a bad situation worse.

2   One aspect of American education too seldom challenged is the lecture system. Professors continue to lecture and students to take notes much as they did in the thirteenth century, when books were so scarce and expensive that few students could own them. The time is long overdue for us to abandon the lecture system and turn to methods that really work.

3   One problem with lectures is that listening intelligently is hard work. Reading the same material in a textbook is a more efficient way to learn because students can proceed as slowly as they need to until the subject matter becomes clear to them. Even simply paying attention is very difficult; people can listen at a rate of four hundred to six hundred words a minute while the most impassioned professor talks at scarcely a third that speed. This time lag between speech and comprehension leads to daydreaming. Many students believe years of watching television have sabotaged their attention span, but their real problem is that listening attentively is much harder than they think.

4   Worse still, attending lectures is passive learning, at least for inexperienced listeners. Active learning, in which students write essays or perform experiments and then have their work evaluated by an instructor, is far more beneficial for those who have not yet fully learned how to learn. Although it's true that techniques of active listening, such as trying to anticipate the speaker's next point or taking notes selectively, can enhance the value of a lecture, few students possess such skills at the beginning of their college careers. More commonly, students try to write everything down and even bring tape recorders to class in a clumsy effort to capture every word.

5   Students need to question their professors and to have their ideas taken seriously. Only then will they develop the analytical skills required to think intelligently and creatively. Most students learn best by engaging in frequent and even heated debate, not by scribbling down a professor's often unsatisfactory summary of complicated issues. They need small discussion classes that demand the common labors of teacher and students rather than classes in which one person, however learned, propounds his or her own ideas.*

■ Vocabulary

Read the following questions about some of the vocabulary words that appear in the previous selection. Circle the letter of the correct answer.

1. In paragraph 1, what does *unenterprising* mean?

   a. not living

   b. not showing initiative

   c. not breathing

   d. not drinking

---

* Adapted from Robert Holkeboer and Thomas Hoeksema, "College Lectures: Is Anyone Listening?" *The College Success Reader* (Boston: Houghton Mifflin co., 1998), 62–65. Copyright © 1998 by Houghton Mifflin Company. Reprinted with permission.

2. In paragraph 1, what does *cosmetic* mean?

    a. true   c. good

    b. superficial   d. makeup

3. In paragraph 3, what does *impassioned* mean?

    a. insensitive   c. emotional

    b. remote   d. demented

4. In paragraph 3, what does *sabotaged* mean?

    a. refunded   c. energized

    b. replaced   d. damaged

5. If something is *beneficial* it _____? (paragraph 4)

    a. hurts you   c. tires you

    b. helps you   d. bores you

■ Reading Skills

Respond to each of the following questions by circling the letter of the correct answer.

1. What is the topic of paragraph 2?

    a. American education   c. methods that really work

    b. the lecture system   d. books that are scarce

2. Which of the following is the topic sentence of paragraph 3?

    a. "One problem with lectures is that listening intelligently is hard work."

    b. "Reading the same material in a textbook is a more efficient way to learn because students can proceed as slowly as they need to until the subject matter becomes clear to them."

    c. "Even simply paying attention is very difficult; people can listen at a rate of four hundred to six hundred words a minute while the most impassioned professor talks at scarcely a third that speed."

    d. "This time lag between speech and comprehension leads to daydreaming."

3. What is the main idea of paragraph 4?

    a. Few students possess good note-taking skills.

    b. Attending lectures is passive learning for inexperienced students.

    c. Students try to write everything down.

    d. Students like to write essays.

4. Which of the following is a *minor* supporting detail in paragraph 5?

    a. Sentence 1   c. Sentence 3

    b. Sentence 2   d. Sentence 4

5. Which of the following is a *major* supporting detail in paragraph 4?

    a. Sentence 1   c. Sentence 3

    b. Sentence 2   d. Sentence 4

Practicing the Active Reading Strategy

■ After You Read

Now that you have read the selection, answer the following questions, using the active reading strategies that you learned in Chapter 1.

1. Identify and write down the point and purpose of this reading selection.

2. Did you circle or highlight any words that are unfamiliar to you? Can you figure out the meaning from the context of the passage? If not, then look up each word in a dictionary and find the definition that best describes the word as it is used in the selection. You may want to write the definition in the margin next to the word in the passage for future reference.

3. Predict any possible questions that may be used on a test about the content of this selection.

■ Questions for Discussion and Writing

Answer each of the following questions based on your reading of the selection.

1. Identify two problems students encounter when trying to learn from a lecture style class format. _____

_____

2. What do students learn by questioning their professors?

_____

3. Do you have any lecture courses? How well do you learn in that course? What could you do to improve your learning in a lecture course?

_____

_____

Practicing the Active Reading Strategy

■ Before and While You Read

You can use active reading strategies before, while, and after you read a selection. The following are some suggestions for active reading strategies that you can employ before you read and as you are reading.

1. Skim the selection for any unfamiliar words. Circle or highlight any words you do not know.

2. As you read, underline, highlight, or circle important words or phrases.

3. Write down any questions about the selection if you are confused by the information presented.

4. Jot notes in the margin to help you understand the material.

TEXTBOOK READING: AGRICULTURE
A Brief History of Agriculture

The food you eat and the clothes you wear depend upon agriculture. The study of agriculture is one of the oldest disciplines to study in schools. This brief history relates how agriculture affected the rise of civilizations.

1   The science of agriculture is almost as old as the human race. In the history of humans on the planet, many civilizations have come and gone. Some were powerful and warlike and some were small and peaceful. Some civilizations, such as the Greeks and Romans, provided the foundation for future civilizations. Architecture, art, literature, and political theories came from these civilizations. Other peoples accomplished great feats of engineering and building. Many aspects of ancient civilizations were different, but they all had one thing in common. Before any civilization could exist and flourish, a strong agricultural base had to be established. The reason for this was simple: Before roads could be built, buildings designed, or works of art created, the people had to be fed.

2   Before the creation of agriculture, people had to spend most of their time hunting and gathering food. These people are known as hunters and gatherers. In order to survive,

they had to find and collect the food nature had to offer. This was a full-time job for all people, and little time could be spent doing anything else. This caused the people to have to travel all the time because food in an area would soon be depleted.

3   When people found they could grow their own food, many of their problems were solved. Now they have a ready supply of food, and could now settle down in one place.

4   Shortly after people began to plant seed and tame animals, they began to search for better ways of growing food. By trial and error they discovered the best time to plant, the best plants to grow, and the best animals to raise. As they got better at growing plants and raising animals, more food could be produced.

As more and more food was produced, it took fewer people to grow the crops and keep the animals. In time, only certain people grew food, and others were then free to accomplish other things. A system of trade was established where goods such as pottery or clothing were traded for the food produced by the farmers. When farmers became really proficient, people could settle in one place and create villages. They could then build roads and towns and create art. This was because other people produced the food needed to feed the workers and builders. The stronger the agriculture of a civilization, the stronger could be the army and groups of workers. Without plenty of food to feed all of the people, little progress can be made by any people.*

■ Vocabulary

Read the following questions about some of the vocabulary words that appear in the previous selection. Before you look up the word, try to use the context of the passage to figure out the meaning. Then circle the letter of the correct answer for each question.

1. If people accomplish *feats*, what have they done? (paragraph 1)

   a. walk a very long way

   b. create products with skill

   c. destroy cities

   d. abandon their homes

2. What is meant by *aspects* in paragraph 1?

   a. people   c. characteristics

   b. religions   d. buildings

---

* Ray V. Herren, *Exploring Agriscience*, 4th ed. (Clifton Park: Delmar, 2011), 24–25. Print.

3. If something will *flourish*, what will it do? (paragraph 1)

    a. grow slowly   c. achieve success

    b. die off   d. stop producing

4. When food is *depleted* (paragraph 2), what has happened to it?

    a. used up   c. moved

    b. solved   d. grown too big

5. What is meant by *proficient* in paragraph 3?

    a. generous   c. abundant

    b. skilled   d. angry

■ Reading Skills

Respond to each of the following questions by circling the letter of the correct answer or by filling in the blank.

1. What is the topic sentence in paragraph 1?

    a. In the history of humans on the planet, many civilizations have come and gone.

    b. Architecture, art, literature, and political theories came from these civilizations.

    c. Many aspects of ancient civilizations were different, but they all had one thing in common.

    d. Before any civilization could exist and flourish, a strong agricultural base had to be established.

2. The topic of paragraph 2 is _____.

    a. people surviving before agriculture

    b. food depletion

    c. collecting ancient foods

    d. hunters and gatherers

3. Identify a major detail from paragraph 2. _____

_____

_____

4. The topic sentence of paragraph 3 is _____.

    a. By trial and error they discovered the best time to plant, the best plants to grow, and the best animals to raise.

    b. As more and more food was produced, it took fewer people to grow the crops and keep the animals.

    c. This was because other people produced the food needed to feed the workers and builders.

    d. Without, plenty of food to feed all of the people, little progress can be made by any people.

5. From the choices in question #4, which sentence is a minor detail in paragraph 3?

_____

Practicing the Active Reading Strategy

■ After You Read

Now that you have read the selection, answer the following questions, using the active reading strategies that you learned in Chapter 1.

    1. Identify and write down the point and purpose of this reading selection.

    2. Did you circle or highlight any words that are unfamiliar to you? Can you figure out the meaning from the context of the passage? If not, then look up each word in a dictionary and find the definition that best describes the word as it is used in the selection. You may want to write the definition in the margin next to the word in the passage for future reference.

    3. Predict any possible questions that may be used on a test about the content of this selection.

■ Questions for Discussion and Writing

Respond to each of the following questions based on your reading of the selection.

    1. What did every civilization need before it could grow? Why? _____

_____

_____

2. Why did hunters and gatherers need to move so often?

_____

3. Identify the ways that agriculture affects your life today. _____

_____

Practicing the Active Reading Strategy

■ Before and While You Read

You can use active reading strategies before, while, and after you read a selection. The following are some suggestions for active reading strategies that you can employ before you read and as you are reading.

1. Skim the selection for any unfamiliar words. Circle or highlight any words you do not know.

2. As you read, underline, highlight, or circle important words or phrases.

3. Write down any questions about the selection if you are confused by the information presented.

4. Jot notes in the margin to help you understand the material.

BIOGRAPHY:
Juan Miguel Fangio: Formula One Race Car Driver

Do you like fast cars? Have you ever watched NASCAR or been to a Formula One race? These can be very exciting and even dangerous events. Juan Manuel Fangio, the subject of the following reading selection, has been called one of the greatest drivers of all time.

1   Born in San Jose de Balcarce, Argentina, in 1911, Fangio left school at the age of 11 and began working as an automobile mechanic. With financial support from the town of Balcarce, he won his first major racing victory driving a Chevrolet in the Gran Premio Internacional del Norte of 1940, a grueling road race between Buenos Aires and Lima, Peru. After a hiatus during World War II, Fangio made it to Europe, where he was invited to race a Simca-Gordini in the French Grand Prix in Reims on July 18, 1948. (Grand Prix are the events that make up a single season on the Formula One circuit, the highest class of European auto racing according to the Federation International de l'Automobile.) Though he retired from both of the races he entered that day, Fangio announced his potential as a worthy rival for his European counterparts.

2   In October 1948, Fangio's Chevrolet rolled over a Peruvian cliff during a road race; though Fangio escaped almost uninjured, his co-driver and friend

Daniel Urrutia was killed in the crash. After briefly considering retirement, Fangio returned to Europe the following summer for his first full European racing season. He won his first four races, and by the end of the season had racked up seven major wins. In 1950, the Formula One World Championship was created. Fangio, who had signed on with the Alfa Romeo team, was just shy of his 39th birthday at the start of that first championship season. He lost the title that year to his Italian teammate, Giuseppe Farina, but stayed with Alfa Romeo and held on to win his first Formula One championship title in 1951.

3   Over the course of his career, Fangio would drive some of the best cars Mercedes-Benz, Ferrari, Maserati, and Alfa Romeo ever produced. In addition to five Formula One titles between 1951 and 1957, he triumphed in an incredible 24 of his 51 Grand Prix races. Perhaps his greatest achievement came in his last full season, at the German Grand Prix in Nurburgring in 1957. Fangio came from 56 seconds behind to overtake the rival Ferrari team, bettering the track record by an incredible 12 seconds on three consecutive laps. The victory gave Fangio his fifth Formula One title. He retired the following year.

4   Known for his spectacular technical ability and for his demure manner, Fangio has been called the greatest driver of all time. He died in July 1995, and was buried in his native Balcarce.*

■ Vocabulary

Read the following questions about some of the vocabulary words that appear in the previous selection. Before you look up the word, try to use the context of the passage to figure out the meaning. Then circle the letter of the correct answer for each question.

1. In paragraph 2 what does *grueling* mean?

    a. lax   c. exhausting; very tiring

    b. a thin porridge   d. hopeful

2. In paragraph 1 what does *hiatus* mean?

    a. interruption in time   c. non-stop work

    b. fall apart   d. continuous

3. In paragraph 2 what does *racked* mean?

    a. release   c. poised

    b. To accumulate or score   d. outwitted

4. In paragraph 3 what does *triumphed* mean?

    a. unsuccessful   c. outlawed

    b. enthusiastic   d. obtain victory

* *Juan Manuel Fangio makes Formula One debut.* History.com. 18 July 2010. Web.

5. In paragraph 4 what does *demure* mean?

   a. cocky   c. shy

   b. boastful   d. modest

■ Reading Skills

Respond to each of the following questions by circling the letter of the correct answer or by filling in the blank.

1. What is the topic of paragraph 1?

   a. Fangio made it to Europe to race

   b. a grueling road race

   c. began working as an automobile mechanic

   d. worthy rival for his European counterparts

2. What is the topic sentence of paragraph 2?

   a. Sentence 1

   b. Sentence 2

   c. Sentence 4

   d. Sentence 5

3. Which of the following is a major supporting detail in paragraph 2?

   a. Sentence 1

   b. Sentence 2

   c. Sentence 3

   d. Sentence 4

4. Write the topic sentence of paragraph 3.

   _____

   _____

5. Which of the following is a major supporting detail in paragraph 3?

   a. Sentence 2

   b. Sentence 3

   c. Sentence 4

   d. Sentence 5

Practicing the Active Reading Strategy

■ After You Read

Now that you have read the selection, answer the following questions, using the active reading strategies that you learned in Chapter 1.

1. Identify and write down the point and purpose of this reading selection.

2. Did you circle or highlight any words that are unfamiliar to you? Can you figure out the meaning from the context of the passage? If not, then look up each word in a dictionary and find the definition that best describes the word as it is used in the selection. You may want to write the definition in the margin next to the word in the passage for future reference.

3. Predict any possible questions that may be used on a test about the content of this selection.

■ Questions for Discussion and Writing

Respond to each of the following questions based on your reading of the selection.

1. Do you believe Fangio could have achieved his goals without the financial support of his town? Explain your reasons. _____

   _____

   _____

2. Why do you believe Fangio considered retirement after his friend's death? Explain your reasons. _____

   _____

   _____

3. Can you think of another athlete who has considered retirement and then come back to achieve greatness like Juan Manuel Fangio? Give examples.

   _____

   _____

   _____

Vocabulary Strategy: Context and Meaning

When you encounter an unfamiliar word as you read and go to the dictionary to look it up, you'll often find several different meanings and variations for that word. How do you know which definition is the right one? You have to look at the **context**—*the words, phrases, and sentences surrounding that word*—to determine which meaning applies.

To figure out the right definition, you may first need to determine the word's part of speech in the sentence. Many words can function as different parts of speech (for example, the word *left* can be a noun, a verb, an adjective, or an adverb), so you'll have to figure out how the word is being used before you can decide which definition applies. For example, the word *interest* is both a noun and a verb. The noun form means both "a state of curiosity" and "a charge for a loan." Which of the noun form meanings is being used in the following sentence?

Finally, the fourth rule to becoming rich is to take advantage of compound *interest*.

This sentence is about becoming wealthy, so you know the word *interest* refers to money.

Vocabulary Exercise

The following sentences all come from paragraphs throughout this chapter. Look up the italicized words in a dictionary and write on the blank provided the definition that best describes how each word is being used.

1. Many people think that the 1950s, an era of breadwinning dads and stay-at-home moms, was the last decade in a long era of *stable* families, but 1950s families actually reversed a 100-year trend of rising divorce rates.

   _____

2. There are two *models* for explaining dropping out of high school.

   _____

3. Always lock car doors and *trunks*—even at home—and keep keys out of children's reach. _____

4. Prompted by our modest exertions, just a few minutes into a walk the body begins to produce endorphins, chemical compounds that reduce pain and stress and enhance memory and judgment as they *course* through the brain. _____

5. Prompted by our *modest* exertions, just a few minutes into a walk the body begins to produce endorphins, chemical compounds that reduce pain and stress and enhance memory and judgment as they course through the brain.

_____

3

Chapter 3 Review

Write the correct answers in the blanks in the following statements.

1. _____ are the specific facts, statistics, examples, steps, anecdotes, reasons, descriptions, or definitions that explain or prove the general _____ stated in the topic sentence.

2. There are two kinds of supporting details: _____ details and _____ details. The _____ details are the main points that explain or support the idea in the topic sentence. _____ details offer more explanation of the major details.

3. _____ are words that assist readers in distinguishing between major and minor details because they make connections and distinctions among the different details.

4. _____ is a technique that involves using lines, boxes, circles, or other shapes to show how sentences in a paragraph are related.

5. An _____ is a list of supporting details labeled with a system of numbers and letters that show the relationships of the details to one another.

6. The best time to _____ is when you are most mentally alert.

7. When there are multiple meanings for a word that you need to look up, you must use the _____ of the sentence or passage to help you determine which definition is the best.

michaeljung@shutterstock.com

CHAPTER

4

Implied Main Ideas

Goals for Chapter 4

- Define the term *implied main idea.*
- Form generalizations based on specific details.
- State the implied main idea of a paragraph.
- Apply the steps of the SQ3R strategy to reading selections.

When you read Chapter 2 of this book, you learned that many paragraphs include a topic sentence that clearly states the main idea. Other paragraphs, however, do not contain a topic sentence. Does that mean they don't have a main point? No, it means that readers must do a little more work to figure out what that point—or the *implied main idea*—is. To see how much you already know about drawing conclusions about a main idea, take the following pretest.

Pretest

The following paragraphs do not include a stated main idea. Read each paragraph and see if you can determine its main point. Circle the letter of the sentence that best states the main idea.

1. As athletic competition and participation mushroomed[1] in the last few decades, the need for specialized care became apparent. The term *sports medicine* began to take on many different connotations[2] and to gain in popularity. Many health professionals began to advertise themselves as "sports medicine specialists." This was done as a marketing tool to gain new business, but these specialists lacked the training needed to ensure proper care for their patients. Even today, many individuals ask how sports medicine differs from the medical treatment nonathletes receive. True sports medicine specialists have training that allows them to specifically address the needs of the athlete.[*]

   a. Proper training is important for treating athletes.

   b. Proper training for treating athletes has developed and changed over the last few decades.

   c. Treating athletes is no different from treating nonathletes.

   d. Marketing is an important tool in treating athletes.

2. For centuries in China, soy has been served as both a food and a drink. In the 1930s, auto magnate[3] Henry Ford used soybeans to make paint enamel. Today, soy can be found in salad dressings, cereals, breads, burgers, energy bars, and frozen desserts. Soy can even be found in moisturizers.[†]

---

1. **mushroomed:** to grow rapidly

2. **connotations:** suggested meanings

3. **magnate:** powerful, influential person

---

[*] Robert C. France, *Introduction to Sports Medicine and Athletic Training,* 2nd ed. (Clifton Park: Delmar, 2011), 4. Print.

[†] Adapted from Lisa Singer, "The Truth About Soy," *Real Simple,* April 2004, 165.

a. Soy beans are delicious.

b. Soy can be used in a variety of ways.

c. Soy may be the key to finding a non-oil based fuel for cars.

d. If you use soy as a moisturizer, you'll see visible results in days.

3. I have clung to a potato cart as it climbed the steep, rugged mountains to Kurdish[1] refugee camps. I have flown in a dark, cold, windowless cargo plane to cover a story in the Mideast desert. I have watched the most graphic and gory bone surgery, standing just inches from the carved limbs. On the other hand, my face flushes hot and my heart races before facing a person with whom I have had a major disagreement. I worry that someone won't like or admire me. I burn with anxiety when I think I'm being talked about behind my back. Nothing unnerves me more than the prospect of being humiliated. Even writing these words, I wonder what friends and family will think when they read them. My sister Leslie, who at least appears fearless, has asked me often over the years: "Why in the world do you care what any of these people think?" I've never had a good answer.*

a. The author has done many dangerous things in her life.

b. The author is not afraid to do dangerous things but is afraid of emotional things.

c. The author is concerned about what her friends and family will think of her writing.

d. The author's sister, Leslie, counsels her on a variety of things.

4. Who is a master student? A master student is a person who has attained[2] a level of skill that goes beyond technique. A master student is curious about everything, and the unknown does not frighten him or her. He or she can take a large body of information and sift[3] through it to discover relationships. Mastery of skills is important to the master student, and work is generally effortless; struggle evaporates. Mastery can lead to flashy results, but often the result of mastery is a sense of profound satisfaction, well-being, and timelessness.†

1. **Kurdish:** related to the Kurds, people inhabiting Kurdistan in Southwest Asia

2. **attained:** achieved

3. **sift:** sort

* "Pulse" by Tracy Chutorian Semler. Reprinted by permission of International Creative Management, Inc. Copyright © 2001 by Tracy Chutorian Semler.

† Adapted from Dave Ellis, "The Master Student," *Becoming a Master Student* (Boston: Houghton Mifflin Co., 2000), 26–27.

4

a. The master student has many different personalities.

b. The master student understands the importance of developing certain critical skills.

c. There are many flashy results that can be attained by a master.

d. The master student feels like he or she needs to be an expert at everything.

5. What do I have planned for the summer? Well, by August, my body fat will match that of a *Survivor*[1] contestant. My abdominal muscles will be flat, my biceps round, my inner thighs carved, and my rear end will be jiggle-free. Oh, and I'll be smarter and far more accomplished, once I finish Plato's *Republic*,[2] watch those French videos, hone[3] my pastry skills, organize my closets, and embrace the power of yoga. It's going to happen. Trust me.*

a. The author is going to change her body type by August.

b. The author is going to organize her closet by August.

c. The author has some very ambitious summer plans.

d. The author has many different skills.

Understanding Implied Main Ideas

Every paragraph contains a main idea. Sometimes that main idea is stated outright in a topic sentence. Sometimes, though, the main idea is implied. An **implied main idea** *is one that is suggested but not stated.* To determine the implied main idea, you examine the details presented and draw from them a conclusion about the overall point.

If you think about it, you figure out implied main ideas quite often in your daily life. Fowr example, look at the following conversation:

Mother: How was your day, honey?

Son: Well, I overslept. As I was rushing to get to class, I slipped and fell in a mud puddle. I left an assignment at home that was due today, so I'll lose points for turning it in late. At lunch, my girlfriend told me she wants to break up with me.

1. *Survivor*: a popular reality television show

2. **Plato's** *Republic*: a philosophical work

3. **hone**: sharpen or improve

* Adapted from Linda Wells, "Better, Stronger, Faster," *Allure*, July 2001, 30.

The son answered his mother's question with a series of specific details. What conclusion can you draw from them? Every incident he reported caused him pain, trouble, or aggravation, so it's safe to conclude that he had a pretty bad day. Here's another example:

> You're in the park. You see a dog. You notice that the dog is not wearing a collar. The dog looks dirty and wet. The dog also appears underfed because you can see its ribs through its skin. The dog appears to be alone, not with a person.

What conclusion do you make? Most people would say that the animal is probably a stray.

You yourself notice details, add them together, and draw conclusions all the time. In Chapter 3 of this book, you practiced recognizing supporting details, the information that proves or explains a main idea. A paragraph with an implied main idea contains *only* supporting details. These details are the clues that you put together to figure out the author's point.

To improve your ability to draw these conclusions while you read, it's helpful to remember what you learned about the terms *general* and *specific* back in Chapter 2.

Figuring out an implied main idea requires you to form a generalization based on a series of specific items or ideas. Look at the following group of words:

coat

pants

dress

shirt

What generalization can you make about this list of items? They're all things you wear, so the general term that describes them is *clothing*.

Now, examine another list:

paper

desk

pencil

toothpick

This group is a little trickier. When you read the first three items, you may have thought they were *things in an office* or *things you use at school*. But the last item isn't in either of those categories. When you add up all the details and look for the similarities, you realize that these are all *products made from wood*.

Exercise **4.1**

Write on the blank above each group of words a general category that includes all of the items listed.

1. **General Idea:** _____

    airplane

    helicopter

    bird

    kite

2. **General Idea:** _____

    leaf blower

    weed eater

    lawn mower

    hedge clipper

3. **General Idea:** _____

    steering wheel

    tire

    hula hoop

    donut

4. **General Idea:** _____

    rap

    hip-hop

    disco

    alternative rock

5. **General Idea:** _____

    ice cream

    cake

    pie

    cookies

6. General Idea: _____

river

ocean

stream

pond

7. General Idea: _____

subway

basement

root cellar

gas station tanks

8. General Idea: _____

cheese

yogurt

cream

butter

9. General Idea: _____

dictionary

magazine

notebook paper

football field

10. General Idea: _____

e-mail

phone

letter

face-to-face

As you remember from Chapter 2, a group of specific sentences can also support a general idea. For example, read the following sentences:

Maggie works seven days a week.

Maggie works over ten hours a day.

Maggie hasn't taken a vacation in three years.

What general statement would include all three of those specific sentences? The answer is Maggie works too much.

Exercise **4.2**

On the blank above each group of sentences, write a general sentence that in-cludes all of the specific details given.

1. **General Sentence:** _____

   Police officers sometimes drive patrol cars in high-speed chases.

   Police officers can be wounded in fights or shot by criminals.

   Police officers have to go into dark buildings or alleys to investigate crimes.

2. **General Sentence:** _____

   Raj has several newspapers delivered to his home every day.

   Raj belongs to several book clubs and attends book club meetings regularly.

   Raj reads six or seven books a month.

3. **General Sentence:** _____

   The sun doesn't shine very much in Seattle.

   Seattle has about 200 rainy days a year.

   Some streets often flood in Seattle.

4. **General Sentence:** _____

   Justin weeds his garden every day.

   Justin has planted four tomato plants in his garden.

   Justin spends a lot of money on flowers for his garden.

5. **General Sentence:** _____

   Jin sends e-mail to many of her friends and family members on a weekly basis.

   Jin does most of her shopping on the Internet.

   Jin surfs the Web for information on movies, books, and other things that interest her.

Determining Implied Main Ideas

To figure out the implied main idea in a paragraph, you can often use a me-thodical, step-by-step approach. Basically, this procedure involves looking for clues in the supporting details, adding them together, and drawing a logical conclusion based on the evidence. These next sections will explain and give you practice with each of the four steps in this process:

Step 1: Find the subject of each sentence.

Step 2: Determine a general topic based on the specific details.

Step 3: State an implied main idea that includes both the topic and what the author is saying about that topic.

As you become a better reader, you will be able to complete all of these steps in your head most of the time.

Step 1: Find the Subject of Each Sentence

The first step in discovering an implied main idea is to closely examine the sup-porting details. The major and minor details in a paragraph will provide you with the clues you need to draw a conclusion about the author's point. For example, read the following paragraph:

(1) "Calvin and Hobbes," a comic strip about a little boy and his ti-ger, often tackles classical, philosophical, and ethical subjects. (2) The "Doonesbury" comic strip takes on political subjects, and even the "Pea-nuts" comic strip included social commentary on the Vietnam War. (3) "The Far Side" cartoons often focus on scientific ethics. (4) The "Dilbert" comic strip points out the illogic and insensitivity within American corpora-tions. (5) The "For Better or Worse" comic strip often examines morality and family issues.*

Here are the subjects in each of the sentences:

Sentence 1: "Calvin and Hobbes"

Sentence 2: "Doonesbury" and "Peanuts"

Sentence 3: "The Far Side"

Sentence 4: "Dilbert"

Sentence 5: "For Better or Worse"

---

* Adapted from *USA Today Newsview*, August 1997, 5.

Exercise **4.3**

On the blanks below each paragraph, write the subject of each sentence.

1. **(1)** Louisiana was named after France's King Louis XIV. **(2)** South Carolina comes from *Carolus*, the Latin word for Charles I, King of England. **(3)** Maryland was named after Queen Mary, wife of England's King harles I. **(4)** Georgia was named in honor of England's King George II. **(5)** Both Virginia and West Virginia were named for Elizabeth I, the "virgin" queen.

   Sentence 1 subject: _____

   Sentence 2 subject: _____

   Sentence 3 subject: _____

   Sentence 4 subject: _____

   Sentence 5 subjects: _____

2. **(1)** Teachers, according to 79 percent of public high school students, are too easy on students when it comes to enforcing rules and assigning homework. **(2)** In addition, half of teens in public schools say their teachers and schools do not challenge them. **(3)** Too many disruptive students in classrooms, according to 70 percent of teenagers, are interfering with learning. **(4)** Schools' standards for graduation, say 70 percent of students, are too low. **(5)** According to three-fourths of students, diplomas are given to students even if they don't learn the required material.*

   Sentence 1 subject: _____

   Sentence 2 subject: _____

   Sentence 3 subject: _____

   Sentence 4 subject: _____

   Sentence 5 subject: _____

3. **(1)** *Latina* is magazine that focuses on beauty, fashion, style, and food for Hispanic women. **(2)** *Essence* magazine contains articles concerning issues of beauty, hair, travel, and lifestyle for African American women. **(3)** *Mode* is a new magazine devoted entirely to issues affecting "plus-size" women. **(4)** *Sport Illustrated* focuses on articles about professional and college sports. **(5)** Men who are interested in fashion and style might read *GQ*.

---

* Adapted from "Teenagers Want More from Public Schools," *USA Today Newsview*, August 1997, 4.

Sentence 1 subject: _____

Sentence 2 subject: _____

Sentence 3 subject: _____

Sentence 4 subject: _____

Sentence 5 subject: _____

4. **(1)** Thomas Jefferson, one of the writers of the Declaration of Independence, was lean, elegant, remote, and a bit sneaky. **(2)** John Adams, who contributed to the Declaration as well, was stout,[1] cheap, and perhaps too honest about himself and everyone else. **(3)** Considered somewhat eccentric, or odd, Benjamin Franklin was a noted inventor and diplomat who was somewhat chubby and messy, but neither of those things interfered with his ability to help write the most important document in American history. **(4)** George Washington was a genius at lifting morale[2] and knowing when to retreat to fight another day, so keeping the Founding Fathers agreeable and on task was his major contribution.

Sentence 1 subject: _____

Sentence 2 subject: _____

Sentence 3 subject: _____

Sentence 4 subject: _____

5. **(1)** Philadelphia is known for its "Philly cheese steak." **(2)** Coney Island in Brooklyn, New York, is known for its hot dogs. **(3)** Miami is famous for its Cuban food, particularly chicken and rice, or "arroz con pollo." **(4)** Chicago has made a name for itself by serving great deep-dish pizza. **(5)** And you can't go to Boston without getting the best clam chowder in the entire United States.

Sentence 1 subject: _____

Sentence 2 subject: _____

Sentence 3 subject: _____

Sentence 4 subject: _____

Sentence 5 subject: _____

1. **stout:** plump
2. **morale:** spirits of a person or group

Step 2: Determine a General Topic Based on the Specific Details

Once you've discovered the supporting details' subjects, you can make a generalization about them. You must make this generalization before you can complete the final step. In using logic to determine an overall category for the details, you are figuring out the overall topic of the paragraph. You'll need to be able to include this topic in your statement of the main idea.

Exercise 4.4

Read each of the following paragraphs and write the correct answers on the blank after each one.

1. **(1)** Saving most of your income may allow you to retire early, like John Greaney, who retired at the age of 38 after saving aggressively in his twenties and early thirties. **(2)** Experts say that living in the smallest, least expensive home that will meet your needs will give you more money to spend during your retirement. **(3)** Other things to do so that you can live well while retired include living more cheaply, tapping into your retirement account sooner, or arranging to work a few hours so that you still have some kind of income to help you live.*

   Sentence 1 subject: _____

   Sentence 2 subject: _____

   Sentence 3 subject: _____

   General topic of paragraph: _____

2. **(1)** At only age sixteen, Mae Jemison entered Stanford University, one of the top colleges in the nation, and earned a bachelor's degree in chemical engineering. **(2)** After earning this degree, she went to medical school at Cornell University in New York and earned a medical degree in 1981. **(3)** Then she joined the Peace Corps, working as a medical officer for more than two years in Africa. **(4)** Next, she entered NASA's astronaut program, and when she rocketed into space aboard the space shuttle *Endeavor* in 1992, she became America's first African-American female astronaut. **(5)** She worked for NASA for six years and then resigned to found her own company, the Jemison Group, which tries to bring advanced technologies to the developing world. **(6)** She is also a college professor and has been a professional dancer.†

---

* Adapted from Linda Stern, "Retire When You Want To," *Reader's Digest*, RD.com, July 17, 2001.

† Adapted from Jim Dawson, "Mae Jemison: Woman of Many Facets," *Star Tribune* (Minneapolis, MN), March 13, 2000.

Sentence 1 subject: _____

Sentence 2 subject: _____

Sentence 3 subject: _____

Sentence 4 subject: _____

Sentence 5 subject: _____

General topic of paragraph: _____

3. **(1)** With wireless networking, you can surf the Web without plugging into the wall. **(2)** Soon, using wireless technologies such as Bluetooth, in addition to embedded computing, all the appliances in your home might be "talking." **(3)** The water heater might hear from the furnace that it's on vacation mode and adjust itself automatically. **(4)** Medical equipment can be miniaturized and even implanted in your body, communicating to doctors via the Web.*

Sentence 1 subject: _____

Sentence 2 subject: _____

Sentence 3 subject: _____

Sentence 4 subject: _____

General topic of paragraph: _____

4. **(1)** What could possibly be on a video made for cats? **(2)** To start, colorful bird sequences filled with stereo chirps and trills are very attractive to cats. **(3)** Gerbils scurrying across reddish desert rocks and a chipmunk darting into a grate rate more highly with other furry viewers, who watch intently from their perches until excitement finally propels them to paw the screen or to look behind the television set to find the critters they've been watching. **(4)** Also popular is the televised aquarium, which makes some kitties jump to the top of the television to try to dip their paws into the image on the screen.†

Sentence 2 subject: _____

Sentence 3 subject: _____

Sentence 4 subject: _____

General topic of paragraph: _____

---

* Greg Anderson, *Connecting with Computer Science,* 2nd ed. (Boston; Course Technology, 2011), 34. Print.

† Adapted from "The Cats' Meow," advertisement, National Syndications, Inc.

4

5. **(1)** On his own, an orangutan[1] named Fu Manchu figured out how to use a wire lock-pick to escape from his cage at the Omaha Zoo, hiding the tool in his mouth each time he was recaptured. **(2)** Another orangutan at a Seattle zoo came up with a ploy,[2] too, by pretending to drop or lose a piece of fruit and then asking for a replacement while actually hiding it. **(3)** A killer whale named Corky let a keeper stand on his head—a trick he had never been taught—to help the man reach a baby whale in danger of dying in a stretcher hanging over the tank. **(4)** An ape named Chantek who learned to earn coins for doing chores and to trade them for treats came up with the idea to try to expand his money supply by counterfeiting extra coins from tinfoil.*

Sentence 1 subject: _____

Sentence 2 subject: _____

Sentence 3 subject: _____

Sentence 4 subject: _____

General topic of paragraph: _____

Broad and Narrow Topic Review

As you complete this step, remember what you learned in Chapter 2 about topics that are too broad or too narrow. Make sure the topic you choose is neither too broad nor too narrow.

Exercise **4.5**

After each paragraph, label each topic by writing *N* on the blank if it's too narrow, *B* if it's too broad, and *T* if it's the correct topic.

1. The mothers of today's "Generation X," the group of Americans born between 1961 and 1981, did 89 percent of the cooking in their homes, but their grown children now tend to divide evening meal preparation equally between the husband and the wife. The parents of Generation Xers usually insisted that their families sit down to eat meals together almost every day, but parents and children today eat only about five

---

1. **orangutan:** a type of ape

2. **ploy:** a sneaky trick

---

* Adapted from Eugene Linden, "What Animals Really Think," *Reader's Digest*, February 2000, 116–123.

meals per week as a family. The length of meals has changed, too: in the homes of most older generation people, mealtimes usually lasted at least thirty minutes, but now only half of Generation Xers stay at the table that long.*

_____ a. Mealtimes

_____ b. Mealtimes in older generation and Generation X homes

_____ c. The length of mealtimes in older generation and Generation X homes

2. Although air conditioning is the invention that keeps us cool and comfortable in the middle of the summer, it also has left many of us psychologically unprepared to deal with the outdoors. People now think that they are incapable of handling the discomfort of high temperatures and humidity. Air conditioning has also been blamed for encouraging urban sprawl and draining the South's energy resources. In 1997, for example, Florida alone spent $1.8 billion just on air conditioning. Furthermore, Southern traditionalists accuse air conditioning of speeding up their lifestyles, encouraging an influx[1] of Northerners, and contributing to a decline in neighborly conduct.[†]

_____ a. Air conditioning

_____ b. Air conditioning's effect on psychology

_____ c. Air conditioning's negative effects

3. The ancient Greeks would tuck rosemary twigs in their hair while studying to help them remember what they were learning. They also wore rosemary garlands to ward off the "evil eye," a look or stare believed to harm others. The popular belief at one time was that only evil people could not grow rosemary. During the Middle Ages, a common practice was to place rosemary under a pillow at night to prevent nightmares. At one time, rosemary was used in almost all wedding ceremonies. Sprigs of rosemary were dipped in scented waters and then woven into a bridal wreath for the bride to wear around her head.[‡]

---

1.   **influx:** flowing in

---

* Adapted from "Who's Cooking in Gen X Households?" *USA Today*, July 1998, 9–10.

† Adapted from Sean Mussenden, "100 Years of Cool Air Change South," *Orlando Sentinel*, June 21, 2002, www.orlandosentinel.com.

‡ Adapted from Tim Haas and Jan Haas, "Using Rosemary," *News Herald* (Morganton, NC), March 28, 2004, 5C.

_____ a. Wedding customs involving rosemary

_____ b. Superstitions

_____ c Historical uses of rosemary

4. Stroll down a country lane. Meander[1] along an ancient footpath. Picnic next to a bubbling stream or a village courtyard. Walking tours will also give you a closer look at a country and its people. You'll get to know your fellow travelers, too. Last but not least, you'll get lots of exercise because walking vacations usually involve several miles of hiking per day.*

_____ a. Vacations

_____ b. Things to see and do on walking tours

_____ c. Meeting people on walking tours

5. Breathing-related sleep disorders, such as chronic snoring and obstructive sleep apnea, increase the risk of high blood pressure, heart attacks, and stroke. Individuals with insomnia, the most common sleep complaint, become irritable and depressed, get into more traffic accidents, develop memory problems, and have difficulties concentrating and doing their jobs. According to recent research, inadequate sleep affects growth hormone secretion, increasing the likelihood of obesity, and impairs the body's ability to use insulin, which can lead to diabetes. Individuals chronically deprived of enough sleep may become more susceptible to certain sicknesses, and researchers speculate that disturbed sleep may be the reason why individuals under stress—such as students taking exams or grieving widows and widowers—may have lower levels of certain infection-fighting cells than normal.[†]

_____ a. Problems due to lack of sleep

_____ b. Lack of sleep

_____ c. Insomnia

---

1. **meander:** walk slowly

---

* Adapted from Judy Hammond, "In Step with the World," _Daily News_, July 15, 2001, Travel Section, 12.

† Dianne Hales, _An Invitation to Wellness: Making Healthy Choices._ Belmont: Thomson Higher Education, 2007, 142. Print.

Step 3: State an Implied Main Idea

If you have successfully completed steps 1 and 2, you have systematically gone through each thinking stage necessary to state the paragraph's main idea. *It is in this last step that you put together all of the clues you have examined to come up with a statement of the main idea in your own words.* This requires you not only to recognize the subjects in the supporting details but also to draw a general conclusion based on *what is being said about each of these subjects.* Then, once more, you decide on a general category of ideas or things that include all of those statements.

Remember what you learned about main ideas and topic sentences in Chapter 2. The main idea has two parts: the topic and the point the author wants to make about that topic. The implied main idea is no different. It, too, should include both of those parts. Your statement will begin with the general topic you discovered in step 2 of this process. Then, it will go on to express the conclusion you drew from adding together the specific supporting details.

As an illustration, let's go through all three steps for the paragraph below:

(1) In 1959, the Mercury astronauts were household names, but today, few Americans can name even one of the 148 Space Shuttle astronauts currently on NASA's roster. (2) In the early days of America's space program, people were interested in astronauts because they were swaggering, bragging, boastful pilots, but now that two-thirds of them are doctors, scientists, and engineers, they're no longer "glamorous." (3) In the 1960s, astronauts were worshipped by the American public as heroes, but today, most Americans are indifferent[1] to them. (4) People used to stop their lives to pay close attention when astronauts went into space, but now, the Space Shuttle goes up and comes back with little fanfare.*

Step 1: *Sentence 1:* Americans' past and present knowledge of astronauts' names

Sentence 2: Americans' past and present interest in astronauts

Sentence 3: Americans' past and present perceptions of astronauts

Sentence 4: Americans' past and present attentiveness to astronauts' missions

---

1. **indifferent:** not interested

---

* Adapted from Traci Watson, "Quick: Name an Astronaut," *USA Today,* July 12, 2001, 1A.

4

Step 2: *Paragraph's topic:* Changes in Americans' attitudes about astronauts

Step 3: *Sentence 1:* Knew names → don't know names

    Sentence 2: Interested → not interested

    Sentence 3: Hero worship → indifference

    Sentence 4: Attentive → not attentive.

    Implied main idea: Between the early days of the space program and now, Americans' attitudes toward astronauts have changed from caring to indifference.

As you can see, determining implied main ideas is not only a necessary reading skill; it also helps you sharpen your thinking skills. You must analyze and apply logic as you complete each step of this process to draw a final conclusion. This kind of practice will lead to better thinking in general.

Exercise 4.6

Write the correct answer on each of the blanks that follow the paragraphs below.

1. **(1)** The cuisine served in Mexico features rice, corn, and beans, which are low in fat and high in nutrients. **(2)** African-American cuisine traces some of its roots to food preferences from West Africa (for examples, peanuts, okra, and black-eyed peas), as well as to traditional American foods, such as fish, game, green, and sweet potatoes. **(3)** The mainland Chinese diet, which is plant-based, high in carbohydrates, and low in fats and animal protein, is considered one of the healthiest in the world. **(4)** Many Indian dishes highlight healthful ingredients such as vegetables and legumes (peas and beans).*

Sentence 1 subject: _____

Sentence 2 subject: _____

Sentence 3 subject: _____

Sentence 4 subject: _____

General topic of paragraph: _____

Implied main idea: _____

2. **(1)** Ever wanted to just up and leave your spouse for an extended—but temporary—period of time? **(2)** Janis Kirstein is a high school art teacher

---

* Dianne Hales, *An Invitation to Wellness: Making Healthy Choices* (Belmont: Thomson Higher Education, 2007), 166. Print.

in Louisville who says she is taking a time-out at the Vermont Studio Center in Johnson, Vermont, to spend a month nurturing[1] her creativity and learning more about art. **(3)** Sally Howald took a leave from her job as a creative director for an ad agency to teach advertising strategies in Holland and to get away from her life as "soccer mom and full-time working mom" and reconnect with the person she was before she married. **(4)** Joan Mister, however, waited until her children were grown and then drove 30,000 miles alone in six months, having her sixty-fifth birthday on the road. **(5)** Her trip, she says, was about self-exploration.*

Sentence 2 subject: _____

Sentence 3 subject: _____

Sentence 4 subject: _____

General topic of paragraph: _____

_____

Implied main idea: _____

_____

3. **(1)** Life satisfaction goes up slightly with age, and emotions become less intense and more stable. **(2)** Education, intelligence, gender, and race do not matter much for happiness. **(3)** African Americans and Hispanics have lower rates of depression than white Americans, but they do not report greater happiness. **(4)** Neither gender is clearly happier, but in different studies women are both happier and sadder than men.[†]

Sentence 1 subject: _____

Sentence 2 subject: _____

Sentence 3 subject: _____

Sentence 4 subject: _____

General topic of paragraph: _____

Implied Main Idea: _____

_____

1. **nurturing:** developing or helping to grow

* Adapted from Karen S. Peterson, "Relationship Respite," *USA Today*, July 19, 2001, 1D.

† Dianne Hales, *An Invitation to Wellness: Making Healthy Choices* (Belmont: Thomson Higher Education, 2007), 136. Print.

4. **(1)** Girls now outnumber boys in student government, honor societies, school newspapers, and debating clubs. **(2)** A recent study found girls ahead of boys in almost every measure of well-being; for example, girls feel closer to their families, have higher aspirations,[1] and even boast better assertiveness skills. **(3)** Boys earn 70 percent of the Ds and Fs that teachers dole out. **(4)** They make up two-thirds of students labeled "learning disabled." **(5)** They account for 80 percent of high school dropouts. **(6)** And they are less likely to go to college than ever before; by 2007, universities are projected to enroll 9.2 million women to 6.9 million men.*

Sentence 1 subject: _____

Sentence 2 subject: _____

Sentence 3 subject: _____

Sentence 4 subject: _____

Sentence 5 subject: _____

Sentence 6 subject: _____

General topic of paragraph: _____

_____

Implied main idea: _____

_____

5. **(1)** Do cops go easy on celebrities? **(2)** Consider the case of a high-profile politician who was linked to the disappearance of his girlfriend. **(3)** Despite evidence linking him to the woman, the police didn't interview him, search his apartment, or give him a lie-detector test early on in the case. **(4)** Or look at the circumstances surrounding a New York City publicist, who some say backed her car into a group of people waiting to get into a famous nightclub. **(5)** By the time the police got around to asking her some questions, her lawyer had arrived and instructed her not to say anything, arranging for her to be released on bail and back at home before dawn. **(6)** Then there's the case of a famous child actor who claims his wife was shot while he went into a restaurant. **(7)** Police declined to name him a suspect despite the fact that he had a gun in his car, and it was clear that the couple was unhappily married.[†]

1. **aspirations:** goals

---

* Adapted from Anna Mulrine, "Are Boys the Weaker Sex?" *U.S. News and World Report,* July 2, 2001.

† Adapted from Rich Hampson, "Do the Cops Go Easy on Celebrities? Maybe Not," *USA Today,* July 19, 2001, 1A. Copyright © 2001, *USA Today.* Reprinted with permission.

Sentence 2 subject: _____

Sentence 4 subject: _____

Sentence 6 subject: _____

General topic of paragraph: _____

_____

Implied main idea: _____

_____

Exercise **4.7**

Read each paragraph and then circle the letter next to the sentence that correctly states the paragraph's main idea.

1. Problems are the cutting edge that distinguishes between success and failure. Problems call forth our courage and our wisdom; indeed, they create our courage and our wisdom. It is only because of problems that we grow mentally and spiritually. When we desire to encourage the growth of the human spirit, we challenge and encourage the human capacity to deal with problems, just as in school we deliberately set problems for our children to solve. It is through the pain of confronting and resolving problems that we learn. As Benjamin Franklin said, "Those things that hurt, instruct."*

   a. Problems have both positive and negative effects.

   b. Problems produce beneficial outcomes for human beings.

   c. Too many people avoid confronting their problems.

   d. Benjamin Franklin had a lot of problems.

2. The state of North Carolina says that 92 percent of its high school students graduate. According to a recent report by the nonprofit Education Trust, though, the actual rate is about 63 percent. The state of California says 87 percent of its students graduate. However, a more accurate estimate is 67 percent. Maryland reports that 85 percent of its students earn their high school diplomas, but the actual rate is more like 74 percent.†

   a. Dropping out of school brings a number of negative consequences.

   b. Several states do not keep accurate records.

---

* Adapted from M. Scott Peck, *The Road Less Traveled* (New York, Simon and Schuster, 1978), 16.

† Adapted from "Major Cause of Joblessness Lies Within U.S. Schools," *USA Today*, March 31, 2004, 22A.

    c. States tend to exaggerate their graduation rates.

    d. Across the nation, graduation rates are steadily rising.

3. Hotels hardly ever clean bedspreads in guest rooms. They never clean the ice buckets or the coffee pots; they merely rinse them and wipe them out. Hotels intentionally install heavily patterned carpets to mask dirt and stains. Hotel maids are likely to have given drinking glasses a quick rinse in the sink, wiped them dry, and returned them to the bathroom for the next guests. If a hotel maid is running late, she may not clean the bathtub at all. And hotel bathroom shower curtains, which are breeding grounds for bacteria and mold, are hardly ever cleaned.*

    a. Hotel rooms are not always cleaned very thoroughly.

    b. Hotels routinely hire maids who don't know how to clean.

    c. Hotel bathrooms are much dirtier than they look.

    d. Hotel maids are overworked and underpaid.

4. When Sir Edmund Hillary and Tenzing Norgay planted the first flag atop Mount Everest on May 29, 1953, they surveyed an utterly pristine[1] place. Nearly fifty years later, dozens of teams line up to take their crack at the sacred Nepalese[2] monolith.[3] Scores of guides jockey to get high-paying clients to the top. Trash on the roof of the world has become so bad that climbers mount expeditions specifically to clean up after past expeditions. At Everest Base Camp, a Nepalese entrepreneur[4] is planning to open a cyber café—perhaps the world's highest at an altitude of 17,000 feet (5,180 meters). And in 2003, not one but two teams of snowboarders rode down Everest from top to bottom.†

    a. Sir Edmund Hillary and Tenzing Norgay were cleaner hikers than today's mountain climbers.

    b. A cyber café will be created on Mount Everest.

    c. Mount Everest is very dirty.

---

1. **pristine:** pure and unspoiled by civilization

2. **Nepalese:** related to Nepal, a country in central Asia

3. **monolith:** a large block of stone

4. **entrepreneur:** a person who starts and operates a new business

---

* Adapted from Peter Greenberg, "What You Should Check Out Before You Check In," *Today Show*, March 15, 2004, http://www.msnbc.msn.com/id/4527495/.

† Adapted from Alex Salkever, "Everest: Now Just Another Tourist Trap?" *National Geographic News*, April 8, 2003.

d. In fifty years, Mount Everest went from being deserted and untouched to being busy and crowded.

5. Why is Harry Potter such a popular and likeable character? Well, for one thing, he is an orphan who was raised by mean, nasty relatives who didn't want him and still manages to succeed in life. He goes from being an abused little boy to being a star athlete at Hogwarts School of Witchcraft and Wizardry almost overnight. He is very self-sufficient, which is a character trait that many people strive to incorporate into their own personalities. He is also a master magician and makes friends and fights mythic battles against the forces of Darkness, all of which appeal to a wide variety of readers. And not once does he blame his miserable aunt and uncle for his troubles. Harry is never a victim, even though he does have the most powerful evil wizard of all time harboring a grudge against him, which makes Harry Potter readers root for the character.[*]

a. Harry Potter was an orphan, which makes a lot of readers identify with him.

b. Harry Potter has had to overcome a lot of adversity[1] and has a lot of positive character traits, so readers identify with him and enjoy reading about him.

c. Harry Potter does not blame anyone for his troubles.

d. The Harry Potter series is very popular.

Reading Strategy: SQ3R

In Chapter 1, you learned how to use active reading techniques to increase your comprehension of the material you read. One specific type of active reading strategy is called the **SQ3R method.** This abbreviation stands for

S urvey

Q uestion

R ead

R ecite

R eview

(Continued)

1. **adversity:** hardship, misfortune

[*] Adapted from Janette Barber, "On Being . . . a Harry Potter Fan," *Rosie*, August 2001, 42–43.

This series of five steps gives you a clear, easy-to-remember system for reading actively.

Step one is to *survey* the text. *To* **survey** means *look over the text to preview it*. Surveying gives you an overall idea of a reading selection's major topics, organizations, parts, and features. When you complete this step, you'll be able to form a mental framework that will allow you to better understand how specific paragraphs, sections, or chapters fit in. At this stage, your purpose is not to read the whole text but to get an overview of what to expect.

If you are preparing to read a longer text, such as a book, read over the title and glance through the table of contents to understand the major topics covered and how they are organized. Flip to one of the chapters and make yourself aware of its important features. A textbook, like this one, for example, may include a list of goals at the beginning of the chapter and a review summary at the end. It will probably also include headings that divide and identify sections of information. It is likely to emphasize key words or concepts with distinctive typeface such as bold print.

Prior to reading a shorter selection—such as one particular chapter, an article, or an essay—survey it by reading any introductory material, the headings throughout, and the first sentence of each paragraph or each section. Read any review summaries or questions at the end of the chapter to get an idea of the major concepts covered in the selection. Also, glance over any illustrations and their captions.

The second step is to **formulate questions**. *Turn the title and the headings into questions*; then, when you read, you can actively look for the answers to those questions. For example, if the heading is "The Medieval Castle," you could turn it into "What was the Medieval Castle like?" If the heading is "The War of 1812," you could create the question "What caused the War of 1812?" or "What happened during the War of 1812?"

The next three steps are the three Rs of the SQ3R process. Step three is **read.** In this step, you *read entire sentences and paragraphs in a section*. However, you read only one section at a time; for example, in a textbook, you'd read from one heading to the next and then stop. As you read, look for the answers to the questions you formed in step two. Mark the text as you go. Highlight or underline those answers and other important information. You may want to write the answers or other details in the margins.

Step four is to *recite*. **Reciting** means *saying something aloud*. After you read a section of material, stop and speak the answers to the questions you created in step two. If you can't answer a question, reread the information until you can. Move on to the next section only when you can say the answers for the section you just read.

The last step of the SQ3R method is *review*. **Review** means *look at again* After you've read the entire selection, go back through it and see if you can still answer all of the questions you formed in step two. You don't have to reread unless you can't answer a particular question.

Practice the SQ3R active reading method with a chapter from one of your textbooks.

 The following links will further explain and demonstrate how to use the SQ3R system. Also included is a link to a form that can help you to organize for SQ3R.

http://www.studygs.net/texred2.htm
http://ccis.edu/departments/writingcenter/studyskills/sq3r.html
http://www.bhsd228.com/reading/docs/pdf/SQ3RReading
Worksheet.pdf

Reading Selections

Practicing the Active Reading Strategy

■ Before and While You Read

You can use active reading strategies before, while, and after you read a selection. The following are some suggestions for active reading strategies that you can employ before you read and as you are reading.

1. Skim the selection for any unfamiliar words. Circle or highlight any words you do not know.

2. As you read, underline, highlight, or circle important words or phrases.

3. Write down any questions about the selection if you are confused by the information presented.

4. Jot notes in the margin to help you understand the material.

BIOGRAPHY
Greatness Knows No Color

by Angela G. King

In the following reading selection, the author shares her insights about discovering what it means to be American.

1   I still remember it vividly. Dozens of small hands shot up into the air throughout packed classrooms and children screamed out the names Martin Luther King Jr., George Washington Carver, and Harriet Tubman, to name a few.

2   The usual short list of well-known blacks was eagerly recited by third-, fourth-, and fifth-graders in response to my query, "Who can name a famous black person in American history?" as I went from school to school in Troy, Michigan.

3   It was 1982, I was 17 years old and, as a debutante for America's oldest black sorority, Alpha Kappa Alpha, I had decided to talk to elementary school kids in my hometown about significant black historical figures.

4   Troy was back then as it is now—a predominately white suburb of Detroit. I happened to be a black girl who lived there, and I figured that all children, not just black children down in the city, needed to know about some of the overlooked Americans who played a pivotal role in pushing this nation forward. Unfortunately, I learned then what still holds true today—that even as we commemorate Black History Month every February, many blacks who made a tremendous contribution in shaping this country languish in obscurity.

5   That's a shame. Knowing about the inventor of the traffic light (Garrett Morgan) or how Elijah McCoy revolutionized the locomotive industry by inventing a self-lubricating oil cap for steam engines or about the partner of Howard Hughes who helped develop the first commercial communications satellite (Frank Mann) isn't just *black* history. It's *American* history.

6   Take the blacks I chose to tell those Troy schoolchildren about as my community-service project. Who has heard of Asa Spaulding, founder of the nation's oldest and largest black life insurance firm? Or Percy Lavon Julian, a chemist who synthesized physostigmine, the drug used to treat glaucoma? Or Mary McCleod Bethune, the educator and promoter of civil and women's rights who founded Bethune-Cookman College, one of this nation's oldest black colleges?

7   I'd never heard of them until I did research for my project back then as a high school senior, and very few of the young students I talked to back then—or, I dare say, their teachers—had heard of them either.

8   I'm sorry to say that it has not been until this year, at age 35, while doing research for a freelance writing project, that I've learned about Dr. Daniel Hale Williams, the first physician to successfully perform open-heart surgery; Jan Ernst Matzeliger, who automated shoe manufacturing with a machine he invented to replace the costly manual method of forming shoes; Julian Francis Abele, one of the nation's first professional black architects, who designed the Philadelphia Museum of Art; and Mary Church Terrell, who founded the National Association of Colored Women to help poor black women fight for women's rights.

9   As the old saying goes, "You can't know where you're going unless you know where you've been." Americans can't move forward together as a nation until we recognize the entire spectrum of people who have helped to shape our nation. That's a lesson not just for February, but all year round.*

■ Vocabulary

Read the following questions about some of the vocabulary words that appear in the previous selection. Before you look up the word, try to use the context to determine the meaning. Then circle the letter of the correct answer for each question.

1. In paragraph 1, the author uses the word *vividly* to describe how she recalls a memory she had about her experience in an elementary school classroom. In this context, what does *vividly* mean?

   a. cloudy   c. shaky

   b. clearly   d. faintly

2. What does the word *query* mean as used in paragraph 2?

   a. eerie   c. explanation

   b. reply   d. question

3. The author describes herself as a former *debutante* (paragraph 3). What do you think the word *debutante* means?

   a. a poor woman

   b. a young woman who makes a formal entrance into society

   c. a college student

   d. an elementary school teacher

---

* "Greatness Knows No Color" by Angela King from *Daily News,* February 25, 2000. Copyright © 2000 New York Daily News, L. P. Reprinted with permission.

4. In paragraph 4, the author writes, "I figured that all children, not just black children down in the city, needed to know about some of the overlooked Americans who played a *pivotal* role in pushing this nation forward." What does the word *pivotal* mean as used here?

   a. significant

   b. not worthy

   c. insignificant

   d. happy

5. What does the word *commemorate* mean as used in paragraph 4?

   a. to begin

   b. to acknowledge and honor

   c. to design

   d. to declare

6. What do you think the phrase to *languish in obscurity* means? In paragraph 4, the author writes that "many blacks who made a tremendous contribution in shaping this country *languish in obscurity*."

   a. are famous

   b. remain fearful

   c. are unknown

   d. stay inside

7. In paragraph 6, the author asks if you know Percy Lavon Julian, a chemist who *synthesized* physostigmine, the drug used to treat glaucoma. What do you think the word *synthesized* means?

   a. shook up

   b. threw out

   c. combined or produced

   d. deleted

8. What does the word *spectrum* mean in paragraph 9? "Americans can't move forward together as a nation until we recognize the entire *spectrum* of people . . . ."

   a. range

   b. cluster

   c. batch

   d. concentration

■ Reading Skills

Respond to each of the following questions by circling the letter of the correct answer or writing your answer on the lines.

1. What is the implied main idea of paragraphs 1 through 3?

   a. Children in Troy, Michigan, are very smart.

   b. The author was a debutante and a member of a black sorority.

    c. Children know a few names of famous African Americans.

    d. The author is from Troy, Michigan, and was a good student.

2. What is the implied main idea of paragraph 6?

    a. There are many significant figures in black history, and students should know about them.

    b. Mary McCleod Bethune founded a famous college long before women were doing things like that.

    c. Asa Spaulding faced racism in founding the oldest and largest black life insurance firm.

    d. Bethune-Cookman College is one of the nation's oldest black colleges.

3. Reread paragraph 8. What is the implied main idea?

    a. The author's research project was very difficult.

    b. These historical figures are not given proper credit for their achievements.

    c. The author wishes she had known about these important black figures in history earlier in her life.

    d. Mary Church Terrell founded the NACW.

4. The topic of paragraph 5 is

    a. traffic lights.   c. communications satellites.

    b. African-American inventors.   d. shameful behaviors.

5. What is the implied main idea of paragraph 9?

_____

_____

_____

Practicing the Active Reading Strategy

■ After You Read

Now that you have read the selection, answer the following questions, using the active reading strategies that you learned in Chapter 1.

1. Identify and write down the point and purpose of this reading selection.

2. Did you circle or highlight any words that are unfamiliar to you? Can you figure out the meaning from the context of the passage? If not, then look up each word in a dictionary and find the definition that best describes the word as it is used in the selection. You may want to write the definition in the margin next to the word in the passage for future reference.

3. Predict any possible questions that may be used on a test about the content of this selection.

■ Questions for Discussion and Writing

Respond to each of the following questions based on your reading of the selection.

1. The author writes in paragraph 5 that "knowing about [important black figures in history] . . . isn't just *black* history. It's *American* history." Do you agree or disagree? Why?

_____

_____

_____

_____

2. Agree or disagree with the statement "You can't know where you're going unless you know where you've been." Explain your answer. Why do you think the author chose to end her essay with that statement?

_____

_____

_____

_____

3. What do you think the author is saying about Black History Month as an event? Do you agree or disagree with her? Why?

_____

_____

_____

_____

Practicing the Active Reading Strategy

■ Before and While You Read

You can use active reading strategies before, while, and after you read a selection. The following are some suggestions for active reading strategies that you can employ before you read and as you are reading.

1. Skim the selection for any unfamiliar words. Circle or highlight any words you do not know.

2. As you read, underline, highlight, or circle important words or phrases.

3. Write down any questions about the selection if you are confused by the information presented.

4. Jot notes in the margin to help you understand the material.

4

TEXTBOOK READING: LAW ENFORCEMENT
Child Neglect

The following excerpt from a juvenile justice textbook used in law enforcement courses discusses the reasons for child neglect in the United States and some of the devastating results.

1   Broadly defined, child neglect is inattention to the basic needs of a child, including appropriate supervision, adequate clothing, and proper nutrition. Often the families from which neglected children come are poor and disorganized. They have no set routine for family activity. The children roam the streets at all hours. They are continually petitioned to juvenile court for loitering and curfew violations. The family unit is often fragmented by death, divorce, or the incarceration or desertion of parents.

2   Some children are stunted in their emotional growth by being raised in a moral vacuum in which parents ignore them. Even more problematic are parents who do not adhere to moral and ethical standards or who have different values than the dominant moral order; they set poor examples for their children. Such parents cannot ignore the probability that their children may model their actions.

3   Some parents deliberately refrain from discipline in the mistaken belief that authoritative restrictions inhibit children's self-expression or unbalance their delicate emotional systems. At the other extreme are parents who discipline their children injudiciously, excessively, and often, weighing neither transgression nor punishment. Parents' warped ideas, selfish attitudes, and twisted values can lead to their children becoming delinquents. Family

policies that are inconsistent or that emphasize too much leniency or excessive punishment may result in retaliation directed at society in general.

4   Children's behavior develops from what they see and understand to be happening around them. If children are exposed to excessive drinking, the use of drugs, illicit sex, gambling, and related vices by parents or adult role models, they may copy these behaviors.

5   Neglected children often lack the food, clothing, shelter, medical care, supervision, education, protection, or emotional support they need to develop appropriate physical, mental, and emotional health. They also may suffer emotional harm through disrespect and denial of self-worth, unreasonable or chronic rejection, and failure to receive necessary affection, protection, and a sense of family belonging. They may suffer ill health because they are not vaccinated against common childhood illness or are exposed to secondhand smoke or lead. They may even die from preventable accidents.*

■ Vocabulary

Read the following questions about some of the vocabulary words that appear in the previous selection. Before you look up the word, try to use the context of the passage to figure out the meaning. Then circle the letter of the correct answer for each question.

1. In paragraph 1, the author states that children are continually being *petitioned* to juvenile court. In this context, what does *petitioned* mean?

   a. asked by an authority to appear

   b. asked for a favor

   c. asked for no punishment

   d. asked for support

2. In paragraph 2, what is the meaning of *vacuum* in the phrase "raised in a moral *vacuum*"?

   a. a tool for cleaning the floors

   b. a black hole in space

   c. a condition where nothing exists

   d. strict religion

---

* Karen M. Hess, Juvenile Justice, 5th ed. (Belmont: Wadsworth, 2010), 137. Print.

3. What does *adhere* mean in paragraph 2?

   a. stray   c. appreciate

   b. support   d. request

4. An example of a lack of *authoritative restrictions* is _____. (paragraph 3)

   a. family vacations   c. no curfew

   b. new clothes   d. homework help

5. An example of a *transgression* would be _____. (paragraph 3)

   a. lying   c. getting a job

   b. making the honor roll   d. buying a gift

■ Reading Skills

Respond to each of the following questions by circling the letter of the correct answer or by writing your answer in the space provided.

1. What is the implied main idea of paragraph 1?

   a. Neglected children come from poor families.

   b. Neglected children come from broken homes.

   c. For many reasons neglected children suffer because they come from homes where their basic needs are not met.

   d. Neglected children become criminals.

2. What is the implied main idea of paragraph 2?

   a. Some parents ignore their children.

   b. Parents who are not good role models may have children who become problems.

   c. Parents who are good role models never have children who become problems.

   d. Children need to have limits set for their behaviors.

3. The topic of paragraph 3 is _____.

   a. the effects of too much punishment

   b. the result of no restrictions

4

    c. family policies causing juvenile delinquency

    d. parental attitudes

4. What is the topic of paragraph 5?

    a. ill health of neglected children

    b. lack of food for neglected children

    c. deaths of neglected children

    d. negative effects on children from being neglected

5. The implied main idea for paragraph 5 is _____

    _____

Practicing the Active Reading Strategy

■ After You Read

Now that you have read the selection, answer the following questions, using the active reading strategies that you learned in Chapter 1.

1. Identify and write down the point and purpose of this reading selection.

2. Did you circle or highlight any words that are unfamiliar to you? Can you figure out the meaning from the context of the passage? If not, then look up each word in a dictionary and find the definition that best describes the word as it is used in the selection. You may want to write the definition in the margin next to the word in the passage for future reference.

3. Predict any possible questions that may be used on a test about the content of this selection.

■ Questions for Discussion and Writing

Respond to each of the following questions based on your reading of the selection.

1. Identify two causes of child neglect from the reading passage.

    _____

2. Who plays the most important role in a child's life? Explain your answer.

    _____

3. Do neglected children always become juvenile delinquents? Why or why not? _____

_____

Practicing the Active Reading Strategy

■ Before and While You Read

You can use active reading strategies before, while, and after you read a selection. The following are some suggestions for active reading strategies that you can employ before you read and as you are reading.

1. Skim the selection for any unfamiliar words. Circle or highlight any words you do not know.

2. As you read, underline, highlight, or circle important words or phrases.

3. Write down any questions about the selection if you are confused by the information presented.

4. Jot notes in the margin to help you understand the material.

WEBSITE READING: SOCIOLOGY
Old Movie Houses Find Audience in the Plains

Do you like to go to the movies? What features of the movie theater do you like best? Many people today do not have access to large movieplexes. In small towns across the country people are working together to revitalize old movie theaters so that everyone in the community can enjoy going to the movies.

1   In an age of streaming videos and DVDs, the small town Main Street movie theater is thriving in North Dakota, the result of a grass-roots movement to keep storefront movie houses, with their jewel-like marquees and facades of careworn utility, at the center of community life. From Crosby (population 1,000), near the Saskatchewan border, to Mayville, in the Red River Valley, tickets are about $5, the buttered popcorn $1.25, and the companionship free.

2   "If we were in Los Angeles or Phoenix, the only reason to go to a movie would be to see it," said Cecile Wehrman, a newspaper editor who, with members of the nonprofit Meadowlark Arts Council, resuscitated the Dakota in Crosby, its plush interiors now a chic black, red, and silver. "But in a small town, the theater is like a neighborhood. It's the

4

see-and-be-seen, bring everyone and sit together kind of place."

3   Today, the Dakota is a star with many roles. It is a destination for high school students on a Saturday night. It is where county employees and local farmers discuss noxious weeds, and where the crowd pours in after football games to watch highlights on the big screen. On Oscar night, the program is shown live. Everyone in town gussies up and walks a red carpet donated by a local furniture company.

4   To Tim Kennedy, a professor of landscape architecture who has traveled across the state to survey little theaters for a book, the communal will of rural towns that keep theaters going represents "buildings as social capital," forged "outside the franchise cinemas and their ubiquitous presence at the malls." Of the 31 operating historic theaters identified by Mr. Kennedy, 19 are community-run, little changed from the days when itinerant projectionists packed their automobile trunks with reels of film and hit the road. Many retain the upstairs soundproof "cry rooms" for fussy babies.

5   To Tom Isern, a professor of history at North Dakota State University Fargo, citizens championing theaters represent "a bounce back from the bottom" for small North Dakota towns. Crosby, for instance, is the seat of Divide County, which lost 14 percent of its population over the past decade but is now rebounding due to oil revenues. Baby boomers are in a position to help. "They are the last picture show generation on the plains," he said, "who can remember that movie theater experience and want to transmit that to their kids."

6   At the Lyric in Park River, a silent-picture-era theater once presided over by Laura McEachern, who dealt with rustling candy wrappers "by stalking the aisles with a pen flashlight and shining it right in your eye," her 81-year-old niece, Lorna Marifjeren, recalled, most of the volunteers are teenagers like Trey Powers. "If the theater wasn't here, a lot more people would be drinking," he said. North Dakota ranked first in the nation for binge drinking in 2009, and some volunteers at the Lyric include teenagers assigned to community service by the court. "Most sure don't mind," said Jim Fish, the juvenile court officer for Walsh, Cavalier, and Pembina Counties. "It's a neat fit. There is a sense of helping the community out."*

---

* Patricia Leigh Brown, "Old Movie Houses Find Audience in the Plains," From *The New York Times,* 07/05/2010, copyright © 2010 The New York Times. All rights reserved. Used by permission and protected by the Copyright Laws of the United States. The printing, copying, redistribution, or retransmission of this Content without express written permission is prohibited.

■ **Vocabulary**

Read the following questions about some of the vocabulary words that appear in the previous selection. Before you look up the word, try to use the context of the passage to figure out the meaning. Then circle the letter of the correct answer for each question.

1. What does the word *façade* mean, as used in paragraph 1?

   a. theory

   b. roofing material

   c. front of a building

   d. inside of a building

2. The author writes that "the nonprofit Meadowlark Arts Council *resuscitated* the Dakota in Crosby." What do you think the word *resuscitated* means?

   a. death

   b. to revive

   c. put a damper on

   d. outlandish

3. In paragraph 3 the author writes "local farmers discuss *noxious* weeds." What does the word *noxious* mean?

   a. harmful or destructive to

   b. weathered

   c. large growth

   d. tangled

4. What does the word *ubiquitous* mean, as used in paragraph 4?

   a. sanctioned

   b. solid

   c. widespread

   d. vintage

5. The word *rebounding* is used in paragraph 5. Using the context of the paragraph, what does the word mean?

   a. to weaken

   b. recover from setback

   c. long term

   d. score a basket

■ **Reading Skills**

Respond to each of the following questions by circling the letter of the correct answer or by writing your answer on the blank provided.

1. What is the topic of paragraph 1?

   a. North Dakota

   b. Crosby

   c. Main Street movie theater

   d. grass-roots movement

4

2. What is the implied main idea of paragraphs 1–3?

   a. Old movie houses are for the elderly.

   b. Tickets and popcorn are always cheaper at old movie houses.

   c. North Dakota is the only state with old movie houses.

   d. Community involvement is vital for old movie houses.

3. The topic of paragraph 4 is

   a. little theaters.   c. Tim Kennedy.

   b. rural towns.   d. cry rooms.

4. "Many retain the upstairs soundproof 'cry rooms' for fussy babies." This statement is an example of a _____ detail.

   a. minor   b. major

5. What is the implied main idea of paragraphs 4–6?

   a. Baby Boomers are in a position to help out.

   b. Crosby is rebounding due to oil revenues.

   c. Small theaters need help from their community; communities need help from small theaters.

   d. Small theaters are a better option than a monstrous movieplex.

Practicing the Active Reading Strategy

■ After You Read

Now that you have read the selection, answer the following questions, using the active reading strategies that you learned in Chapter 1.

1. Identify and write down the point and purpose of this reading selection.

2. Did you circle or highlight any words that are unfamiliar to you? Can you figure out the meaning from the context of the passage? If not, then look up each word in a dictionary and find the definition that best describes the word as it is used in the selection. You may want to write the definition in the margin next to the word in the passage for future reference.

3. Predict any possible questions that may be used on a test about the content of this selection.

■ Questions for Discussion and Writing

Respond to each of the following questions based on your reading of the selection.

1. Do you feel old movie houses are an important part of small-town America? Why or why not? _____

    _____

2. Would you rather see a movie at an old movie house or at a more modern movie facility? What are your reasons? _____

    _____

3. The author talks about a "grass-roots movement to keep storefront movie houses." What do you think is involved in keeping old movie houses? Be specific in your examples. _____

    _____

4

Vocabulary Strategy: The Definition/Restatement Context Clue

When you encounter an unfamiliar word as you read, you may be able to figure out its meaning by using context clues. The context of a word is its relationship to the other words, phrases, and sentences that surround it. Sometimes these nearby elements offer clues you can use to get a sense of what a particular word means.

One type of context clue is **definition** or **restatement.** *In this type of clue, either the word's meaning is directly stated, or synonyms are used to restate it.* The following sentence, which comes from one of the paragraphs in this chapter, uses restatement:

> Considered somewhat *eccentric*, or odd, Benjamin Franklin was a noted inventor and diplomat who was somewhat chubby and messy, but neither of those things interfered with his ability to help write the most important document in American history.

The word *odd* is a synonym for *eccentric*; therefore, it tells you what *eccentric* means.

Vocabulary Exercise

The following sentences all come from paragraphs in Chapters 2, 3, and 4. In each one, underline the definition or restatement context clue that helps you understand the meaning of the italicized word.

1. You can also use *visualization*, _____ how to manage a stressful situation more successfully.

2. Research has revealed that regular aspirin use may protect against the risk of colon cancer by as much as 40 to 50 percent; *esophageal* _____ cancer by about 80 to 90 percent; and ovarian cancer by some 25 percent.

3. The mothers of today's "*Generation X*," _____ _____, did 89 percent of the cooking in their homes, but their grown children now tend to divide evening meal preparation equally between the husband and the wife.

4. Doctors now have several new treatments that alter the soft *palate* _____ and help quiet nighttime snoring.

5. In 1872, therefore, the Time-Table Convention searched for a solution, and Charles F. Dowd proposed the creation of *time zones*, _____ _____.

6. Prompted by our modest exertions, just a few minutes into a walk the body begins to produce *endorphins*, _____ _____

7. If you find that *procrastination*, _____, hurts your progress, here are some ways to break the habit.

8. They also wore rosemary garlands to ward off the "*evil eye*," _____ _____

9. Teenagers using the Internet today, however, are *multitasking*; that is, as they are online, they are also _____.

10. In the early days of America's space program, people were interested in astronauts because they were *swaggering*, _____pilots, but now that two-thirds of them are doctors, scientists, and engineers, they're no longer "glamorous."

Chapter 4 Review

Write the correct answer in each of the blanks in the following statements.

1. An _____ main idea is one that is suggested but not stated.

2. An implied main idea paragraph contains specific supporting details but no _____.

3. To determine the implied main idea of a paragraph, you can follow four steps.

   a. Find the _____ of each sentence.

   b. Determine the _____ of supporting details in the paragraph.

   c. Determine a general _____ based on the specific details.

   d. Draw a _____ from the supporting details and state an implied main idea in your own words.

4. An implied main idea, like one that's stated in a topic sentence, includes both the _____ and what is being said about that topic.

5. SQ3R stands for _____, _____, _____, _____, and _____.

6. The type of context clue where the meaning of the word is directly stated is called a _____ or _____ context clue.

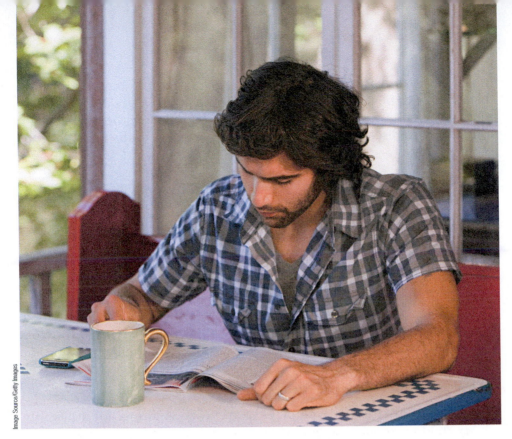

Image Source/Getty Images

Transitions

Goals for Chapter 5

- ■ Define the term *transition*.

- ■ Recognize common transitions used to indicate a list of items.

- ■ Recognize common transitions used to indicate a sequence.

- ■ Recognize common transitions used to indicate cause/effect.

- ■ Recognize common transitions used to indicate comparison/contrast.

- ■ Recognize common transitions used to indicate definition and examples.

- ■ Recognize transitions in paragraphs organized according to more than one pattern.

- ■ Practice the steps involved in summarizing a reading selection.

In Chapters 3 and 4, you learned how to recognize supporting details within paragraphs. To help you understand how those details are related to one another, paragraphs include transitions that help you follow the author's train of thought. To discover what you already know about transitions, take the following pretest.

Pretest

Circle the transition words and phrases in the following paragraphs.

1. Starting a vegetable garden can be a rewarding experience, but you have to spend a lot of time tending your plants in order to be able to have a crop at the end of summer. At first, your plants will be small and will not yield any vegetables or fruit. But don't get discouraged! Before long, you will begin to see small sprouts growing, which means that the work you have done is paying off. Eventually, after spending time weeding and trimming your garden, you are sure to have many things to eat from your garden, and you will understand the joys of gardening.

2. Five minutes after I arrive home, I have to cook dinner for my family. My children are old enough to boil a pot of water, yet dinner has become my nightly duty. Consequently, we end up getting take-out on many nights because I am just too tired to cook. As a result, I feel like our diet is not as healthy as it should be.

3. When Janis Klein became a school nurse fifteen years ago, one-sixth of the children in her elementary school had head lice.[1] As a result, they couldn't go to school. So Klein, who has worked in hospitals and summer camps, quickly became an expert in recognizing head lice. In time, she started her own business to help families throughout the area recognize, treat, and deal with head lice.*

4. You and your dog can do more together than go on long walks, chase balls, and share a bowl of popcorn while watching Saturday-morning cartoons. Take Heidi, for instance. Heidi is an English springer spaniel who volunteers with her owner as a therapy dog at a residential treatment school for children who suffer from emotional disorders. Another example is Sophie the bull terrier, who works with her owner at a Connecticut-area nursing

---

1.   **head lice:** small insects that can be parasites on animals and humans

---

* Adapted from M. K. Fottrell, "No Nits Here," *Westchester Parent*, August 2001, 16.

home whose residents all seem to comment, "She reminds me of a dog I used to have when I was young." Also, there are dogs that help the blind or hearing-impaired live a productive life by being good and responsible companions.*

5. There are several types of headaches that signal more serious disorders. First is "the worst headache of your life" (arterial bleeding). In addition, there are the headaches with weakness or loss of vision (stroke), headaches accompanied by blackout (seizures), and headaches associated with fever (meningitis).[1] However, not all headaches require medical attention. Some result from missed meals or muscle tension. Therefore, they are easily remedied with a cold pack applied directly to the scalp over the angry nerve endings. Aspirin, too, works by interfering with enzymes[2] that inflame the nerves.[†]

Transitions

Transitions *are words and phrases whose function is to show the relationships between thoughts and ideas.* The word *transition* comes from the Latin word *trans*, which means "across." Transitions bridge the gaps across sentences and paragraphs and reveal how they are related.

Transitions make sentences clearer, so they help readers understand the ideas in a passage more easily. Without them, the readers have to figure out relationships on their own. For example, read these two sentences:

> She was afraid of guns. She bought a gun and learned to use it to protect herself.

When you read these two sentences, which are not connected, the second one seems to contradict the first one. If someone fears guns, why would she buy one? In the absence of a transition, the reader has to pause and mentally fill in that gap on his or her own. Now look at how the addition of a transition more clearly reveals the contrast between the two thoughts:

> She was afraid of guns. **But** she bought a gun and learned to use it to protect herself.

---

1. **meningitis:** disease characterized by fever, vomiting, headache, and stiff neck
2. **enzymes:** proteins in living organisms

---

* Adapted from "Healing Partners," *AKC Family Dog, New Puppy Edition,* Fall/Winter 2003, 6.
† Adapted from Marc Siegel, "What Is a Headache?" *New York Daily News,* February 23, 2004, 44.

Characteristics of Transitions

You should be aware of three characteristics of transitions:

1. Some of them are synonyms. In other words, they mean the same thing. For instance, the transitions *also, in addition,* and *too* all have the same meaning. Therefore, they are usually interchangeable with one another.

2. Some transitions can be used to show more than one kind of relationship between details. For example, you may see the word *next* in both a list of items and in a paragraph that explains the steps in a process.

   > The **next** component of love is commitment. (list of items)
   > **Next,** prepare an agenda for the meeting. (steps in a process)

3. Different transitions can create subtle but significant changes in the meanings of sentences. For example, reread an earlier example that includes a contrast transition:

   > She was afraid of guns. **But** she bought a gun and learned to use it to protect herself.

   The transition *but* suggests that she bought a gun *in spite of* her fear. Notice, however, how a different transition changes the relationship between the two sentences.

   > She was afraid of guns. **So** she bought a gun and learned to use it to protect herself.

   Substituting the transition *so,* which is a cause/effect word, suggests that she bought the gun to *overcome* her fear. Altering that one transition significantly alters the meaning of those two sentences.

As you read, then, you'll need to pay attention to transitions so you can accurately follow the train of thought within a reading selection. The remainder of this chapter explains and illustrates the different types of transition words that accompany various patterns of organization.

Transition Words That Indicate a List

Certain transition words show readers that the sentence will *add another item* to a list. A list may consist of examples, reasons, or some other kind of point. Here are some common list transitions:

List Transitions

also	furthermore	finally
in addition	first, second, third	lastly
too	first of all	most importantly
another	and	moreover
one	for one thing	next

The following pairs of sentences illustrate the use of list transitions:

When you travel in a recreational vehicle, kids feel at home no matter where you go. **And** parents love the freedom, the conveniences, and the relatively low cost.

Hummingbirds are among the smallest warm-blooded animals on earth. **Also,** they are among the meanest.

A sincere apology can have a tremendous amount of healing power. **In addition,** it can set the stage for better communication in the future.

Now, read a paragraph that includes list transition words (boldfaced and italicized). Notice how each transition indicates the addition of another item in the list.

Your credit score is determined by five factors. **The first factor** is your payment record. Thirty-five percent of your score depends on whether you pay your bills on time. **The second factor** is the amount you owe. Your total amount of debt accounts for 30 percent of your score. **The third determinant**[1] of your score is your credit history. The length of time you've been borrowing and paying back money influences 15 percent of your score. Your credit application history is **the fourth factor.** Ten percent of your score is based on how much new debt you try to acquire. **The fifth and final factor** is your credit mix. This last ten percent of your score is based on what kinds of debts you have incurred.[2]*

---

1. **determinant:** influencing factor

2. **incurred:** acquired

---

* Adapted from Paul J. Lim, "They Know Your Credit Score," *Reader's Digest,* July 2001, 164–166.

5

This paragraph presents a list of five factors that determine an individual's credit score. The list transitions *first, second, third,* and so on indicate each new factor.

Exercise **5.1**

Fill in the blanks in the following sentences and paragraphs with appropriate list transitions. Choose words or phrases from the box on page 179. Try to vary your choices.

1. Pet ownership requires a lot of your time and effort. _____, having a pet costs money.

2. You'll need a few things to bake a cake. _____, you will need the right ingredients. _____, you will need the proper baking dish. And _____, you will need an oven.

3. A low-fat diet has many benefits. _____, it can help you stay at a weight that is appropriate for your height and age. _____, it can reduce your risk of heart disease.

4. _____ example of an Alfred Hitchcock movie is *Vertigo,* starring Jimmy Stewart and Kim Novak. _____ example is *The Birds,* which made Tippi Hedren a big star.

5. Buddha gave some good advice about what to say and what not to say to others. The founder of Buddhism[1] recommended that a person ask three vital questions before saying anything to another person. _____, ask yourself if the statement is *true.* _____, ask if the statement is *necessary.* _____, ask if the statement is *kind.* If a statement falls short on any of these counts, Buddha advised that we say nothing.*

6. My mother always gave me a lot of tips before I went out on a date. _____, I was never to order spaghetti. She thought that eating spaghetti on a date was too messy and had the potential for disaster. _____, I was never to wear patent-leather[2] shoes. She was so

1. **Buddhism:** religion that focuses on eliminating desire to end suffering and on meditating to obtain spiritual enlightenment

2. **patent-leather:** black leather finished to a hard, glossy surface

---

* Adapted from Barry L. Reece and Rhonda Brandt, *Effective Human Relations in Organizations,* 7th ed. (Boston: Houghton Mifflin Co., 1999), 213.

old-fashioned that she thought that patent-leather shoes could reflect what you were wearing under your dress or skirt! _____, I was always supposed to let my date open the door for me. _____, her last tip was to never let a boy kiss me on the first date. My mother was certainly behind the times!

Transition Words That Indicate Sequence

Some transition words signal that the sentence is providing *another event, step, or stage within a chronological order of details.* Here is a list of common **sequence** transitions:

<table>
<tr><td colspan="4" align="center">**Sequence Transitions**</td></tr>
<tr><td>first, second, third</td><td>next</td><td>as</td><td>finally</td></tr>
<tr><td>before</td><td>soon</td><td>when</td><td>over time</td></tr>
<tr><td>now</td><td>in the beginning</td><td>until</td><td>in the end</td></tr>
<tr><td>then</td><td>once</td><td>later</td><td>during, in, on,</td></tr>
<tr><td>after</td><td>today</td><td>eventually</td><td>*or by (followed*</td></tr>
<tr><td>while</td><td>previously</td><td>last</td><td>*by a date)*</td></tr>
<tr><td></td><td>often</td><td>meanwhile</td><td></td></tr>
</table>

The following pairs of sentences illustrate the use of sequence transitions:

On July 29, 1981, Diana Spencer married England's Prince Charles and became the Princess of Wales. *In 1992,* Charles and Diana officially separated.

High-fiber foods take longer to eat and increase your satisfaction. *Then,* when they get to the intestines, fiber-rich foods act as an appetite suppressant.[1]

During the Great Depression, Wal-Mart founder Sam Walton sold magazine subscriptions door-to-door. *After* serving in World War II and *then* managing a Ben Franklin variety store *from 1945 to 1950*, Walton and his wife, Helen, opened their own Walton's Five and Dime in Bentonville, Arkansas.*

---

1. **suppressant:** something that puts a stop to something else

---

* Adapted from Paul Boyer et al., *The Enduring Vision,* 5th ed. (Boston: Houghton Mifflin Co., 2004), 935.

5

Now, read a paragraph that uses sequence transition words (boldfaced and italicized). Notice how each transition indicates another event in the timeline.

> The famous Leaning Tower of Pisa has been tilting for over eight hundred years, and recent improvements should allow it to continue tilting for another three hundred more. ***On August 9, 1173***, construction began on this well-known Italian bell tower. ***Almost immediately***, it began leaning because it was being erected on the soft silt of a buried riverbed. ***Between 1178 and 1360***, work stopped and started two more times as workers tried to continue the project and figure out how to compensate for the tilt. ***Over the next six centuries***, the tower's lean continued to increase, although tourists were still allowed to visit. ***Then, in 1990***, Italy's prime minister feared the tower would collapse and closed it to the public. ***From 1999 to 2001***, engineers excavated soil from beneath the tower. ***Now***, the tower still leans out about fifteen feet beyond its base, but it should remain stable for several more centuries.*

This paragraph tells the story of the Leaning Tower of Pisa, arranging the details using a sequence of events. Each new detail is introduced with a sequence transition to help the reader easily follow the progression of those events.

Exercise 5.2

Fill in the blanks in the following sentences and paragraphs with appropriate sequence transitions. Choose words or phrases from the box on page 181. Try to vary your choices.

1. Twenty years ago, patients got most medical information from their doctors. _____ they can access some 70,000 health-care-related Internet sites.

2. Summer in Arizona starts out very hot and dry. _____, the monsoon rains of July and August create cooler temperatures.

3. Yesterday, I had my eyes checked at the eye doctor's office. _____, I get the results of my eye exam.

4. _____ colonial times, many children died due to disease and poor medical care.

---

* Adapted from Richard Covington, "The Leaning Tower Straightens Up," *Smithsonian*, June 2001, 41–47.

5. You just won big money in the lottery. Now what do you do? _____, protect your ticket. Seal it in an envelope and stash it in a safe deposit box until you can claim your prize. _____, contact lottery head-quarters within the time limit. You probably have from 180 days to one year to show up with your winning ticket. _____, you'll have to decide how you want to receive your money. You can either get one lump-sum[1] payment, or you can arrange to be paid a portion every year for, say, twenty years. _____, hire a financial advisor and an accountant to help you manage and invest your money. _____, you'll need to decide whether or not you want to keep your job. Many people think they'd quit right away, but to make the money last through wise invest-ments, you may need to keep on working.*

6. Franklin Roosevelt[2] was not eager to enter World War II, according to many historians. _____ December 7, 1941, however, his position changed. _____ the Japanese invaded the military base at Pearl Harbor, FDR found that he had no choice but to enter the war. _____ much thought, he addressed the American people and gave them his decision.

7. _____, the volunteer program known as "Friends for Life" was a small organization run by four people. _____, it is a successful pro-gram that pairs senior citizens with dog friends and has a staff of more than one hundred people nationwide. _____, the head of "Friends for Life," John Baker, wants to expand the program overseas. _____ 2010, he hopes to have programs operating in France, Belgium, and Germany.

Transition Words That Indicate Cause/Effect

Certain transition words indicate that an occurrence about to be presented in a sentence is either **a cause** (*a reason for*) or **an effect** (*a result of*) an occurrence presented in a previous sentence. These are the transitions that reveal cause or

1. **lump-sum:** paid all at once
2. **Franklin Roosevelt:** 32nd president of the United States

* Adapted from Jack R. Fay, "Wow! I Just Won the Lottery: Now What Do I Do?" *USA Today*, November 2000, 26–27.

5

effect relationships between thoughts. The most common cause/effect transition words are listed below.

Cause Transitions	
because of	due to
for this reason	since
led to	caused by

Effect Transitions		
therefore	so	as a result
in response	hence	thus
consequently	as a consequence	

The following pairs of sentences illustrate the use of cause/effect transitions:

High-protein/low-carbohydrate diets produce dramatic weight loss. **As a result,** many people are cutting bread, pasta, and cereal out of their meals.

Most head-on vehicle collisions occur when distracted drivers drift into oncoming traffic. **So** to reduce your risk of such an accident, drive more on divided highways with medians.

Many Americans choose to live in urban and suburban neighborhoods. **Consequently,** they separate themselves from a deep connection to the land and become indifferent to the environment.

Next, read a paragraph that uses cause/effect transition words (boldfaced and italicized). Notice how each transition indicates another effect.

Mother England made the mistake of withholding liberty too long from her "children" in the American colonies. They grew to be rebellious "teenagers" who demanded their freedom. **In response**, their "mother" refused to release them, and a war had to be fought. **As a consequence**, though, England did learn a valuable lesson from a painful experience, which is why she later granted a peaceful and orderly transfer of power to another tempestuous[1] offspring named India.*

---

1.   **tempestuous:** stormy; agitated

---

* Adapted from Dr. James Dobson, "Focus on the Family," *News Herald* (Morganton, NC), July 22, 2001, 11C.

This paragraph is arranged according to the chain-reaction type of cause/effect paragraphs. Each transition indicates that the detail is the result of a previous occurrence.

Fill in the blanks in the following sentences and paragraphs with appropriate cause/effect transitions. Choose words or phrases from the box on page 184. Try to vary your choices.

1. Female elected officials are gaining more political power along with the public's trust. _____, the United States will probably elect its first woman president during the twenty-first century.

2. There have been a few incidents involving children slipping under the water at the town pool this year. _____, the town representatives are making it mandatory[1] for children to wear safety vests at all times while at the pool.

3. _____teenagers' natural tendency to go to bed later and awake later, several school districts around the country have adjusted high school starting times.*

4. I have been eating more than I should, especially when it comes to dessert. _____, I have gained five pounds!

5. Many Americans are locked into a work-and-spend cycle. Their debts increase. _____, they give up leisure time to make more money. The treadmill continues to roll, and some people become too tired to enjoy active leisure activities such as hiking, swimming, or playing a round of golf. _____, they engage in less satisfactory activities such as sitting passively in front of the television set. _____, this work-and-spend cycle reduces quality of life.†

6. My grandfather's name was Charlie Bundrum, a tall, bone-thin man who worked with nails in his teeth and a roofing hatchet in his fist. He died

1. **mandatory:** required

* Adapted from Desda Moss, "Science Confirms What Parents Know," *USA Today*, March 12, 2004, 15A.
† Adapted from Barry L. Reece and Rhonda Brandt, *Effective Human Relations in Organizations*, 7th ed. (Boston: Houghton Mifflin Co., 1997), 462.

5

in the spring of 1958, one year before I was born. _____, I knew almost nothing about him growing up because nobody in my mother's family talked about him. _____, I made it my life's work to try to find out what kind of man Charlie Bundrum was.*

7. I was in high school when I realized my own possibilities. I had started a volunteer organization that matched students with senior citizens, and my teacher told me I was a good person. _____, I felt very good about myself, and those few words literally changed how I saw myself. _____, I try to help young people understand the power they have to change the world. I cofounded the national organization Do Something based on the idea that life is most rewarding when we're helping others.†

Transition Words That Indicate Comparison/Contrast

Paragraphs include **comparison** transitions to help readers see *similarities* between two or more things. They include **contrast** transitions to point out *differences*.

First, let's examine the comparison transitions, which appear in the list below.

Comparison Transitions		
also	similarly	similar to
too	in like manner	in the same way
likewise	just like, just as	along the same line
		in both cases

The following pairs of sentences illustrate the use of comparison transitions:

When you shop for a car, you look for the color, style, and features you want. ***Similarly,*** new genetic[1] research may allow future parents to choose the characteristics they want in their children.

---

1. **genetic:** related to genes, the units that determine the particular characteristics of an organism

---

* Adapted from Rick Bragg, "Charlie and the River Rat," from "Ava's Man," *Reader's Digest*, August 2001, 149.

† Adapted from Andrew Shue, "A Message from Andrew Shue," Special Advertising Section, *Reader's Digest*, August 2001, 160.

In the nineteenth century, large numbers of Irish, Italian, and Jewish immigrants struggled to blend into American society. *__Likewise,__* today's Latinos and Asians are weaving themselves into this country's diverse[1] cultural mix.

Today's parents are objecting to the skimpy, skin-baring clothes their pre-teens are wearing. *__In the same way,__* 1960s parents were horrified by their girls' hip-huggers and halter tops.

The following paragraph uses comparison transition words (bold-faced and italicized). Notice how each transition indicates another point of comparison.

The disputed[2] presidential elections of 1876 and 2000 shared some striking similarities. The 1876 election between Samuel Tilden and Rutherford B. Hayes was so close that the victory hinged upon just a few electoral votes. *__Likewise,__* in 2000, the race between Al Gore and George W. Bush depended upon only a handful of electoral votes.[3] In 1876, the state of Florida played a major part in the election's outcome. *__Similarly,__* Florida was cast into the national spotlight in 2000 when the election depended upon that state's poll results. The media of 1876 prematurely[4] assumed that Hayes had won. The media in 2000, *__too,__* presumed George W. Bush the winner before they had all of the facts. *__In both cases,__* the Supreme Court had to get involved to help settle the matter.*

Exercise 5.4

Fill in the blanks in the following sentences and paragraphs with appropriate comparison transitions. Choose words or phrases from the box on page 186. Try to vary your choices.

1. World War I changed the nature of war by introducing gas, trench warfare, tanks, submarines, and aircraft. _____, World War II changed fighting by adding rockets and atomic bombs.

---

1. **diverse:** different

2. **disputed:** argued about

3. **electoral votes:** votes from the body chosen to elect the president and vice president of the United States

4. **prematurely:** occurring before the right time

---

* Adapted from Jeremy F. Plant, "Déjà vu: Revisiting the 1876 Presidential Election," *USA Today,* May 2001, 16–18.

5

2. Many antibiotics and drugs have been discovered in European rivers and tap water. _____, low levels of three antibiotics are present in West Virginia waters.

3. My biology textbook is colorful and breaks down information into small sections. _____, my economics textbook offers a chapter summary and beautiful illustrations to make the concepts easier to understand.

4. _____ you, I try to exercise at least a half an hour every day.

5. Many observers feared for the future of America's families at the ends of both the nineteenth and twentieth centuries. In the 1890s, the U.S. divorce rate was the highest in the world. _____, the 1990s divorce rate was very high. In the 1890s, there was an epidemic[1] of sexually transmitted diseases. Such diseases were a problem in the late 1990s. Late nineteenth-century urban areas were plagued[2] by drug abuse. _____, many late twentieth-century Americans struggled with drug addiction and the crime it caused.*

6. Born in the Bronx and reared in a humble household on Long Island, Billy Joel[3] attended school by day and worked odd jobs at night to help support his single mother. _____ half of the rest of the teenage world in the 1960s, he _____ played in a rock and roll band. Unlike most of the others, he stayed with it, developing a solo act and taking it to whatever places would hire him.†

7. Although the positions they play couldn't be more different, pitchers and catchers share many of the same traits and characteristics. _____ a pitcher can hold the fate of the whole ball game in his hands, a catcher can do the same by either tagging someone out at home and preventing a run from scoring or just the opposite—dropping the ball and letting the

1. **epidemic:** a disease affecting large numbers of people

2. **plagued:** afflicted; affected

3. **Billy Joel:** a popular singer/musician

* Adapted from Stephanie Coontz, "The American Family," *Life*, November 1999, 79.

† Adapted from Shanti Gold, "When the Ship Comes In: Downtown Man, Uptown Girl," *New York Daily News*, March 16, 2003, 39.

run score. _____, pitchers and catchers share the pain of sustaining major injuries, pitchers to their arms and shoulders, and catchers to any part of their body that can be hit by a bat or a ball. And _____ that pitchers are lifelong pitchers and never play another position, catchers are very loyal to the position, only moving if injury or the team manager makes them move.

Now, let's look at the contrast transitions.

Contrast Transitions

however	nevertheless	unfortunately
but	on the one hand	in contrast
yet	on the other hand	conversely
although	unlike	even though
instead	rather	still
in opposition	on the contrary	nonetheless
in spite of	actually	whereas
just the opposite	despite	in reality
though	while	as opposed to

The following pairs of sentences illustrate the use of contrast transitions:

Scientists agree that exercising the mind keeps it functioning well. **However,** they disagree about the best way to go about achieving mental fitness.

For a while, eggs fell out of favor because of their high cholesterol content. **But** the latest studies show they are both healthy and nutritious.

Photos of President John F. Kennedy's family at play only looked casual and spontaneous. **In reality,** they were professionally lit, and the people in them were styled and posed.

Next, read a paragraph that includes contrast transition words (boldfaced and italicized). Notice how each transition indicates another point of contrast.

Interactive and independent teaching styles differ in a number of various ways. The instructor whose style is independent is usually formal and businesslike with students and places more importance on individual effort than on group effort. **On the other hand,** the instructor whose style is interactive is usually informal with students and places more importance on group effort than on individual effort. The preferred teaching method of the independent instructor is lecturing, and he or she will often call on students rather than ask for volunteers. The interactive instructor, **_though,_** prefers small group activities and large group discussions. Rather than calling on students, he or she will usually ask for volunteers. Students usually feel competitive in the independent instructor's class. **_Conversely,_** they feel cooperative in the interactive instructor's class.*

Exercise **5.5**

Fill in the blanks in the following sentences and paragraphs with the appropriate contrast transition. Choose words or phrases from the box on page 189. Try to vary your choices.

1. Friendship ranks with marriage and kinship as one of the most important relationships in our lives. _____, it can be the most neglected.

2. _____ being one of the most beautiful and admired women in the world, Marilyn Monroe[1] suffered from depression.

3. You would think that a team with the high salary budget of the New York Rangers hockey team would have many championships in its history. _____ the Rangers have only won four Stanley Cup championships in the last one hundred years.

4. Charles called to see if I was available to go to dinner. _____, I had another commitment.

5. Golf is really more of a game than a sport. Sports—such as basketball or tennis—require aerobic activity that increases the heart rate and makes players sweat. Golf, _____, requires about the same physical conditioning necessary for stamp collecting. In sports like soccer and hockey, fans cheer, boo, and scream at the players. _____, in golf, the announcers whisper, and the spectators have to be quiet, clapping politely when a player hits a good shot. Sports—such as baseball and football—require uniforms, cheerleaders, and most importantly, real opponents. Golf, _____, has none of these things.[†]

1. **Marilyn Monroe:** a famous actress who committed suicide

---

* Adapted from Carol C. Kanar, _The Confident Student,_ 5th ed. (Boston: Houghton Mifflin Co., 2004), 51.
† Adapted from Bill Geist, "Planet Golf," _Reader's Digest,_ August 2001, 121–22.

6. Some people say that reading the newspaper is a better way to get information than watching television. _____, studies have shown that people who get their news exclusively from television news shows know almost as much about current affairs as people who read newspapers. _____, the debate rages on with some people favoring newspapers and some favoring television news shows.

7. Struggling students see themselves as victims, believing that what happens to them is determined mostly by external forces such as fate, luck, and powerful people. Successful students, _____, accept personal responsibility, seeing *themselves* as the primary cause of their outcomes and experiences. Struggling students have difficulty sustaining motivation and often feel depressed, frustrated, or resentful about the lack of di rection in their lives. _____ successful students are self-motivated because they have discovered meaningful goals and dreams that give them purpose. Struggling students seldom identify specific actions needed to accomplish a desired outcome. Successful students, _____, are good at self-management. They consistently plan and take purposeful actions in pursuit of their goals and dreams.*

5

Transition Words That Indicate Definition

One final set of transition words are those that signal *definitions* and *examples*. This pattern usually includes two parts—*a definition of a term and the examples that illustrate that term*. Because the definition pattern or organization often includes one or more examples, this type of transition will often appear in definition paragraphs. However, transitions that indicate example can appear in other types of paragraphs, too. Anytime that authors want to illustrate an idea or make it clearer, they often identify the beginning of an example with one of the following transitions.

Definition Transitions	
is	defined as

---

* Adapted from Skip Downing, *On Course*, 4th ed. (Boston: Houghton Mifflin Co., 2005), 1.

<table>
<tr><td colspan="3" align="center">**Example Transitions**</td></tr>
<tr><td>for example</td><td>as an illustration</td><td>in one case</td></tr>
<tr><td>for instance</td><td>in one instance</td><td>more precisely</td></tr>
<tr><td>to illustrate</td><td>such as</td><td>specifically</td></tr>
</table>

The following pairs of sentences illustrate the use of example transitions:

Volcanic explosions can be devastating. **One illustration** is Indonesia's Tambora Volcano, which killed 10,000 people when it exploded in 1815.

An autoimmune disease **is** one in which a person's immune system attacks the body's healthy tissue and organs. Lupus, **for instance,** is one of about eighty such diseases.

Thousands of employers are attempting to reduce the cost of employee health insurance by regulating their employees' lifestyles. **For example,** many companies require that employees don't smoke.

Now, read a paragraph that includes example transition words (boldfaced and italicized). Notice how the transition introduces the example.

When you reveal wrongdoing within an organization to the public or to those in positions of authority, you *are* a whistle-blower. Whistle-blowers are sounding alarms in industries from tobacco companies to airlines. ***For example,*** Sylvia Robins reported that she knew about a procedural flaw at Unisys, a National Aeronautics and Space Administration subcontractor that produces software programs for the space shuttle program. Robins came forward to stop any further endangerment of space shuttle crews.*

This definition paragraph explains the meaning of the term *whistle-blower.* After defining the term, it presents an illustration of one specific person who acted as a whistle-blower.

Exercise **5.6**

Fill in the blanks in the following sentences and paragraphs with appropriate example transitions. Choose words or phrases from the box on pages 191 and 192. Try to vary your choices.

---

* Adapted from Barry L. Reece and Rhonda Brandt, *Effective Human Relations in Organizations,* 7th ed. (Boston: Houghton Mifflin Co., 1999), 139–40.

1. One study of multivitamins found that one-third of brands don't contain what the label promises. _____, two brands of multivitamins for adults contained only 40 percent of the amount of vitamin A listed on the package.

2. Today many available cars are considered safe. _____, the Ford Explorer scored extremely well in crash tests, making it one of the safest cars you can buy.

3. Dolphins have been shown to have superior thinking abilities and more than a little extrasensory perception, or ESP.[1] _____, a dolphin swimming beside a young woman sensed that the woman was pregnant by nudging her abdomen, even though the woman herself did not know she was carrying a baby at the time!

4. Many American manufacturers of various products have facilities overseas. Dell, a Texas company that makes computers, _____, owns a large plant in Ireland. Microsoft software runs computers all over the world. McDonald's franchises are operated in many foreign cities, including Moscow and Tokyo.*

5. I'm a nerd. Although the Internet boom has lent some respectability to the term, narrow-minded stereotypes of nerds still linger. _____, nerds are supposed to be friendless bookworms who suck up to authority figures. _____, we're sissies.†

6. The categories of people to which you see yourself belonging and to which you always compare yourself are called *reference groups*. The performance of people in a reference group can influence your self-esteem. _____, if being a good swimmer is very important to you, knowing that someone in your reference group swims much faster than you do can lower your self-esteem.‡

7. Exporting is selling and shipping materials and products to other nations. _____, the Boeing Company exports its airplanes to a number of countries for use by their airlines. Importing is purchasing materials

1. **ESP:** knowing information that comes from outside of the normal range of senses

* Adapted from Carol C. Kanar, *The Confident Student*, 5th ed. (Boston: Houghton Mifflin Co., 2004), 357.
† Adapted from Tom Rogers, "My Kids Are Smarter Than Yours," *Reader's Digest*, August 2001, 69.
‡ Adapted from Douglas A. Bernstein et al., *Psychology*, 5th ed. (Boston: Houghton Mifflin Co., 2000), 605. Copyright © 2000 by Houghton Mifflin Company. Reprinted with permission.

5

or products from other nations and bringing them into one's own country. _____, American stores may purchase rugs in India or raincoats in England and have them shipped back to the United States for resale.*

Transition Words in Combinations of Patterns

Supporting details in paragraphs can be organized according to more than one pattern. For example, a paragraph may include both *sequence* details and *effect* details. In such paragraphs, it will be particularly important for you to notice transition words and phrases, because they will provide clues about the various relationships among different kinds of details. For an example of a paragraph that includes more than one pattern and, therefore, different kinds of transitions, read the following.

> Xenotransplantation *is* the use of animal organs as replacement for human organs. *For example,* surgeons have removed diseased livers from human patients and substituted livers taken from baboons. Such animal-to-human transplants began *in the 1900s* when doctors tried but failed to transplant kidneys from pigs, goats, apes, and lambs. *In the 1960s,* a number of primate[1]-to-human transplants were attempted, and several patients who received chimpanzee or baboon kidneys lived up to nine months following the operation. *In 1983,* a baby received a baboon heart, but her body rejected it twenty days later. *During the early 1990s,* doctors made three more attempts at liver xenotransplantation. *Today,* researchers are still studying xenotransplants and trying to make them a viable[2] option for people suffering from organ failure.[†]

This paragraph begins with the definition pattern, including an example. Then, it switches to the sequence pattern as it explains the history of

---

1. **primate:** mammals like apes and monkeys

2. **viable:** capable of success; workable

---

* Adapted from William Pride, Robert Hughes, and Jack Kapoor, *Business,* 6th ed. (Boston: Houghton Mifflin Co., 1999), 60.

† Adapted from John J. Fung, "Transplanting Animal Organs into Humans Is Feasible," *USA Today,* November 1999, 54–55.

xenotransplant attempts. Therefore, it includes both definition/example and sequence transitions.

Exercise **5.7**

Read each of the following paragraphs and then circle the transition words or phrases. Then, in the list below the paragraph, place a check mark next to each of the two patterns used to organize the details.

1. Although Columbus[1] was a great navigator and sailor, he was not a particularly good leader. Spanish officials and settlers were never loyal to him, and King Ferdinand and Queen Isabella of Spain eventually tired of him. However, unlike Columbus, Hernando Cortés[2] was a great leader and was able to help Ferdinand and Isabella realize their goals. In 1519, he and an army of six hundred Spanish soldiers landed in Mexico. Within three years, Cortés and his small force had defeated the mighty Aztec[3] empire. Establishing themselves in Mexico City, the Spanish took over the empire, bringing the Indian groups to the south under their rule.*

   _____ list

   _____ sequence

   _____ cause/effect

   _____ comparison/contrast

   _____ definition/example

2. If you feel like giving up when you encounter a very long or hard assignment, you probably have a low tolerance for unpleasant tasks. However, you can change your attitude toward unpleasant tasks so that you can concentrate and get them done. First, remind yourself that the sooner you start, the sooner you will finish. Next, remind yourself that your attitude toward studying may be causing you to lose concentration and may be keeping you from doing your work as well as you can. Third, make long or difficult assignments easier to handle by breaking them into smaller

1. **Columbus:** the first historically important European discoverer of the New World

2. **Hernando Cortés:** Spanish adventurer who conquered Mexico's Aztec empire

3. **Aztec:** an ancient civilization of Central Mexico

* Adapted from Carol Berkin et al., *Making America*, Brief 2nd ed. (Boston: Houghton Mifflin Co., 2001), 26.

segments that you can complete in one sitting. Then reward yourself for doing the work.*

_____ list

_____ sequence

_____ cause/effect

_____ comparison/contrast

_____ definition/example

3. Readers fall into two categories: active readers and passive readers. *Active readers* control their interest level and concentration. They read with a purpose. They know what information to look for and why. Active readers constantly question what they read. They relate the author's ideas to their own experience and prior knowledge. On the other hand, *passive readers* are not in control of their reading. They read the same way they watch television programs and movies, expecting others to engage them and keep their attention. A common passive reading experience is to "wake up" in the middle of a paragraph, wondering what you have just read. Active readers control the process of reading; passive readers are unaware that reading is a process that they can control.†

_____ list

_____ sequence

_____ cause/effect

_____ comparison/contrast

_____ definition/example

4. Because so many children play at the Lexington Avenue Park every day, many children lose the toys they bring to play with, such as trucks, dolls, and balls. You can do a few things to avoid losing your children's toys at the park. Before you come to the park, label everything with your child's name and address. It is also a good idea to bring as few toys as you can and to make a list of the things that you bring with you. While you are at the park, keep your child's toys in a pile where he or she is playing, if possible. Before you leave, make a quick sweep of the park to see if your child has left anything behind. This will ensure that you leave with your child's toys.

---

* Adapted from Carol C. Kanar, *The Confident Student*, 5th ed. (Boston: Houghton Mifflin Co., 2004), 258.

† Carol Kanar, *The Confident Student*, 7th ed. (Boston: Wadsworth, 2011), 162. Print.

_____ list

_____ sequence

_____ cause/effect

_____ comparison/contrast

_____ definition/example

5. The Spanish Crown supported many exploratory ventures[1] to the "New World" by hiring _conquistadors._ A _conquistador_ was the name given to a Spanish explorer who set out to overtake parts of the New World both in Mexico and what is now the United States. For example, Ponce de Leon, Hernando de Soto, and Francisco Pizarro were all conquistadors. In 1513 and again in 1521, Juan Ponce de Leon led expeditions to Florida. In 1539, the Spanish sent Hernando de Soto to claim the Mississippi River. In 1533, Francisco Pizarro conquered the Inca Empire, an advanced civilization that glittered with gold.*

_____ list

_____ sequence

_____ cause/effect

_____ comparison/contrast

_____ definition/example

Exercise **5.8**

The following groups of sentences have been scrambled. Number them in the order they should appear (1, 2, 3, and so on) so that they make sense. Use the transitions to help you figure out the right order. Then, in the list below each group, place a check mark next to the pattern or patterns used to organize the details.

1. _____ First, write your positive statements—sentences like "I am intelligent," "I can handle my problems," and "I am creative"—on 3 × 5 index cards.

   _____ One technique for improving self-esteem is designing positive self-talk statements.

1. **ventures:** daring or dangerous undertakings

---

* Adapted from Carol Berkin et al., _Making America_, Brief 2nd ed. (Boston: Houghton Mifflin Co., 2001), 26.

_____ Then, each time you see one of these cards, review its message and believe the words.

_____ Next, attach your cards to your bathroom mirror, your refrigerator, your car dashboard, and your desk.*

Pattern of organization:

_____ list

_____ sequence

_____ cause/effect

_____ comparison/contrast

_____ definition/example

2. _____ The catalog will also tell you whether a fee is involved in applying for a degree and under what conditions you can get your money back if you withdraw from a course.

_____ The calendar in your catalog, for example, is one of the items you will use most frequently.

_____ Your college catalog is a publication that contains a wealth of information about your college's programs, policies, requirements, and services.

_____ It shows when classes begin and end, when holidays occur, when the drop-and-add period is over, when final exams are scheduled, and when you should apply for a degree.†

Pattern of organization:

_____ list

_____ sequence

_____ cause/effect

_____ comparison/contrast

_____ definition/example

3. _____ Consequently, town residents who want to swim will have to join either the Silver Lake swim club or the Charles Cook Pool in Cortlandt Manor.

---

* Adapted from Barry L. Reece and Rhonda Brandt, *Effective Human Relations in Organizations*, 7th ed. (Boston: Houghton Mifflin Co., 1997), 111.

† Adapted from Carol C. Kanar, *The Confident Student*, 5th ed. (Boston: Houghton Mifflin Co., 2004), 20.

_____ As a result, no swimming will be allowed during July and August.

_____ Due to high levels of algae, the Duck Pond in the center of town has tested positive for a dangerous microbe.[1]

_____ Because swimming won't be allowed, the Duck Pond in the center of town is being closed for the summer.

Pattern of organization:

_____ list

_____ sequence

_____ cause/effect

_____ comparison/contrast

_____ definition/example

4. _____ In the early 1960s, Irving refined his storytelling skills at the University of Iowa, where he got a master's degree in creative writing.

_____ John Irving[2] grew up in Exeter, New Hampshire, where his stepfather taught at the exclusive Phillips Exeter Academy.

_____ He took up wrestling at age fourteen to provide a much-needed outlet for his energy.

_____ In 1964, he married photographer Shyla Leary, whom he met in college, and became a father at the age of 23.*

Pattern of organization:

_____ list

_____ sequence

_____ cause/effect

_____ comparison/contrast

_____ definition/example

5

1. **microbe:** a tiny life form

2. **John Irving:** American writer whose novels include *The World According to Garp*

* Adapted from Kim Hubbard and Natasha Stoynoff, "Hands Full," *People* Magazine, July 30, 2001, 96–97.

Reading Strategy: Summarizing

When you **summarize** *a reading selection, you briefly restate, in your own words, its most important ideas.* A summary usually focuses on the most general points, which include the overall main idea and some of the major supporting details. As a result, summaries are much shorter than the original material. A paragraph can usually be summarized in a sentence or two, an article can be summarized in a paragraph, and a typical textbook chapter can be summarized in a page or two.

Summarizing is an important reading skill that you will use for three specific academic purposes: studying, completing assignments and tests, and incorporating source material into research projects.

Studying. Writing summaries is an effective way to gain a better understanding of what you read. If you need to remember the information in a textbook chapter, for instance, you will know it more thoroughly after you have summarized its main ideas. Also, the act of writing down these ideas will help reinforce them in your memory.

Completing assignments and tests. Summaries are one of the most common types of college writing assignments. Professors in a variety of disciplines often ask students to summarize readings such as journal articles. Also, "summarize" is a common direction in tests that require written responses.

Incorporating source material into research projects. You will use summaries of other sources to support your ideas in research projects such as term papers. *To write a summary, follow these three steps:*

1. Using active reading strategies, read and reread the original material until you understand it.

2. Identify the main idea and major supporting points. In particular, underline all of the topic sentences. You might also want to create an outline or map that diagrams the general and specific relationships among sentences (in a paragraph) or paragraphs (in an article or chapter).

3. Using your own words, write sentences that state the author's main idea along with the most important major details. Your paraphrase should be accurate; it should not add anything that did not appear in the original or omit anything important from the original. It should also be objective. In other words, don't offer your own reactions or opinions; just restate the author's points without commenting on them. If you use a phrase from the original, enclose it in quotation marks to indicate that it is the author's words, not yours.

Follow the three steps described above to write a one-paragraph summary of the following textbook passage.

Your Diverse Campus

Diversity means variety, pure and simple. Diversity on campus—and in society at large—refers to the variety of races, ethnic groups, cultures, religions, sexual orientations, nationalities, and other constituencies and perspectives that are represented. Colleges have responded to student diversity by offering services and opportunities to meet a variety of needs. Moreover, diversity has many benefits. Exposure to different customs and ways of thinking challenges your ideas and broadens your worldview. Because your campus is a small slice of our larger society, it provides you with an opportunity to hone your interpersonal skills and to develop intercultural communication skills that will prepare you for a career in an increasingly diverse workplace.

Creating a learning environment where all are treated with respect and where all are free to pursue their educational goals is everyone's responsibility. Do your part by being open to ideas and customs that may differ from your own. If you harbor any stereotypical thinking that prevents cross-cultural communication, now is the time to let it go. Look around you at your classmates and instructors. They are individuals—first.

Embrace diversity by reaching out to others in a spirit of friendship and community. Make all students feel welcome, just as you want to be welcomed. Accept other's differences, listen without being critical, and establish friendships based on shared interests and values. As you form your support group, think of others' differences not as barriers to communication but as bridges to understanding. Let your support group ring with the harmony of different voices.*

 The following web links will provide you with additional information and practice with the very important skills of summarizing.

http://users.drew.edu/~sjamieso/summary.html
http://www.tc.umn.edu/~jewel001/CollegeWriting/
WRITEREAD/Summary/samples.htm

* Kanar, Carol. *The Confident Student,* 7th ed. (Boston: Wadsworth, 2011), 11. Print.

Reading Selections

Practicing the Active Reading Strategy

■ Before and While You Read

You can use active reading strategies before, while, and after you read a selection. The following are some suggestions for active reading strategies that you can employ before you read and as you are reading.

1. Skim the selection for any unfamiliar words. Circle or highlight any words you do not know.

2. As you read, underline, highlight, or circle important words or phrases.

3. Write down any questions about the selection if you are confused by the information presented.

4. Jot notes in the margin to help you understand the material.

5

BIOGRAPHY:
Sonia Sotomayor: Celebrity Status
for a Supreme Court Justice

Sonia Sotomayor was born on June 25, 1954, in the Bronx borough of New York City, New York, to Juan Sotomayor and the former Celina Baez. Both of her parents were born in Puerto Rico, where she visits relatives once or twice a year on average. As a child, Sotomayor grew up in a bilingual household and did not learn to speak English fluently until after the death of her father, who only spoke Spanish, when she was 9 years old. Sotomayor's mother, a retired nurse, raised Sonia and her brother Juan, a physician who lives in Syracuse, New York, as a single working mother.

Sotomayor was attracted to the law at an early age. She says she was inspired to become a prosecutor by an episode of the legal drama Perry Mason in which a character playing a prosecutor claimed that serving justice meant losing cases where the defendant was innocent. "I noticed that Perry Mason was involved in a lot of the same kinds of investigative work that I had been fascinated with reading Nancy Drew, so I decided to become a lawyer."

As the first Hispanic Supreme Court Justice, Sotomayor made history with her confirmation on August 6, 2009. She is only the third woman to serve on the nation's highest court.

1   Apparently, no one told Sonia Sotomayor that Supreme Court justices are supposed to be circumspect, emerging from their marble palace mainly to dispense legal wisdom to law schools, judges 'conferences and lawyers' meetings. Since becoming the first Hispanic justice, Sotomayor has mamboed with movie stars, exchanged smooches with musicians at the White House and thrown

out the first pitch for her beloved New York Yankees. A famous jazz composer even wrote a song about her: "Wise Latina Woman." In short, Sotomayor has become a celebrity—all without having made a single major decision at the nation's highest court.

2   Few Americans can name most of the justices. "Many, many, many more Americans can name the Seven Dwarfs than they can the people on the Supreme Court," said Bob Thompson, professor of television and popular culture at Syracuse University. Not so for Sotomayor. Autograph seekers, picture takers, and well-wishers hound her wherever she goes, months after her confirmation hearing, swearing-in, and first appearance in the courtroom. In fact, apart from a C-SPAN program that interviewed all the justices, she is refusing television, magazine, and newspaper interview requests, including a request for comment from The Associated Press for this story. Sotomayor even nixed plans by famed photographer Annie Liebowitz to shoot her for a photo spread in *Vogue* magazine.

3   She did allow *Latina* magazine to photograph her inside the Supreme Court building, but wouldn't submit to a formal interview even though a friend wrote the accompanying article. Wearing her black robe, the justice appeared on the cover of the latest issue prominently displaying her bright red fingernails, which White House aides had persuaded her to repolish in a demure neutral shade last July for her Senate confirmation hearing. Even though she's avoided interviews, people recognize her everywhere. "There are people who can identify her in a line of pictures who couldn't identify some of the people who are big movie stars," Thompson said.

4   Part of the adulation stems from the historic nature of her appointment: the first Hispanic on the court, and only the third female, after retired Justice Sandra Day O'Connor and current Justice Ruth Bader Ginsburg. "She is the first Latino, Latina to sit on the Supreme Court and that's powerful. She's a powerful role model," said Thomas Saenz, president and general counsel of the Mexican American Legal Defense and Educational Fund. "She will have an effect on Latino children akin to the effect that the election of the first African-American president has had and will have on African American childcare and that's encouraging. And for all of that she deservedly gets treated like a rock star."

5   Sotomayor is also only the third non-white justice. The late Thurgood Marshall joined the court in 1967, the court's first African-American justice and first non-white. Justice Clarence Thomas, who replaced Marshall, still serves on the court with Sotomayor. Times were much different when Marshall arrived. The justice would tell stories of being mistaken for an elevator operator inside the Supreme Court, recalled one of his former clerks, Mark Tushnet. These days, Thomas says he's recognized as a justice wherever he goes. "It's easier to recognize…to pick one person out who's different," Thomas told C-SPAN. Thompson, the Syracuse professor, said it could be a

5

good thing for Sotomayor's fame to linger if it draws attention away from reality television stars and the like and toward the court. Supreme Court justices "should be the celebrities," Thompson said. "Given the nature of our governmental system, these are the people that every citizen should know. These are important people."*

■ Vocabulary

Read the following questions about some of the vocabulary words that appear in the previous selection. Before you look up the word, try to use the context of the passage to figure out the meaning. Then circle the letter of each correct answer.

1. In the introduction what does the word *fluently* mean?

   a. capable of using a language easily

   b. unable to speak

   c. capable of talking loudly

   d. the process of learning a language

2. The author uses the word *circumspect* to describe Supreme Court justices. What does it mean? (paragraph 1)

   a. loose, out of control   c. flashy

   b. strict   d. careful, cautious

3. In paragraph 3 the author uses the word *prominently*. What does it mean?

   a. held back   c. standing out or projecting

   b. obnoxious   d. done with intent

4. The author uses the word *demure* to describe a nail polish color. What does the word mean? (paragraph 3)

   a. flashy   c. outlandish

   b. reserved, modest   d. expensive

5. "Part of the *adulation* stems from the historic nature of her appointment." (paragraph 4) What does *adulation* mean?

   a. disgust   c. excessive admiration or flattery

   b. insulting   d. massive security

---

* Holland, Jesse J. *Sonia Sotomayor Has Achieved Celeb Status As Supreme Court Justice*, Used with permission of The Associated Press Copyright © 2011. All rights reserved.

■ Reading Skills

Respond to each of the following questions by circling the letter of the correct answer.

1. What is the main idea of paragraph 1?

   a. sentence 1   c. sentence 3

   b. sentence 2   d. sentence 4

2. What sequence transition is used in sentence 2 in paragraph 1?

   _____

3. Which sentence in paragraph 3 begins with a contrast transition?

   a. sentence 1   c. sentence 3

   b. sentence 2   d. sentence 4

4. Paragraph 4 includes the sentence: "She will have an effect on Latino children akin to the effect that the election of the first African-American president has had and will have on African American childcare and that's encouraging." This sentence uses the cause/effect transition "effect". Which sentence in paragraph 4 includes the cause?

   a. sentence 1   c. sentence 3

   b. sentence 2   d. sentence 5

5. What is the implied main idea of paragraph 5?

   a. African-American judges came before Sonia Sotomayor.

   b. Sotomayor will make an outstanding judge.

   c. Sonia Sotomayor will be easy to recognize as a Supreme Court justice.

   d. Thurgood Marshall was the first African-American Supreme Court justice.

Practicing the Active Reading Strategy

■ After You Read

Now that you have read the selection, answer the following questions, using the active reading strategies that you learned in Chapter 1.

1. Identify and write down the point and purpose of this reading selection.

2. Did you circle or highlight any words that are unfamiliar to you? Can you figure out the meaning from the context of the passage? If not,

then look up each word in a dictionary and find the definition that best describes the word as it is used in the selection. You may want to write the definition in the margin next to the word in the passage for future reference.

3. Predict any possible questions that may be used on a test about the content of this selection.

■ Questions for Discussion and Writing

Answer the following questions based on your reading of the selection.

1. How would you feel being the first Hispanic Supreme Court justice? Have you ever been the first person to accomplish something? _____

_____

2. The author states, "Few Americans can name most of the justices." Why do you think this is true? _____

_____

3. The author describes how Sonia Sotomayor was "attracted to law at an early age." Do you think what you are influenced by as a child impacts your career choices? Explain your answer and give details. _____

_____

Practicing the Active Reading Strategy

■ Before and While You Read

You can use active reading strategies before, while, and after you read a selection. The following are some suggestions for active reading strategies that you can employ before you read and as you are reading.

1. Skim the selection for any unfamiliar words. Circle or highlight any words you do not know.

2. As you read, underline, highlight, or circle important words or phrases.

3. Write down any questions about the selection if you are confused by the information presented.

4. Jot notes in the margin to help you understand the material.

TEXTBOOK READING: HEALTH CARE
The First Trimester

Have you thought about a career in the medical field or perhaps in education? Perhaps you have taken a course in biology. Understanding the growth and development of an embryo to a baby is an important part of these courses.

1   The first trimester is sometimes considered the most critical. Because of the embryo's rapid differentiation and development of tissue, the embryo is exceptionally vulnerable to the mother's intake of noxious[1] substances and to aspects of the mother's health.

2   By the end of the first month, a primitive heart and digestive system have developed. The basic imitation of a brain and nervous system is also apparent. Small buds that will eventually become arms and legs are appearing. In general, development starts with the brain and continues down through the body. For example, the feet are the last to develop. In the first month, the embryo bears little resemblance to a baby because its organs have just begun to differentiate.

3   The embryo begins to resemble human form more closely during the second month. Internal organs become more complex. Facial features including eyes, nose, and mouth begin to become identifiable. The 2-month-old embryo is approximately an inch long and weighs about one-third of an ounce.

4   The third month involves the formation of arms, hands, legs, and feet. Fingernails, hair follicles, and eyelids develop. All three basic organs have appeared, although they are still underdeveloped. By the end of the third month, bones begin to replace cartilage. Fetal movement is frequently detected at this time.*

5

■ Vocabulary

Read the following questions about some of the vocabulary words that appear in the previous selection. Before you look up the word, try to use the context of the passage to figure out the meaning. Then circle the letter of the correct answer for each question.

1.   **noxious:** poisonous

* Charles Zastrow and Karen K. Kirst-Ashman, *Understanding Human Behavior and the Social Environment*, 7th ed. (Belmont: Thomson Higher Education, 2007), 53. Print.

1. The author uses the word *differentiation* in paragraph 1 to describe an embryo's development. What does *differentiation* mean?

   a. same

   b. to become distinct or different

   c. understated

   d. disfigured, damaged

2. The author uses the word *vulnerable* to describe an embryo in paragraph 1. What does the word *vulnerable* mean?

   a. lifelike   c. open to attack or damage

   b. small, tiny   d. gullible

3. What does the word *trimester* mean in paragraph 1?

   a. three weeks   c. three years

   b. three days   d. three months

4. Paragraph 2 includes the word *primitive*. What does the word mean?

   a. early stage of development

   b. modern

   c. apelike

   d. outlandish

■ Reading Skills

Respond to each of the following questions by circling the letter of the correct answer or by writing your answer on the blank provided.

1. What is the cause/effect transition used in paragraph 1?

   _____

2. Paragraph 2 begins with a transition: "By the end of the first month, a primitive heart and digestive system have developed." What type of transition is the author using?

   a. list   c. sequence

   b. definition   d. cause/effect

3. What is the minor detail transition in paragraph 2? _____

4. What sentence states the main idea of paragraph 3?

   a. sentence 1   c. sentence 3

   b. sentence 2   d. sentence 4

5. Which sentence in paragraph 4 includes a sequence transition?

a. sentence 2   c. sentence 4

b. sentence 3   d. sentence 5

Practicing the Active Reading Strategy

■ After You Read

Now that you have read the selection, answer the following questions, using the active reading strategies that you learned in Chapter 1.

1. Identify and write down the point and purpose of this reading selection.

2. Did you circle or highlight any words that are unfamiliar to you? Can you figure out the meaning from the context of the passage? If not, then look up each word in a dictionary and find the definition that best describes the word as it is used in the selection. You may want to write the definition in the margin next to the word in the passage for future reference.

3. Predict any possible questions that may be used on a test about the content of this selection.

■ Questions for Discussion and Writing

Respond to each of the following questions based on your reading of the selection.

1. The author begins by saying that, "the first trimester is sometimes considered the most critical." Do you agree or disagree with the author? Defend your answer. _____

_____

2. What did you learn about the first trimester? What was the most surprising, or something you did not know? _____

_____

Practicing the Active Reading Strategy

■ Before and While You Read

You can use active reading strategies before, while, and after you read a selection. The following are some suggestions for active reading strategies that you can employ before you read and as you are reading.

5

1. Skim the selection for any unfamiliar words. Circle or highlight any words you do not know.

2. As you read, underline, highlight, or circle important words or phrases.

3. Write down any questions about the selection if you are confused by the information presented.

4. Jot notes in the margin to help you understand the material.

TEXTBOOK READING: FIRE SCIENCE
Wildland Firefighters

Have you ever seen a house fire or watched as firefighters put out a large fire? Fighting fires is an extremely challenging career. When forests burn, special firefighters called "wildland firefighters," are called to help put out these dangerous fires. The following textbook excerpt will help you to understand the training needed for these special men and women.

1   Fires set by lightning or careless human behavior consume thousands of acres of our precious wildlands annually. For example, in October 2007, more than 500,000 acres in California burned, and this is a small percentage of the total acres burned in 2007. In national forests and parks, non-firefighters are the first line of defense against these fires. Forest rangers patrol assigned areas to ensure that travelers and campers comply with fire regulations. Forest fire inspectors and prevention specialists spot fires from watchtowers and report their findings to headquarters by telephone or radio. When a fire is reported, wildland firefighters are brought in to suppress the blaze. In addition to basic firefighting training, these specialists study fire ecology, the science of how fire behaves in natural environments and how it affects both living and nonliving things in the environment.

2   The work is physically demanding and can be emotionally taxing. Wildland firefighters are frequently required to work for days at a time—sometimes up to 14 days straight, without a day off or home leave. A typical shift is 16 hours or longer, and shifts over 24 hours are not unknown. In addition to the long hours, the crews must brave hazardous environments, enduring extremes of heat as well as smoky, dirty, and dusty conditions.

3   A wildland firefighter may not always work directly in the front lines of an advancing fire. Other assignments might include creating fire lines—cutting down trees and digging out grass and other combustible vegetation in the path of the fire—to deprive it of fuel. This is one of the most efficient means of battling a blaze. Wildland firefighters may also work at setting and monitoring

prescribed fires. These are fires purposely ignited by fire personnel or agencies under controlled conditions for specific management objectives. For example, setting a prescribed fire is a good, natural way to help put nitrates back into the soil. Furthermore, a prescribed burn can help decrease wildfires because it removes dead and dying trees to prevent heavy fuel loads during dry sessions.

4   There are a number of challenging specialist careers within the wildland firefighting field. Helicopter attack teams, or helitack, dump enormous buckets or belly tanks of water onto the fire. Some helitack crews rappel out of helicopters, gaining access the only way possible to fires in remote areas or in rugged terrain. Smoke jumpers parachute out of planes to reach areas not otherwise accessible, and hotshot crews hike into the area where the fire is burning to begin extinguishment.*

■ Vocabulary

Read the following questions about some of the vocabulary words that appear in the previous selection. Before you look up the word, try to use the context of the passage to figure out the meaning. Then circle the letter of the correct answer for each question.

1. When a fire *consumes* a forest, what does is the fire doing? (paragraph 1)

   a. eating

   b. dying out

   c. destroying

   d. burning slowly

2. In paragraph 1, how do firefighters *suppress* a blaze?

   a. put it out

   b. let it burn

   c. watch it carefully

   d. call for more help

3. In paragraph 2, how can emotions be *taxing*?

   a. needing money

   b. exhausting

___

* Loyd, Jason B. *Fundamentals of Fire and Emergency Services.* Upper Saddle River: Pearson Education Inc., 2010, 20–21. Print.

5

   c. burning

   d. happy

4. Vegetation that is *combustible*, will do what? (paragraph 3)

   a. burn easily

   b. not burn easily

   c. grow very large

   d. be eaten by deer

5. When helitack crews *rappel* out of helicopters, what are they doing? (paragraph 4)

   a. jumping

   b. using a basket

   c. descending by using a rope

   d. parachuting

■ Reading Skills

Respond to each of the following questions by circling the letter of the correct answer or by writing your answer on the blank provided.

1. List the two major transitions that are used in paragraph 1.

   a. _____

   b. _____

2. The topic sentence for paragraph 2 is

   a. sentence 1.

   b. sentence 2.

   c. sentence 3.

   d. sentence 4.

3. The general topic of paragraph 3 is

   a. setting prescribed fires,

   b. other duties of wildland firefighters.

   c. creating fire lines.

   d. setting up a base camp.

4. List the three transitions used in paragraph 3.

   a. _____

   b. _____

   c. _____

5. Write the topic sentence of paragraph 4.

   _____

   _____

   _____

   _____

Practicing the Active Reading Strategy

■ After You Read

Now that you have read the selection, answer the following questions, us-ing the active reading strategies that you learned in Chapter 1.

1. Identify and write down the point and purpose of this reading selection.

2. Did you circle or highlight any words that are unfamiliar to you? Can you figure out the meaning from the context of the passage? If not, then look up each word in a dictionary and find the definition that best describes the word as it is used in the selection. You may want to write the definition in the margin next to the word in the passage for future reference.

3. Predict any possible questions that may be used on a test about the content of this selection.

■ Questions for Discussion and Writing

Respond to each of the following questions based on your reading of the selection.

1. What ways do non-firefighting personnel help to fight forest fires?

   _____

   _____

   _____

   _____

2. Why do wildland firefighters set prescribed burns?

_____

_____

_____

_____

3. Would you be interested in a career as a wildland firefighter? Why or why not?

_____

_____

Vocabulary Strategy: The Explanation Context Clue

In Chapter 4, you learned about the definition/restatement context clue. A second type of context clue is **explanation.** In this type of clue, *the words, phrases, or sentences near an unfamiliar word will explain enough about that word to allow you to figure out its meaning.* For example, read this next sentence, which comes from one of the paragraphs in this chapter:

Almost immediately, it began leaning because it was being erected on the soft *silt* of a buried riverbed.

What is *silt*? Well, you get several explanation clues in this sentence. First of all, it's soft, and secondly, it's found in buried riverbeds. It also caused the tower to lean. Therefore, you can conclude that it must be some type of wet, unstable sand.

Vocabulary Exercise

The following examples all come from paragraphs in Chapters 4 and 5. In each one, use the explanation context clue to help you determine the meaning of the italicized word and write a definition for this word on the blank provided.

1. From 1999 to 2001, engineers *excavated* soil from beneath the tower.

_____

2. So to reduce your risk of such an accident, drive more on divided high-ways with *medians*.

_____

3. Mother England made the mistake of withholding liberty too long from her "children" in the American colonies. They grew to be rebellious "teenagers" who demanded their freedom. . . . As a consequence, though, England did learn a valuable lesson from a painful experience, which is why she later granted a peaceful and orderly transfer of power to another *tempestuous* offspring named India.

_____

4. The *disputed* presidential elections of 1876 and 2000 shared some strik-ing similarities. The 1876 election between Samuel Tilden and Rutherford B. Hayes was so close that the victory hinged upon just a few electoral votes. Likewise, in 2000, the race between Al Gore and George W. Bush depended upon only a handful of electoral votes.

_____

5. Sports—such as basketball or tennis—require *aerobic* activity that increases the heart rate and makes players sweat.

_____

6. The ancient Greeks would tuck rosemary twigs in their hair while studying to help them remember what they were learning. They also wore rosemary *garlands* to word off the "evil eye," a look or stare believed to harm others.

_____

7. He is also a master magician and makes friends and fights *mythic* battles against the forces of Darkness, which appeals to a wide variety of readers.

_____

Chapter 5 Review

Write the correct answer in each of the blanks in the following statements.

1. _____ are words and phrases whose function is to show the relationships between thoughts and ideas.

2. Some transitions are _____; in other words, they mean the same thing.

3. Some transitions can be used in more than one _____ of organization.

4. Different transitions can create subtle but significant changes in the _____ of sentences.

5. _____ transitions indicate the addition of another reason, example, type, or other point.

6. _____ signal another event, step, or stage within a chronological order of details.

7. _____ transitions indicate either a reason for or a result of an occurrence presented in a previous sentence.

8. _____ transitions point out similarities, and _____ transitions point out differences.

9. _____ transitions illustrate ideas in definition paragraphs as well as in other types of paragraphs.

10. _____ organized according to more than one pattern will often include different kinds of transitions.

11. Summaries are usually _____ than the original material.

12. An _____ context clue will describe or give further information about an unfamiliar word in the sentences just before or after that word.

Erik Dreyer/Getty Images

Patterns of Organization

Goals for Chapter 6

- ■ Define the term *pattern* as it relates to paragraphs.
- ■ Name the five broad patterns for organizing supporting details in paragraphs.
- ■ Recognize words in topic sentences that indicate certain patterns.
- ■ Recognize supporting details within a list pattern.
- ■ Recognize supporting details within a sequence pattern.
- ■ Recognize supporting details within a cause/effect pattern.
- ■ Recognize supporting details within a comparison/contrast pattern.
- ■ Recognize supporting details within a definition pattern.
- ■ Take notes on a reading selection.

Now that you've practiced examining supporting details and transitions, you're ready to look at some common patterns for arranging details. A **pattern** *is a consistent form or method for arranging things.* To find out what you already know about patterns of organization in paragraphs, take the pretest below.

Pretest

Read each of the following paragraphs and decide which pattern of organization arranges the details. Write a check mark on the blank next to the correct pattern.

1. Smoking is the single most preventable risk factor for fatal illnesses in the United States. Indeed, cigarette smoking accounts for more deaths than all other drugs, car accidents, suicides, homicides, and fires combined. Further, nonsmokers who inhale smoke from other people's cigarettes face an elevated risk for lung cancer and other illnesses related to the lungs, a fact that has given rise to a nonsmokers' rights movement in the United States.*

   _____ list

   _____ sequence

   _____ cause/effect

   _____ comparison/contrast

   _____ definition

2. Therapists often teach clients desirable behaviors by demonstrating those behaviors. In modeling, the client watches other people perform desired behaviors to learn new skills without going through a lengthy process. In fear treatment, for example, modeling can teach the client how to respond fearlessly while getting rid of the fear responses the patient has.†

   _____ list

   _____ sequence

   _____ cause/effect

   _____ comparison/contrast

   _____ definition

---

* Adapted from Douglas Bernstein et al., *Psychology,* 5th ed. (Boston: Houghton Mifflin Co., 1999), 473.

† Adapted from Douglas Bernstein et al., *Psychology,* 5th ed. (Boston: Houghton Mifflin Co., 1999), 572.

3. The newly redesigned $20 bill, which was released in 2003, includes a number of enhanced security features that make it harder to counterfeit. For one thing, it includes an embedded plastic security thread that is visible from both sides. Also, it is printed with color-shifting ink. When the bill is tilted up and down, the color-shifting ink in the number *20* in the lower-right corner changes from copper to green and back to copper. Finally, the bill includes a watermark.[1] When the bill is held up to the light, there appears to the right side of the portrait of Andrew Jackson a faint image that is similar to the portrait. It's part of the paper itself, and it can be seen from both sides.*

_____ list

_____ sequence

_____ cause/effect

_____ comparison/contrast

_____ definition

4. Just before I went to college, I remember telling my father that I wanted to be an actress and to major in speech and drama. My father grew up poor in rural Mississippi, where being a teacher was the highest calling—the most honorable position a black person could hold, other than being a doctor, so he was not happy with my choice. Before I left, I got a scholarship so that my daddy wouldn't have to pay my tuition—and so that I would have control over my decision. Then, I attended college and majored in speech and drama. From there, I went on to become a newscaster and host of my own television show.[†]

_____ list

_____ sequence

_____ cause/effect

_____ comparison/contrast

_____ definition

1. watermark: a design impressed upon paper

* Adapted from U.S. Department of the Treasury Bureau of Engraving and Printing, "New $20 Bill: Security Features," 2003, http://www.moneyfactory.com/newmoney/main.cfm/learning/interactivebilltext.

[†] Adapted from Oprah Winfrey, "Set Yourself Free," *O* Magazine, April 2001, 37.

6

5. My two children are so different that it surprises me every day. For one thing, my older child is a girl, and my younger child is a boy. My daughter loves reading, going to the movies, and writing in her journal. My son, on the other hand, loves running, jumping, and swimming—anything that requires using energy. My daughter loves all different kinds of foods, but my son likes to eat only pizza. And although my son can't go a day without watching some kind of sporting event on television, my daughter will only watch a baseball game if nothing else is on.

_____ list

_____ sequence

_____ cause/effect

_____ comparison/contrast

_____ definition

Patterns of Organization

To help readers find and comprehend supporting details more easily, paragraphs are usually organized according to at least one particular pattern. A **pattern** *is a consistent, predictable form or method of putting something together.* If you learn the most common patterns found within paragraphs, you'll be able to:

1. Recognize supporting details more quickly and accurately.

2. Better understand the relationships among supporting details.

Both of these skills are essential to good reading comprehension.

This chapter presents five broad patterns of organization: *list, sequence, cause/effect, comparison/contrast,* and *definition.* Each pattern type is illustrated by itself first, but it's important to realize that paragraphs often combine two or more of these patterns. The end of this chapter presents some examples of paragraphs that are organized according to two or more patterns.

Topic Sentences and Patterns of Organization

As you read the example paragraphs and learn to recognize each pattern, note how the **topic sentence** *often indicates the paragraph's pattern of organization.* Alert readers know how to watch for clues within topic sentences, clues that indicate how the information is arranged. When you can see these clues, you'll be able to predict the paragraph's framework and see more easily how the details fit into it as you read.

List

Many paragraphs organize supporting details as a list of items. *A **list** is a number of things that come one after the other.* Lists within paragraphs are often in the form of examples, reasons, types, or some other kind of point. Lists of items all equally support the paragraph's topic sentence. For example, read the following paragraph:

> I hit the beach with my new electronic book in hand, but e-books and the outdoors don't mix. They're impossible to read because bright sun reflects off the glass screen, turning it into a mirror. ***And*** they're fragile, too. I had to shield mine from sand and surf, but a computer just doesn't belong on the beach. ***Plus,*** I had to worry about my e-book being stolen while I took a dip in the ocean.*

The details in this paragraph are organized into a list of reasons. The main idea is "E-books and the outdoors don't mix," and the paragraph gives three reasons to support that idea.

Reason #1: They're difficult to read in a sunny setting.

Reason #2: They're too fragile.

Reason #3: They might be stolen.

If you were to map this paragraph, it might look like this:

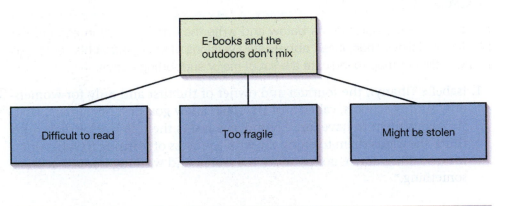

---

* Adapted from Jim Louderback, "E-books: Hot or Not?" *USA Weekend,* July 13–15, 2001, 4.

Lists of supporting details all equally develop the topic sentence, so they can often be presented in any order. Authors, however, may choose to arrange them according to their order of importance so they can emphasize one of the points by either presenting it first or saving it for last.

A paragraph's topic sentence will often indicate that the details will appear as a list of items. For example:

> We should eliminate pennies for a **number of reasons**.

> There are **four major forms** of child abuse.

> I began the New Year with **three major goals** in mind.

As you read, look for the following topic sentence words that indicate that a list will follow.

Words and Phrases That Indicate a List Pattern

Quantity word	*plus*	*List word*	
several		examples	kinds
many		reasons	characteristics
two, three, four, etc.		points	methods
a number of		classes	advantages
numerous		types	ways
		categories	forms
		groups	tips
		goals	

Exercise 6.1

Read each of the paragraphs below and write the correct word in each of the blanks that follow. Then, insert abbreviated versions of the paragraph's sentences in the outline or map to indicate the list of *major* supporting details.

1. Isabelle Tihanyi, the founder and owner of the first and only for-women-only surfing schools, called Surf Diva, has a few goals for her surfers. First, she wants them to have fun. Second, she wants them to learn to surf. And third, she wants them to enjoy the whole process of learning to surf, which means falling down, going under the water, and working hard to achieve something.*

---

* Adapted from David Leon Moore, "Surf Divas," *USA Today*, 1C.

6

Word(s) in the topic sentence that indicate a list: _____

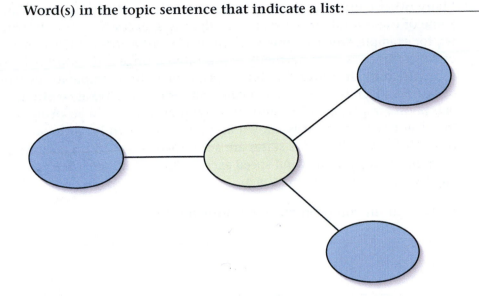

2. Several animated[1] programs on television today are designed to appeal specifically to adults. One example, *The Simpsons,* which started as short animated segments on *The Tracy Ullman Show,* is the oldest of the animated situation comedies for adults and deals with adult themes but in a lighthearted manner. Another example is *King of the Hill,* which focuses on a family and, again, deals with its problems and adult themes in a comedic way. Finally, *South Park,* although originally designed to appeal to and be viewed by adults, has found a following with the preteen and teen set who memorize and recite lines from the program.

Word(s) in the topic sentence that indicate a list: _____

_____

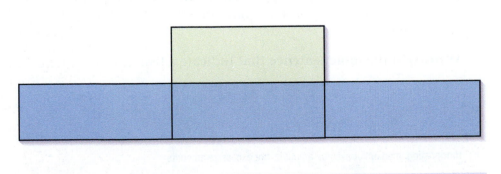

_____
1. **animated:** not live action; cartoons

6

3. Many other winds can bring extreme weather conditions to a region. Some of these winds are extremely cold; others, excessively hot. In winter, for example, when an intense storm tracks east across the Great Plains of North America, cold northerly winds often plunge southward behind it. As the cold air moves through Texas, it may drop temperatures tens of degrees in a few hours. Such a cold wind is called a **Texas norther**, or *blue norther,* especially if accompanied by snow. If the cold air penetrates into Central America, it is known as a *norte.* Meanwhile, if the strong, cold winds over the plains states are accompanied by drifting, blowing, or falling snow, and the wind speed exceeds 35 mi/hr, the term *blizzard* is applied to this weather situation.*

Word(s) in the topic sentence that indicate a list: _____

I. _____

   A. _____

   B. _____

   C. _____

4. Joining a weight loss program or group like Weight Watchers or Jenny Craig has four advantages. First, if you choose a program suited to your personality and lifestyle, your chances of success are much higher. For instance, if you like to eat out a lot, a program that requires that you buy its food may not be for you, but one in which you can eat what you like, in moderation,[1] may be the answer. Second, some weight loss programs often offer different classes on portion control, exercise, and eating habits that may help you understand why you overeat at times. Third, weight loss programs are attended by a lot of different people, so you may find a built-in support group that can help you overcome the tough times when you are dieting. Finally, studies have shown that people who join weight loss programs often have greater success at losing weight and often keep the weight off longer than those who diet on their own.

Word(s) in the topic sentence that indicate a list: _____

---

1. moderation: medium or average amounts, not excessive amounts

---

* C. Donald Ahrens, *Extreme Weather and Climate* (Belmont: Brooks/Cole, 2011), 231. Print.

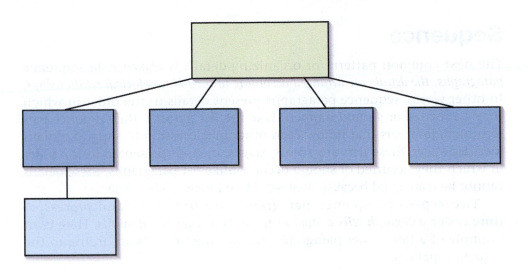

5. Family rules typically fall into five categories. The first category is safety rules such as "Stay in your car seat while riding in the vehicle." The second category is health, which includes hygiene and nutrition. For example, a common hygiene rule might be "Brush your teeth every morning." A third category of rules covers appropriate and inappropriate behaviors such as "Don't burp at the table." Next is the rights category, which includes rules like "Knock before you enter the bathroom." Finally, the fifth category concerns values. "We respect people's feelings" is an example of a values-type rule.*

Word(s) in the topic sentence that indicate a list: _____

6

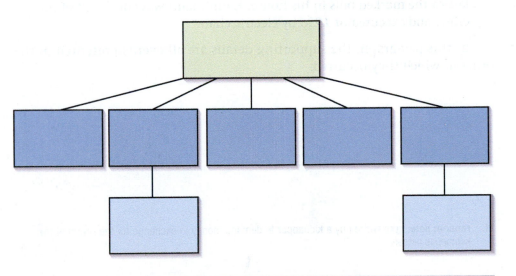

---

* Adapted from Nancy Seid, "How to Set Rules Your Kids Won't Break," *Parents*, August 2001, 109.

Sequence

The next common pattern for organizing details is *sequence. In* **sequence** *paragraphs, the details are arranged according to their chronological relationships.* In other words, sequence paragraphs present details in the order in which they happened or should happen. Like the list pattern, the sequence pattern includes items that follow each other in succession to support a main idea. However, these lists are events, stages, or steps presented in the order in which they occurred or should occur. Unlike list paragraphs, these details cannot be rearranged because they would no longer make sense.

Two types of sequence paragraphs are *time order* and *process.* A **time order** *paragraph tells a story or recounts a sequence of events.* Here is an example of a time order paragraph that arranges details according to the sequence pattern:

> The Lindbergh baby kidnapping was one of the biggest crime stories of the twentieth century. On **March 1, 1932,** Charles Lindbergh, Jr., the beloved twenty-month-old son of the flying ace, was put to bed, as usual, at **7:30 PM.** But when a nurse checked on the blond, curly-haired boy at **10 PM,** his crib was empty, and the window to his second-floor bedroom was open. Police found a ransom note[1] on the sill. Whoever took the child wanted $50,000 to bring him back. Charles Lindbergh paid the money in marked bills. But on **May 12,** the baby's body was found in the woods near the Lindbergh house, and police believed he was killed the night he was kidnapped. In **September 1934,** detectives arrested Bruno Richard Hauptmann after finding thousands of dollars of the marked bills in his house. Hauptmann was convicted of the crime and executed **in 1936** by electric chair.*

In this paragraph, the supporting details are all events presented in the order in which they occurred:

---

1. **ransom note:** note written by a kidnapper to demand money in exchange for the return of the kidnapped person

---

* Adapted from Angie Cannon and Kate V. Forsythe, "Crime Stories of the Century," *U.S. News and World Report,* December 6, 1999, 41ff.

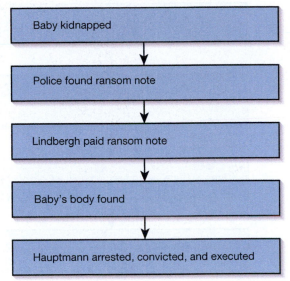

LINDBERGH BABY KIDNAPPING

Baby kidnapped

Police found ransom note

Lindbergh paid ransom note

Baby's body found

Hauptmann arrested, convicted, and executed

The second type of sequence paragraph is *process. A **process** paragraph explains how something is done or could be done.* Its details are organized in the steps or stages, in the order in which they occur. Here is an example:

The new gasoline-electric hybrid[1] cars work by transferring power back and forth between a gasoline engine and an electric motor. *First,* the car's batteries feed power to the electric motor to start the car. *When* the car accelerates to about 15 miles per hour, the gasoline engine takes over. It also sends backup power to a generator, which either feeds it back to the electric motor or sends it to recharge the batteries. *As* the car continues to accelerate, the batteries contribute power to the electric motor to help the gasoline engine. *When* the car slows down, the electric motor captures the energy from the spinning axles[2] and sends it to recharge the batteries.*

1. **hybrid:** something containing mixed parts

2. **axles:** shafts on which wheels revolve

---

* Adapted from William Holstein, "Green Cars and Red Ink," *U.S. News and World Report,* November 6, 2000, 42.

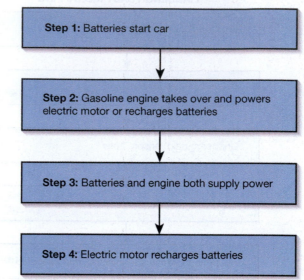

HOW A HYBRID CAR WORKS

Step 1: Batteries start car

Step 2: Gasoline engine takes over and powers electric motor or recharges batteries

Step 3: Batteries and engine both supply power

Step 4: Electric motor recharges batteries

Topic sentences in sequence paragraphs will often indicate that a chronology will follow:

To cope with stress more effectively, follow *six steps*.

According to William Shakespeare,[1] a person's life moves through *seven stages*.

Over the last one hundred years, women's swimwear has undergone *several developments*.

As you read, look for topic sentence words that indicate a sequence pattern.

Words and Phrases That Indicate a Sequence Pattern		
Quantity Word	*plus*	*Sequence Word*
several		events
two, three, four, etc.		steps
a number of		stages
over time		developments
in just one year		procedures
		processes

---

1. **William Shakespeare:** 17th century English writer of plays and poetry

Exercise **6.2**

Read each of the paragraphs below and fill in the blanks that follow. Then, write abbreviated versions of the paragraph's sentences in the outline or map to indicate the *major* sequence details.

1. As the 1960s progressed, the United States would be struck by a series of major natural disasters. The Ash Wednesday storm in 1962 devastated more than 620 miles of shoreline on the East Coast, producing more the $300 million in damages. In 1964, an earthquake measuring 9.2 on the Richter scale in Prince William Sound, Alaska, became front-page news throughout America and the world. This quake generated a tsunami that affected beaches as far down the Pacific Coast as California and killed 123 people. Hurricane Betsey struck in 1965, and Hurricane Camille in 1969, killing and injuring hundreds of people and causing hundreds of millions of dollars in damage along the Gulf Coast.*

   Word(s) in the topic sentence that indicate sequence: _____

   _____

   I. _____

      A. _____

      B. _____

      C. _____

      D. _____

2. To maintain the sharpness of kitchen knives by using a steel rod, follow several easy steps. First, with one hand, hold the sharpening steel rod, point down, on a flat, stable surface like a cutting board. Second, with the other hand, angle the knife blade so that it is about 15 degrees from the rod. Third, pull the knife down the rod in a slight arc, pulling the knife handle toward you, stroking the entire blade edge from base to tip. Fourth, repeat this procedure on the other side of the blade. Repeat the entire process three to five times, alternating the right and left sides of the knife's cutting edge.†

   Word(s) in the topic sentence that indicate sequence: _____

---

* George Haddow, Jane Bullock, and Damon Coppola, *Introduction to Emergency Management*, 3rd ed. (Burlington: Butterworth-Heinemann, 2008), 3–4. Print.

† Adapted from "Sharpening Can Make Knives Safer," *Charlotte* (NC) *Observer*, February 11, 2004, 2A.

SHARPENING A KNIFE

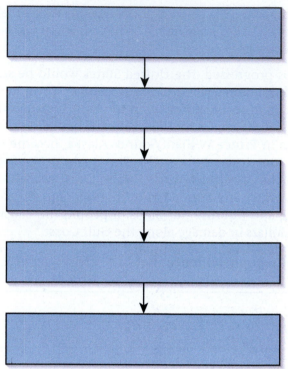

3. Many experienced cooks shy away from baking bread because it is a time-consuming task with many steps. The first step is to buy all of the necessary ingredients, including yeast and flour, the two main ingredients in any bread. The second step is to put your ingredients together. Then, the time-consuming part begins because the dough, or the combination of all of your ingredients, must sit for an extended period of time—anywhere from one hour to four hours—to allow the yeast in the dough to rise. After the dough-rising step has been completed, you must take the time to knead[1] the dough, which can also take a long time, depending on how much dough you have prepared. Finally, your risen, kneaded dough should be shaped and baked at the appropriate temperature for the period of time specified in your recipe.

Word(s) in the topic sentence that indicate sequence : _____

---

1. **knead:** to work the dough with your hands and knuckles

I. _____

  A. _____

  B. _____

  C. _____

  D. _____

  E. _____

4. Building on the disillusionment of the 1960s, Americans' distrust of the federal government has deepened over the last several decades. In the 1970s, the Watergate scandal and Richard Nixon's resignation from the presidency convinced many that politics was inherently[1] corrupt. In the 1980s, the administration of Ronald Reagan added the Iran-Contra scandal to the public's concerns about government corruption and cover-ups. And in the 1990s, Bill Clinton's White House was tainted[2] by a variety of special investigations and trials as well as allegations[3] about his character, like the one that he had extramarital affairs.*

Word(s) in the topic sentence that indicate sequence : _____

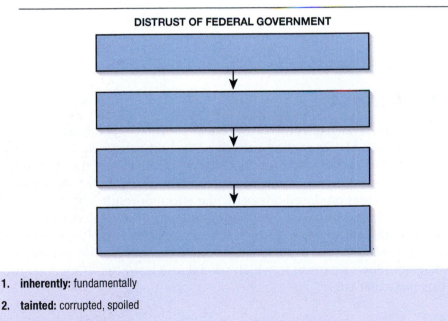

DISTRUST OF FEDERAL GOVERNMENT

1. **inherently:** fundamentally

2. **tainted:** corrupted, spoiled

3. **allegations:** accusations

* Adapted from Mary Beth Norton et al., *A People and a Nation*, Vol. II, 5th ed. (Boston: Houghton Mifflin Co., 1998), 1002.

5. Christopher Columbus's[1] journey to the New World took just over two months. On August 3, 1492, in command of three ships—the *Pinta,* the *Niña,* and the *Santa Maria*—Columbus set sail from the southern Spanish port of Palos. The first part of the journey must have been very familiar, for the ships steered down the Northeast Trades to the Canary Islands. There Columbus refitted his square-rigged ships, adding triangular sails to make them more maneuverable.[2] On September 6, the ships weighed anchor and headed out into the unknown ocean. Just over a month later, pushed by the favorable trade winds, the vessels found land approximately where Columbus had predicted. On October 12, he and his men landed on an island in the Bahamas, which its inhabitants called Guanahani, but which he renamed San Salvador. Later he went on to explore the islands now known as Cuba and Hispaniola.*

Word(s) in the topic sentence that indicate sequence: _____

_____

I. _____

    A. _____

    B. _____

    C. _____

    D. _____

Cause/Effect

When details are arranged in the **cause/effect** *pattern, the paragraph intends to show how the details relate to or affect each other.* Like a list paragraph, a cause/effect paragraph presents a series of occurrences. However, unlike a list, the cause/effect pattern reveals how one occurrence led to another. It might also demonstrate how a series of causes produced one particular effect, or result. The diagram on page 233 will help you visualize some common types of cause/effect patterns.

The first diagram shows a chain reaction of causes and effects, whereas the second one indicates a separate series of effects that are not related. The third diagram shows a pattern in which several unrelated causes together produce one particular effect.

1.   Christopher Columbus: the first historically important European discoverer of the New World

2.   maneuverable: able to move

---

* Adapted from Mary Beth Norton et al., *A People and a Nation,* Vol. I, 5th ed. (Boston: Houghton Mifflin Co., 1998).

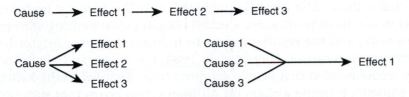

For an example of the cause/effect pattern, read the following paragraphs:

Several outcomes depend upon *the results* of the population census conducted in the United States every ten years. Political representation is *affected by* the census because population determines how many congressional representatives each state can have. The census numbers are also given to local governments, which *determine* how many schools, hospitals, and firehouses to build to accommodate the number of people living in the area. The census *results* are given to businesses, too. They use the data to *decide* where to open businesses, where to close them, and even what kind and how many products to put on stores' shelves.*

In this paragraph, one cause produces three different effects.

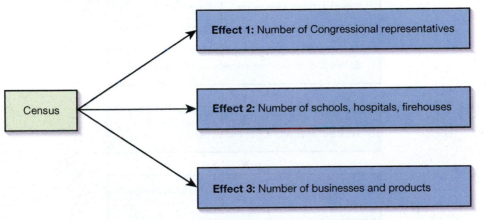

Here's a second example that is arranged according to a different cause/effect pattern:

The saga[1] of fiber and its protection against colon cancer *reveals* how uncertain science can lead to consumer confusion. In 1971, a British surgeon observed that Africans in rural areas had fewer bowel[2]

---

1. **saga:** long report or story

2. **bowel:** related to the intestines in the digestive system

---

* Adapted from Calvin Baker, "The Uncounted," *Life,* March 2000, 64.

disorders than Americans. He theorized[1] that the Africans' high-fiber diet made the difference. So, scientists began experimenting with rats and mice, and the ***results*** seemed to indicate that fiber might help prevent colon cancer. Therefore, in 1984, the American Cancer Society recommended that people eat more fiber. That ***led to*** the Kellogg Company's printing a claim on All-Bran cereal boxes that suggested its product could reduce the risk of colon cancer. Other cereals followed suit even though it wasn't clear that *cereal* fiber was responsible. In the late 1980s and early 1990s, however, more clinical trials found that fiber's protection was much weaker than earlier studies had predicted.*

This paragraph explains a chain reaction. The British doctor's observation about Africans was the cause, and then a series of effects occurred as a result. You might map this paragraph as follows:

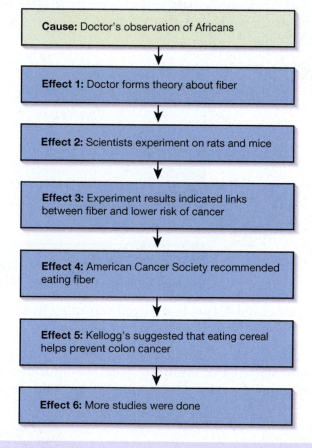

Cause: Doctor's observation of Africans

Effect 1: Doctor forms theory about fiber

Effect 2: Scientists experiment on rats and mice

Effect 3: Experiment results indicated links between fiber and lower risk of cancer

Effect 4: American Cancer Society recommended eating fiber

Effect 5: Kellogg's suggested that eating cereal helps prevent colon cancer

Effect 6: More studies were done

1.   theorized: proposed as being true

* Adapted from Linda Kulman, "Food News Can Get You Dizzy, So Know What to Swallow," *U.S. News and World Report,* November 13, 2000, 70.

Topic sentences in cause/effect paragraphs will often indicate that an explanation of related occurrences will follow:

Stereotyping often **leads to** prejudice and discrimination.

The **results** of hypnosis can be fascinating.

A **chain reaction** of events **led to** the Great Depression of the 1930s.

As you read, look for the following topic sentence words that signal a cause/effect pattern.

Words and Phrases That Indicate a Cause/Effect Pattern

consequences	was caused by
effects	causes
results	chain reaction
outcomes	leads to
affect	factors
because	

Exercise **6.3**

Read the paragraphs below and fill in the blanks that follow. Then, write abbreviated versions of the paragraph's sentences in the map to indicate the cause/effect relationships among the *major* supporting details.

1. Because of their negative effects, multiple births are frowned upon even by fertility doctors. One of the drawbacks to having four, five, or six babies at one time is poor health for the infants. Multiple births are often premature,[1] and premature babies usually require long periods of intensive care. Even if the babies are not born prematurely, they are more likely to suffer from afflictions,[2] such as heart problems or genetic[3] disorders, that can affect their lifelong health. These health problems lead to a second disadvantage: financial problems. Multiple birth babies can run up expensive medical bills. These bills, along with the daily demands of caring for several infants at one time, usually result in high levels of stress for the whole family.*

---

1. **premature:** occurring before the right time

2. **afflictions:** causes of suffering

3. **genetic:** related to genes, the units that determine the particular characteristics of an organism

---

* Adapted from Rita Rubin, "Little Safety in Numbers," *USA Today,* July 19, 2001, 8D.

Word(s) in the topic sentence that indicate cause/effect order:

_____

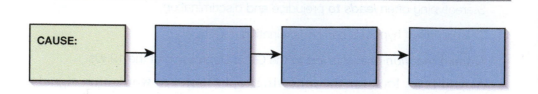

2. Negative beliefs lead to negative behaviors. For example, after a disappointing test score, a struggling student thinks, "I knew I couldn't do college math!" This belief will likely lead the student to miss classes and neglect assignments. These self-defeating behaviors lead to even lower test scores, reinforcing the negative beliefs. This student, caught in a cycle of failure, is now in grave[1] danger of failing math.*

Word(s) in the topic sentence that indicate cause/effect order: _____

_____

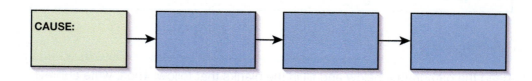

3. A number of factors may be contributing to your getting sunburned every summer. If you wear sunscreen but still get sunburned, you may not be using a sunscreen with enough SPF, the ingredient that shields your skin and indicates how long you can stay in the sun with protection. For instance, if you wear a sunscreen with SPF 30, you can stay in the sun thirty times longer than you could without protection. Second, you may not be reapplying sunscreen after every dip in the pool, ocean, or lake, and after intense physical activity. Third, in addition to sunscreen, you may not be wearing a hat and sunglasses to protect your face and eyes.

Word(s) in the topic sentence that indicate cause/effect order: _____

_____

1.   **grave:** serious

* Adapted from Skip Downing, *On Course*, 4th ed. (Boston: Houghton Mifflin Co., 2005), 5.

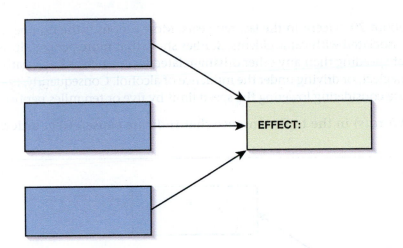

4. If companies shipped just 25 percent of their freight on trains instead of big trucks, traffic on America's overcrowded roads would decrease significantly. As a result, drivers' commuting time could decrease by 86 hours per year by 2020; commuters would gain two full workweeks' worth of personal time. In addition, they would each save $1,127 in annual commuting costs. Plus, getting more big trucks off the roads would significantly reduce harmful emissions[1] that pollute our air.*

Word(s) in second sentence that indicate cause/effect order: _____

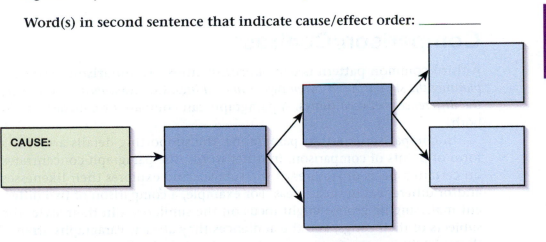

5. Researchers have found that the average American is driving fifteen to twenty miles per hour faster than he or she did ten years ago, with serious consequences. As a result, the number of speeding tickets issued has risen by

---

1. **emissions:** substances discharged into the air

* Adapted from Wendall Cox, "Consider Shifting Truck Freight to Trains," *USA Today*, February 24, 2004, 12A.

about 20 percent in the last ten years. More serious is the number of deaths associated with car accidents. Studies show that more people die as a result of speeding than any other driving-related factor such as bad weather, driver neglect, or driving under the influence of alcohol. Consequently, many states are considering lowering the speed limit by five or ten miles per hour.

Word(s) in the topic sentence that indicate cause/effect order:

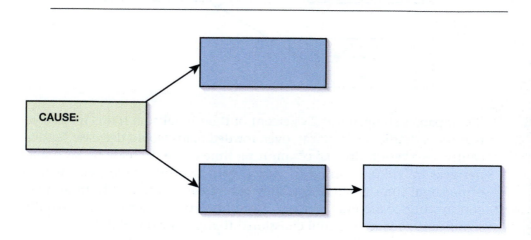

Comparison/Contrast

A third common pattern is comparison/contrast. **Comparison** *means explaining the similarities between two or more things.* **Contrast** *means examining the differences between things.* A paragraph can compare or contrast, or do both.

In comparison/contrast paragraphs, the supporting details are in the form of points of comparison. In other words, the paragraph concentrates on certain aspects or features of the subjects and explores their likenesses and/or differences in those areas. For example, a comparison of two different male singing groups might focus on the similarities in their style, the subjects of their songs, and the audiences they attract. Paragraphs arrange these details in one of two ways. One option is to focus on each subject in turn. The following paragraph, which deals only with similarities, provides an example of this pattern.

Abraham Lincoln was *similar* in many ways to Benjamin Franklin. Franklin received little schooling, dropping out at age ten to work. Yet he loved to read and write, and he wrote everything from articles to poetry. Franklin is famous for his inventions such as the Franklin stove and for his world-famous experiments with electricity. In addition, he was an able politician who helped to win America's independence and form its new government. Franklin was also an outspoken opponent of slavery. *Like* Franklin, Lincoln received little schooling, attending for only a year. However, he, too, loved to read and write, and he is famous for his eloquent[1] speeches such as The Gettysburg Address. Lincoln, like Franklin, was also an inventor; he is the only president to hold a patent.[2] And he is also known for his ability as a politician and his hatred of slavery.*

This paragraph groups the points of comparison by subject, discussing first Benjamin Franklin and then Abraham Lincoln. It would be outlined like this:

I. Similarities between Benjamin Franklin and Abraham Lincoln

    A. Benjamin Franklin
       1. Received little schooling
       2. Loved to read and write
       3. Inventor
       4. Able politician
       5. Opponent of slavery

    B. Abraham Lincoln
       1. Received little schooling
       2. Loved to read and write
       3. Inventor
       4. Able politician
       5. Opponent of slavery

A comparison/contrast paragraph can also be arranged so that it focuses on the points of comparison, alternating back and forth between the two subjects.

Even in preschool, boys and girls fall into very *different* play patterns. Boys tend to gather in larger groups, *whereas* girls, early on, gather in small groups. Boys play games that have clear winners and losers and bluster[3] through them, boasting about their skills.

---

1. **eloquent:** vivid and expressive

2. **patent:** government grant giving sole rights to an invention to its creator

3. **bluster:** speak loudly and arrogantly

---

* Adapted from "Remarkable Similarities Between President Abraham Lincoln and Benjamin Franklin," http://www.theamericans.us/poparticle-Lincoln-Franklin.html.

Girls play theatrical games, such as playacting roles as members of a pretend family, that don't feature hierarchy[1] or winners. One study of children aged three to four found they were already resolving conflict in *separate* ways—boys resorting to threats, girls negotiating verbally and often reaching a compromise.*

This paragraph contrasts three aspects of preschool play groups: their size, type of games played, and ways conflict is resolved. You could outline the organization of these three points of comparison as follows:

I. Play patterns of boys and girls

    A. Size of play groups
      1. Boys
      2. Girls

    B. Types of games
      1. Boys
      2. Girls

    C. Conflict resolution
      1. Boys
      2. Girls

Topic sentences in comparison/contrast paragraphs often indicate that an explanation of similarities and/or differences is to follow:

Public schools and private schools **differ** in four significant aspects.

Although they share a few **similarities**, football and rugby are more **different** than **alike**.

In comparison to Japanese cars, American cars give you more for your money.

As you read, look for the following topic sentence words that indicate a comparison/contrast pattern.

Words and Phrases That Indicate a Comparison/Contrast Pattern

similarities	differences
alike	different
likenesses	

---

1. **hierarchy:** groupings according to rank

---

* Adapted from Deborah Blum, "What's the Difference Between Boys and Girls?" *Life*, March 1999, 52.

Exercise **6.4**

Read the following comparison/contrast paragraphs and answer the questions that follow by circling the letter of correct response or filling in the blanks.

Although there are some differences between today's teenagers and those of previous generations, they are very much the same in many respects. It's true that modern teens must deal with problems—such as school shootings and AIDS—unknown to teens in other eras. Anorexia, bulimia,[1] and teen suicide are more prevalent,[2] too. But the teens of today still struggle with the same emotions and daily dramas as teens of yesterday. Teens still see adults as too critical. They still define themselves as different through their outward appearance. In previous generations, it was bell-bottoms and long hair. Today, it's green hair and body piercings. But what was true then and is today is that to be a teen is to be on the search for self. "Who am I?" and "How do others perceive me?" are two big questions for teenagers of any era.*

1. This paragraph (circle the letter of one answer):

   a. compares.

   b. contrasts.

   c. compares and contrasts.

2. What two subjects are being compared and/or contrasted?

   _____ and _____

3. On what four similarities between the two subjects does the paragraph focus?

   1. _____

   2. _____

   3. _____

   4. _____

Although *USA Today* and the *New York Times* are both daily newspapers, they couldn't be more different. For one thing, *USA Today* caters[3] to the reader who wants lots of news about a lot of different subjects and who doesn't have

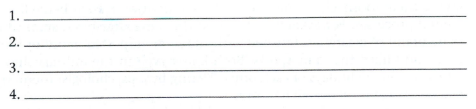

1. **anorexia** and **bulimia:** two types of eating disorders

2. **prevalent:** widespread; common

3. **caters:** attends to the needs or desires

* Adapted from Kimberly Kirberger, "Are Today's Teens That Different?" *Life*, March 1999, 48.

a lot of time to devote to reading. The *New York Times* features in-depth articles on fewer subjects and is known for its ground-breaking stories on news in the United States and abroad. *USA Today* is heavy on sports and entertainment reporting, whereas the *New York Times* is noted for its number of articles on political issues. Finally, *USA Today* is a daily paper that is only published Monday through Friday, whereas the *New York Times* is published seven days a week, with an extensive weekend supplement most noted for its magazine section.

4. This paragraph (circle the letter of one answer):

    a. compares.   c. compares and contrasts.

    b. contrasts.

5. What two subjects are being compared and/or contrasted? _____

   and _____

6. On what three differences between the two subjects does the paragraph focus?

    1. _____

    2. _____

    3. _____

Mark and John—identical twins separated at birth—met for the first time at twenty-four years of age. They were physically alike; the same molars were giving them toothaches. There were also similarities in their behavior and mental processes. For example, they used the same aftershave, smoked the same brand of cigarettes, brushed with the same imported brand of toothpaste, and liked the same sports. Both had served in the military, having joined within eight days of each other. Testing by a psychologist found they had nearly identical overall IQ scores.*

7. This paragraph (circle the letter of one answer):

    a. compares.   c. compares and contrasts.

    b. contrasts.

---

* Adapted from Douglas Bernstein and Peggy Nash, *Essentials of Psychology*, 2nd ed. (Boston: Houghton Mifflin Co., 2002), 30.

8. What two subjects are being compared and/or contrasted?

_____ and _____

9. On what four similarities between the two subjects does this paragraph focus?

1. _____

2. _____

3. _____

4. _____

There were two types of cotton—upland and Sea Island cotton. Sea Island cotton was the most widely gown. The fibers were longer (called *staple length*), and the seed could be easily removed from the fibers. The problem with upland cotton was that the fibers seemed to be glued to the seeds and were extremely difficult to remove. Even though it was a slow process, the seeds from the Sea Island cotton separated from the seeds by hand very easily. The problem was that this type of cotton would only grow along the coasts of the southern colonies.*

10. This paragraph (circle the letter of one answer):

a. compares.   c. compares and contrasts.

b. contrasts.

11. What two subjects are being compared and/or contrasted?

_____ and _____

12. What three differences does the paragraph discuss?

1. _____

2. _____

3. _____

Swimming in a lake and swimming in a pool are two different experiences. For one thing, swimming in a lake does not involve swimming in chemicals like chlorine, which you need in a pool to keep it clean. Another thing that makes the swimming experience different is that lake water is often very cold whereas pool water can get warm and stay warm due to the fact that it is in

* Ray V. Herren, *Exploring Agriscience*, 4th ed. (Clifton Park: Delmar, 2011), 27. Print.

a closed container or area. Lake water is often very clear, whereas pool water, if you don't maintain it properly, can get cloudy and full of leaves and bugs. Finally, often you can see small fish and eels swimming with you in a lake, which is something you would never see in a pool!

13. This paragraph (circle the letter of one answer):

    a. compares.   c. compares and contrasts.

    b. contrasts.

14. What two subjects are being compared and/or contrasted?

    _____ and _____

15. On what four differences between the two subjects does the paragraph focus?

    1. _____

    2. _____

    3. _____

    4. _____

Definition

One last pattern you should learn to recognize is the definition pattern. **Definition** *usually states the meaning of a particular word, term, or concept, and then goes on to illustrate it with one or more examples.* Textbooks often use this pattern to explain a term being introduced for the first time. The following paragraph is organized according to the definition pattern.

> *Job sharing* (sometimes referred to as *work sharing*) *is* an arrangement whereby two people share one full-time position. One job sharer may work from 8 AM to noon and the other from 1 to 5 PM, or they may alternate workdays. For example, at a financial institution in Cleveland, two women share the position of manager of corporate communications. One works Tuesdays and Thursdays, and the other works Mondays, Wednesdays, and Fridays. They communicate daily through computers, voice mail, and fax machines to handle their challenging administrative position.*

---

* Adapted from William M. Pride et al., *Business*, 6th ed. (Boston: Houghton Mifflin Co., 1999), 237.

The example or examples within a definition paragraph may be arranged according to one of the other patterns. For example, the definition might be followed by an example that contains details organized with a sequence pattern. Or the definition might be followed by a list of two or more examples. This next paragraph is a good example:

> Punishment *involves* the presentation of an unpleasant stimulus[1] or the removal of a pleasant stimulus in order to decrease the frequency of an undesirable behavior. One example is shouting "No!" and swatting your dog when it begins chewing on the rug. That illustrates a negative stimulus that follows a behavior you want to eliminate. Another example is taking away a child's TV privileges following a demonstration of rude behavior. This is a punishment, or penalty, that removes a positive stimulus.*

Topic sentences will often indicate that a definition will follow:

> Money *can be defined* as anything a society uses to purchase products, services, or resources.

> Personality *is* an individual's unique pattern of psychological and behavioral characteristics.

> To understand what a Republican believes, you must first know what the word conservative *means*.

As you read, look for the following topic sentence words that may indicate a definition pattern.

Words That Indicate a Definition Pattern

means	definition
meaning	is/are
define	

---

1. **stimulus:** something that causes a response

* Adapted from Douglas A. Bernstein, *Psychology,* 4th ed. (Boston: Houghton Mifflin Co., 1997), 209.

6

Exercise **6.5**

Read each of the following definition paragraphs and then respond to the questions that follow by writing your answers on the blanks provided.

(1) People learn a lot from personal experience, but they can also learn by observing what others do and what happens to them when they do it. (2) Learning by watching others—a process called *observational learning*—is efficient and adaptive.[1] (3) We don't have to find out for ourselves that a door is locked or that an iron is hot if we have just seen someone else try to open the door or suffer a burn.*

1. What term is defined in this paragraph? _____

2. Which sentence states the definition? _____

3. How many examples are given as illustrations? _____

(1) In a zoo, a "landscape immersion" exhibit is one that mimics[2] the natural habitats of animals. (2) This type of exhibit brings together different animals and vegetation from similar climate zones and allows the animals to interact as they do in the wild. (3) Also, zoos are extending the plants, rocks, and other natural features of the exhibits into areas where visitors walk, stand, and sit. (4) The jaguar habitat at Seattle's Woodland Park Zoo, for example, is designed so that the big cats can creep into tree branches and lurk over the heads of visitors. (5) The "Absolutely Apes" exhibit at the San Diego Zoo mocks an Asian rain forest, complete with fallen tree trunks. (6) And the National Aquarium in Baltimore includes a simulation of an Australian river canyon, complete with waterfall.†

4. What term is defined in this paragraph? _____

5. Which sentence states the definition? _____

6. How many examples are given as illustrations? _____

7. Which pattern organizes the examples? _____

---

1. **adaptive:** capable of changing in response to new situations

2. **mimics:** copies

---

* Adapted from Douglas Bernstein and Peggy Nash, *Essentials of Psychology*, 2nd ed. (Boston: Houghton Mifflin Co., 2002), 167.

† From Tracey Harden, "Improving the Environment for Creatures of Two and Four Legs," *New York Times*, March 31, 2004, http://www.nytimes.com.

(1) A *nutraceutical* (a combination of the words *nutrition* and *pharmaceutical*) is either a pill or another pharmaceutical product that has nutritional value, or a food that has had its nutritional value enhanced by drugs. (2) One nutraceutical that has been in the news is beta-carotene, which is used as a dietary supplement[1] to prevent heart attacks. (3) The term also describes a number of vegetables that have been altered to contain elevated levels of naturally occurring substances believed to ward off cancer. (4) Many natural remedies that have been known for centuries—such as herbal teas—are also considered to be nutraceuticals.*

8. What word is defined in this paragraph? _____

9. Which sentence states the definition? _____

10. How many examples are given as illustrations? _____

11. Which pattern organizes the examples? _____

(1) Many companies in the United States are adopting a "business casual policy" regarding how their employees dress. (2) What is *business casual*? (3) Business casual means that employees, who formerly wore suits and ties in the case of men, and suits and dresses in the case of women, are now permitted to wear more comfortable, less formal attire to the office. (4) An example of this would be khaki pants and a polo shirt for men. (5) For women, perhaps linen pants and a blouse would be appropriate.

12. What term is defined in this paragraph? _____

13. Which sentence states the definition? _____

14. How many examples are given as illustrations? _____

15. Which pattern organizes the examples? _____

(1) *Better* is a retail-fashion term that describes clothing lines that are not as expensive as designer collections—by implication,[2] those would be the "best"—and are affordable for most middle-class consumers. (2) Calvin Klein and Realities, for example, are two mid-priced lines at Lord and Taylor. (3) That store will also showcase the new Michael line from Michael Kors. (4) "Better is affordable luxury," says LaVelle Olexa, senior vice president of fashion merchandising at Lord and Taylor.†

1. **supplement:** something added to complete something else

2. **implication:** suggestion

---

* Adapted from Michael Quinion, "Nutraceutical," *World Wide Words*, http://www.quinion.com/words/turnsofphrase/tp-nut1.htm.

† Adapted from Isabel C. Gonzalez, "Turn for the Better," *Time*, March 22, 2004, 76.

16. What word is defined in this paragraph? _____

17. Which sentence states the definition? _____

18. How many examples are given as illustrations? _____

Combination of Patterns

Often, paragraphs include more than one pattern of organization. The major supporting details may be arranged according to one pattern, and minor details may be arranged according to another. For example, read the following paragraph:

> Quitting smoking is difficult because of the *effects* of nicotine in cigarettes. Nicotine *produces* pleasurable feelings and acts as a depressant.[1] As the nervous system adapts to nicotine, smokers tend to increase the number of cigarettes they smoke and, thus, the amount of nicotine in their blood. *Therefore,* when a smoker tries to quit, the absence of nicotine *leads to* two types of withdrawal. The *first type* of withdrawal is physical, which may include headaches, increased appetite, sleeping problems, and fatigue. The *second type* of withdrawal is psychological. Giving up a habit can *result* in depression, irritability, or feelings of restlessness.*

This paragraph begins with the *effects* of nicotine and ends with a *list* of two types of nicotine withdrawal.

Here is one more example:

> There are very *different* ways that men and women handle stress. *Because* women have a very *different* hormonal balance from men, researchers are finding that women are more prone to take on more stress in their daily living than men. The *reasons* are varied, but one reason is that women seem to have more stress in their lives. They "multitask," or do many things at once, to keep their family life coordinated and running smoothly. Men, *on the other hand*, focus on one task at a time. *Another reason* women have more stress than men is that women worry a lot more than men and about more things. *Although* men may worry about one or two things in a day—their immediate family or money—women worry about their own families, their friends' families, their extended families, and other things.

---

1. **depressant:** substance that lowers the rate of bodily activities

---

* Adapted from American Cancer Society, http://www.cancer.org/tobacco/quitting.html.

Most of the details in this paragraph are arranged using the comparison/contrast pattern of organization. However, the paragraph also includes the causes of stress for both men and women, so the paragraph combines the comparison/contrast and cause/effect patterns.

Exercise **6.6**

In the list following each paragraph, write a check mark in the blank before each pattern used to organize the supporting details.

1. *Retrograde amnesia* involves a loss of memory for events prior to some critical injury. Often, a person with this condition is unable to remember anything that took place in the months, or even years, before the injury. In most cases, the memories return gradually. For example, one man received a severe blow to the head after being thrown from his motorcycle. After regaining consciousness, he claimed that he was eleven years old. Over the next three months, he gradually recalled more and more of his life. He remembered when he was twelve, thirteen, and so on—right up until the time he was riding his motorcycle the day of the accident. But he was never able to remember what happened just before the accident.*

   _____ list   _____ comparison/contrast

   _____ sequence   _____ definition

   _____ cause/effect

2. It was evident in the early 1970s that the United States was beginning to suffer economic decline. Recessions—which economists define as at least two consecutive quarters of no growth in the gross national product[1]—began to occur more frequently. An eleven-month recession struck the country in 1969 and 1970, the first recession in almost a decade. Between 1973 and 1990, there were four more, and two were particularly long and harsh.†

   _____ list   _____ comparison/contrast

   _____ sequence   _____ definition

   _____ cause/effect

---

1. gross national product: the total market value of all of the goods and services produced in a nation

---

* Adapted from Douglas Bernstein, *Psychology*, 4th ed. (Boston: Houghton Mifflin Co., 1997), 242.

† Adapted from Mary Beth Norton et al., *A People and a Nation*, Vol. II, 5th ed. (Boston: Houghton Mifflin Co., 1998), 958.

3. Three tools can help you better manage your time. The first one is a monthly calendar, which provides an overview of upcoming commitments, appointments, and assignments. The second self-management tool is a "next actions" list. On this list, record everything you want to do that day or as soon as possible, and as you complete each item on the list, cross it off. The third self-management tool is a tracking form, which allows you to schedule actions that need to be done repeatedly to reach a short-term goal. For example, if your short-term goal is to get an *A* in your sociology class, you could note on your tracking form to "Read the textbook one or more hours" and then check a box each time you complete that action. Researchers at the University of Georgia have found that engaging in these kinds of self-management activities positively affects college grades.*

_____ list   _____ comparison/contrast

_____ sequence   _____ definition

_____ cause/effect

4. Photographs sent back to Earth from the Mars rovers indicate that the Mars landscape is very similar to Earth's dry deserts. The Martian landscape, like deserts on Earth, is dry and has a mixture of rocks on the surface. Also, in both places there are channels that were formed by rain in the past. Scientists have concluded, therefore, that Mars may have been through the same kind of alternating wet and dry climate cycles that have affected our own planet's desert regions. And because scientists have discovered groundwater beneath deserts in Egypt, they wonder if there might be water beneath the Martian surface.†

_____ list   _____ comparison/contrast

_____ sequence   _____ definition

_____ cause/effect

5. The police can search you under two circumstances—when they have a search warrant and when they have lawfully arrested you. A search warrant is an order from a judge authorizing the search of a place; the order must describe what is to be searched and seized, and the judge can issue it only if he or she is persuaded by the police that a good reason exists to believe that a crime has been committed and that the evidence bearing

---

* Adapted from Skip Downing, *On Course*, 4th ed. (Boston: Houghton Mifflin Co., 2005), 82–84.

† Adapted from "Scientist: Mars Rovers Show Deserts Similar to Earth," CNN.com, March 11, 2004, http://www.cnn.com/2004/TECH/space/03/11/mars.deserts.ap/.

on that crime will be found at a certain location. In addition, you can be searched if the search occurs when you are being lawfully arrested.*

_____ list   _____ comparison/contrast

_____ sequence   _____ definition

_____ cause/effect

Exercise **6.7**

In each of the following topic sentences, circle the clue word or words that suggest a particular pattern of organization. Then write a check mark next to the pattern indicated by the clue word(s).

1. Long-term overuse of aspirin can cause significant health risks.

   _____ list   _____ comparison/contrast

   _____ sequence   _____ definition

   _____ cause/effect

2. For three reasons, fly-fishing is a great hobby.

   _____ list   _____ comparison/contrast

   _____ sequence   _____ definition

   _____ cause/effect

3. The personal computer's thirty-year history can be divided into four major eras.

   _____ list   _____ comparison/contrast

   _____ sequence   _____ definition

   _____ cause/effect

4. Biometeorology is the new science of studying how the human body interacts with the weather.

   _____ list   _____ comparison/contrast

   _____ sequence   _____ definition

   _____ cause/effect

---

* Adapted from James Q. Wilson, and John J. DiIulio Jr., *American Government: The Essentials*, 9th ed. (Boston: Houghton Mifflin Co., 2004), 452.

5. Hearing and listening are very different actions.

_____ list   _____ comparison/contrast

_____ sequence   _____ definition

_____ cause/effect

6. Shopping online and shopping in a mall differ significantly.

_____ list   _____ comparison/contrast

_____ sequence   _____ definition

_____ cause/effect

7. A rude cell phone user exhibits three inconsiderate behaviors.

_____ list   _____ comparison/contrast

_____ sequence   _____ definition

_____ cause/effect

8. A search engine is defined as a program that searches the Internet for documents that contain certain specified keywords.

_____ list   _____ comparison/contrast

_____ sequence   _____ definition

_____ cause/effect

9. Canning your own vegetables requires following six steps.

_____ list   _____ comparison/contrast

_____ sequence   _____ definition

_____ cause/effect

10. MTV's effects on the music industry cannot be underestimated.

_____ list   _____ comparison/contrast

_____ sequence   _____ definition

_____ cause/effect

Reading Strategy: Taking Notes

Learning how to take notes effectively is a vital skill for college students. You will often be tested on the information in reading selections such as textbook chapters, so you will need to make sure you're using all of the tools at your disposal to understand and retain this information. One of those tools is an active reading technique known as *note taking*. **Taking notes** *means recording in writing the major information and ideas in a text.* You might choose to take these notes in the margins of the book itself, or in a notebook, or on separate sheets of paper.

Regardless of where you write them, notes offer two important benefits. First of all, writing down information and ideas helps you to remember them better. For many people, taking the extra time to write the main points by hand helps implant those points in their memory more securely. As a result, retention and test performance tend to improve. Second, good notes are often easier to study because they provide you with a condensed version of the main points.

Good notes always begin with highlighting or underlining main ideas or key terms as you read, just as you learned to do in Chapter 1. When you write notes, they might take one or more of the following forms:

- **A list of the main ideas in all of the paragraphs.** Put them in your own words and condense them whenever possible. Don't try to include all of the details, just the most important points.

- **A summary of the chapter or article** (for an overview of this strategy, see Chapter 5).

- **An outline.** In previous chapters of this book, you've practiced filling out outlines that reveal the relationships among the details. You can use a Roman numeral outline, but the notes are usually for your eyes only, so you could also adopt or create a more informal system. No matter what kind of outline you use, though, make sure it clearly demonstrates the general and specific relationships among the ideas.

No matter what form they take, effective notes always possess three important characteristics. They should be:

1. *Neat.* Skip lines between points and write legibly.

2. *Clearly organized.* Group related points together so they're easier to remember.

3. *Factual and objective.* Like summaries, notes should be free of your own opinions.

6

Actively read "A History of Theme Parks" in the Reading Selections. Then, take notes by creating a list of the paragraphs' main ideas, by writing a summary, or by outlining the selection.

The following websites will help you to learn more about taking better notes in college—both in class and in your textbooks.

http://www.howtostudy.org/resources_skill.php?id=9
http://www.studygs.net/booknote.htm

Reading Selections

Practicing the Active Reading Strategy

■ Before and While You Read

You can use active reading strategies before, while, and after you read a selection. The following are some suggestions for active reading strategies that you can employ before you read and as you are reading.

1. Skim the selection for any unfamiliar words. Circle or highlight any words you do not know.

2. As you read, underline, highlight, or circle important words or phrases.

3. Write down any questions about the selection if you are confused by the information presented.

4. Jot notes in the margin to help you understand the material.

BIOGRAPHY
Jumping Jack's Still a Flash

by Rick Reilly

Are you addicted to sugar? How much do you like to exercise? Jack LaLanne, who was known as "the godfather of fitness," was addicted to sugar as a child, but grew up to invent much of the exercise equipment we use today. Before his death at age 96 in 2011, Jack LaLanne endorsed his own brand of power juicers and worked out every morning. The following article from Sports Illustrated *shares some of the amazing accomplishments of this icon of fitness.*

1   Here it comes, the festive day in this country, Sunday, February 1, when all Americans—men and women, young and old—gather together

and give up on their New Year's resolutions. Your promise to eat right gets left. Your resolution to work out doesn't work out. Your solemn vow to lose weight dies somewhere between the Ding Dongs and the Domino's. And the last person you want to call to celebrate with is Jack LaLanne, the jerk who has ruined it for everybody by not missing a single daily workout in seventy-four years.

2   Remember *The Jack LaLanne Show*? Your mom doing jumping jacks in the family room? Jack in his short-sleeved jumpsuit? His German shepherd, Happy? Well, Happy's dead, but LaLanne is still at it. At 89, the 5'4" LaLanne has a 46-inch chest and a 31-inch waist and can still do 100 push-ups without turning so much as light pink. His ninetieth birthday is coming up in September, and he wants to celebrate by swimming the 30 miles from Catalina Island to Long Beach, California, underwater, using air tanks. It'll take about 22 hours. (For my ninetieth, I also plan to use air tanks, at home in a hospital bed, gumming rice cakes.)

3   And when LaLanne looks out at this Cheez Doodle country of ours, most of us doing impressions of three-days-dead walruses, he wants to cry into his juicer. "We have no pride, no discipline in this country!" rants LaLanne. "We're serving junk food in schools! People think they can eat anything and just sit on their big, fat butts! Athletes are selling their souls to advertise crap that they know is no good for kids—milk and cheeseburgers and candy! Why can't people see that it's killing them! Any stupid ass can die! Living is hard! You've got to work at living!"

4   He's not a fan of the Atkins diet:[1] "It's a gimmick! All that meat! You need whole-grain bread and cereals!" Or dairy products: "Am I a suckling calf? No other creature uses milk after they wean." Or our eating habits: "Would you get your dog up in the morning and give him a cup of coffee, a cigarette, and a doughnut?"

5   Against all the unprincipled blowhards[2] and liars in this country, LaLanne stands out like a nun in a paddy wagon.[3] He works out every day from 5 AM to 7, pumping iron the first hour, swimming the next. His daily diet never sways: a protein soy drink for breakfast, five pieces of fruit and four egg whites for lunch, and a salad with ten raw vegetables, brown rice, and three ounces of grilled fish for dinner. And a glass of wine. Party!

6   He says he hasn't had a sweet since he was 15, and his wife and staff confirm it. "I tell him, 'A piece of carrot cake once in a while can be a very good thing,'" says his secretary, Liz, "but he'll never go for it."

---

1. **Atkins diet:** a diet that consists mainly of proteins and vegetables

2. **blowhards:** braggarts; people who boast

3. **paddy wagon:** van used by police for taking suspects into custody

6

7   Jack, are you nuts? "Yeah, I guess I am," he says. You don't know the half of it.

8   At 40, he swam from Alcatraz to Fisherman's Wharf handcuffed. At 60, he did it again, towing a rowboat with 1,000 pounds of sand. At 70, he jumped into Long Beach Harbor handcuffed and towed 70 people in 70 boats for a mile and a half. One birthday he did 1,000 chin-ups and 1,000 push-ups in 82 minutes.

9   Doesn't sound like a guy who once wanted to kill himself, does it?

10   A sugar addict at 15, he'd get splitting headaches and bang his head against the wall trying to get rid of them. He was so skinny the girls at his school beat him up. He set fire to his parents' house, tried to attack his older brother with an ax. "I considered suicide many times," LaLanne says. "I couldn't stand [my life] anymore."

11   And then his mom took him to a lecture by a nutritionist, who told him he was a human garbage can. That day, LaLanne resolved to eat right and start exercising—which is like saying, "That day, young Bill Shakespeare[1] resolved to try a little writing." LaLanne became captain of the high school football team and an all-conference wrestling champion, and he was offered a pro baseball contract. He opened America's first health club, in 1936 in Oakland, and wound up with more than 100 clubs, which he eventually licensed to Bally. In 1951, he invented the television exercise program, *The Jack LaLanne Show*. People called him a crackpot[2] and said it would die in six weeks. It lasted 34 years.

12   Look around. Health clubs, health-food stores, jogging, Pilates, yoga, and personal trainers. It all started with Jack LaLanne.

13   To honor him, each one of us needs to wash-and-vac our bodies, give up sweets, get in shape, demand that our kids get gym class and healthy foods in schools, and rid this country of the plague of obesity.

14   First thing next year.*

■ Vocabulary

Read the following questions about some of the vocabulary words that appear in the previous selection. Before you look up the word, try to use the context of the passage to figure out the meaning. Then circle the letter of each correct answer.

1.   **Bill Shakespeare:** William Shakespeare, a great seventeenth-century writer of plays and poetry

2.   **crackpot:** an odd or eccentric person

* Reprinted courtesy of *Sports Illustrated:* "Jumping Jack's Still a Flash" by Rick Reilly, January 26, 2004. Copyright © 2004 Time Inc. All rights reserved.

1. In paragraph 1, the author states: "Here it comes, the *festive* day in this country, Sunday, February 1, when all Americans—men and women, young and old—gather together and give up on their New Year's resolutions." What does *festive* mean?

   a. joyful

   b. unhappy

   c. distorted

   d. unwrapped

2. What is a *solemn vow*? "Your *solemn* vow to lose weight dies somewhere between the Ding Dongs and the Domino's" (paragraph 1).

   a. a sad song

   b. a serious promise

   c. a broken promise

   d. a depressed friend

3. What is a *gimmick*? "It's a *gimmick*," the author writes of LaLanne's opinion of the Atkins diet in paragraph 4.

   a. serious commitment

   b. publicity stunt

   c. serious illness

   d. deadly concept

4. What does it mean to *wean*? "No other creature uses milk after they *wean*." (paragraph 4).

   a. to give up breastfeeding from one's mother

   b. to start using a fork and knife

   c. to start eating red meat

   d. to stop eating red meat

5. What is a *plague*? "[A]nd rid this country of the *plague* of obesity." (paragraph 13).

   a. happy occurrence

   b. disease

   c. cure

   d. misgiving

6

■ Reading Skills

Respond to the following questions by circling the letter of the correct answer.

1. What pattern organizes the details in paragraph 8?

   a. cause/effect   c. comparison

   b. sequence   d. definition

2. What is the implied main idea of paragraph 8?

   a. Jack LaLanne is insane.

   b. Jack LaLanne does everything for his wife.

   c. Jack LaLanne is incredibly strong.

   d. Jack LaLanne enjoys swimming.

3. What pattern organizes the details in paragraph 11?

   a. list

   b. definition

   c. cause/effect

   d. sequence

4. Which of the following paragraphs begins with a list transition?

   a. paragraph 3   c. paragraph 8

   b. paragraph 5   d. paragraph 10

5. What is the implied main idea of paragraph 11?

   a. LaLanne's visit to a nutritionist changed his life.

   b. LaLanne's mother was worried about him.

   c. LaLanne was a human garbage can.

   d. LaLanne was too short to play professional sports.

Practicing the Active Reading Strategy

■ After You Read

Now that you have read the selection, answer the following questions, using the active reading strategies that you learned in Chapter 1.

1. Identify and write down the point and purpose of this reading selection.

2. Besides the vocabulary words included in the exercise on page 257, are there any other vocabulary words that are unfamiliar to you? If so, write a list of them. When you have finished writing your list, look up each word in a dictionary and write the definition that best describes the word as it is used in the selection.

3. Predict any possible questions that may be used on a test about the content of this selection.

■ Questions for Discussion and Writing

Answer the following questions based on your reading of the selection. Write your answers on the blanks provided.

1. LaLanne's visit to a nutritionist changed his life. Have you ever had a life-changing experience? If so, what was it?

_____

_____

_____

_____

2. What kind of commitment do you think it takes to live a life like Jack LaLanne's? Why do you think he was so driven to live a healthy lifestyle? What motivated him, in your opinion?

_____

_____

_____

_____

3. Do you think that Americans are in better shape or worse shape than people in the rest of the world? Why?

_____

_____

_____

_____

6

Practicing the Active Reading Strategy

■ Before and While You Read

You can use active reading strategies before, while, and after you read a selection. The following are some suggestions for active reading strategies that you can employ before you read and as you are reading.

1. Skim the selection for any unfamiliar words. Circle or highlight any words you do not know.

2. As you read, underline, highlight, or circle important words or phrases.

3. Write down any questions about the selection if you are confused by the information presented.

4. Jot notes in the margin to help you understand the material.

TEXTBOOK READING: HOSPITALITY INDUSTRY
History of Theme Parks

Have you ever been to Disney World? Or maybe just a local amusement park for a day of summer fun? Modern theme parks and amusement parks can trace their beginnings back hundreds of years.

1 The historical roots of theme parks originate in the fair. Historians note that fairs have existed for thousands of years, and the earliest fairs were probably agricultural shows. Today the agricultural fair is still the most common type held in the United States and Canada. Fairs also usually offer musical entertainment, sports events, and carnival rides and games. In addition to agricultural fairs, international expositions like the World's Fair highlight scientific, industrial, and artistic contributions from various countries.

2 From the temporary, seasonal operation of the local fair sprang the idea for the development of permanent amusement parks. One of the earliest known amusement parks was Vauxhall Gardens in England, created in the 1600s. Copenhagen's Tivoli Gardens, which celebrated its 150th anniversary in August 1993, is probably the world's most famous amusement park. Tivoli contains twenty acres of gardens, twenty-five rides, and more than twenty-five restaurants. One roller-coaster ride, called the Flying Trunk, takes travelers through a fairy-tale world of Hans Christian Andersen characters. The Tivoli Gardens, visited by Walt Disney, provided some of the inspiration for his Disneyland development.

3 Amusement parks were first built in the United States in the 1800s

at popular beaches. The major attraction was often a roller coaster, originally called a "sliding hill." The establishment of Coney Island in 1895, however, took amusement parks to a new level. Located in Brooklyn, New York, on the Atlantic Ocean, Coney Island was (and still is) a popular tourist attraction known for its amusement facilities, boardwalk, beaches, and the New York Aquarium.

4   Such amusement parks were, of course, the predecessors to modern-day theme parks. Today's theme parks have exploited the thrills of amusement park rides and combined them with the educational entertainment of fairs. A theme park differs from an amusement park in two distinct ways. First, theme parks are based on a particular setting or artistic interpretation such as "Frontierland" or "Old Country." Second, theme parks usually operate on a much larger scale than amusement parks, with hundreds or thousands of acres of parkland and hundreds or thousands of employees running the operation.

5   The primary purpose of a theme park was best described by the father of theme parks, Walt Disney. He thought that theme parks should be clean, friendly places where people could have a good time. In July 1955, Disney opened the world's first theme park, Disneyland, in Anaheim, California. The face of family recreation has never been the same. Legend has it that Walt Disney conceived his theme park idea while sitting on a park bench watching his daughters ride a merry-go-round. He thought that adults should have the chance to enjoy themselves, too, rather than just pay the tab. Accordingly, Disney found a way to manufacture and market fun for every age. Today, Walt Disney's vision has taken his original theme park concept into the international marketplace with Disney World locations in Paris, France; Toyko, Japan; and Hong Kong.*

6

■ Vocabulary

Read the following questions about some of the vocabulary words that appear in the previous selection. Before you look up the word, try to use the context of the passage to figure out the meaning. Then circle the letter of the correct answer for each question.

1. In paragraph 1, what is meant by *"international expositions"*?

    a. a public show   c. a wheat field

    b. a park   d. a nightclub

---

* Kaye (Kye-Sung) Chon, and Thomas A. Maier, *Welcome to Hospitality: An Introduction,* 3rd ed. (Clifton Park: Delmar, 2010), 349–50. Print.

2. What are *predecessors* in paragraph 4?

   a. professors

   b. something that comes before

   c. something new

   d. something that comes after

3. If something has been *exploited* (paragraph 4), what has happened to it?

   a. a great adventure

   b. gotten old

   c. blown up

   d. used to greatest advantage

4. In paragraph 5, what did Walt Disney do when he *conceived* the idea of a theme park?

   a. had the idea for

   b. threw out

   c. drew pictures of

   d. paid for

5. To "*pay the tab*" in paragraph 5, means to pay what?

   a. tuition

   b. cost of the rides

   c. buttons on a coat

   d. top of a folder

■ Reading Skills

Respond to each of the following questions by circling the letter of the correct answer or by writing your answer on the blank provided.

1. List the two major transition words in paragraph 1 and identify what pattern of organization they describe.

   a. _____

   b. _____

2. The last three sentences in paragraph 2 are examples of _____.

   a. major details

   b. minor details

3. What type of transition is used in paragraph 3?

   a. definition

   b. list

   c. contrast

   d. sequence

4. In paragraph 4 what two things are being contrasted?

_____ and _____.

5. Which sentence in paragraph 5 best states the main idea?

a. sentence 1

c. sentence 5

b. sentence 2

d. sentence 8

Practicing the Active Reading Strategy

■ After You Read

Now that you have read the selection, answer the following questions, using the active reading strategies that you learned in Chapter 1.

1. Identify and write down the point and purpose of this reading selection.

2. Did you circle or highlight any words that are unfamiliar to you? Can you figure out the meaning from the context of the passage? If not, then look up each word in a dictionary and find the definition that best describes the word as it is used in the selection. You may want to write the definition in the margin next to the word in the passage for future reference.

3. Predict any possible questions that may be used on a test about the content of this selection.

■ Questions for Discussion and Writing

Respond to each of the following questions based on your reading of the selection.

1. What type of fair is the oldest? Have you ever been to a state fair? What was it like? _____

_____

2. Why is the Tivoli Garden in Copenhagen probably the world's most famous amusement park? _____

_____

3. Which amusement park is your favorite? Why? Is there an amusement park or theme park that you would like to visit? _____

_____

6

Practicing the Active Reading Strategy

■ Before and While You Read

You can use active reading strategies before, while, and after you read a selection. The following are some suggestions for active reading strategies that you can employ before you read and as you are reading.

1. Skim the selection for any unfamiliar words. Circle or highlight any words you do not know.

2. As you read, underline, highlight, or circle important words or phrases.

3. Write down any questions about the selection if you are confused by the information presented.

4. Jot notes in the margin to help you understand the material.

NEWSPAPER READING: PSYCHOLOGY
Birth Order

by Doreen Nagle

Behavioral scientists and researchers at the Child Development Institute say there are enough similar patterns in oldest, youngest, and middle children that show birth order really can play a role in behavior. Do the following traits ring true in your family?

6

Firstborn

1 New parents generally worry more than experienced parents. As novices, first-time parents are unsure about what to expect (even with the advice and warnings of experienced parents as well as experts) and treat each new phase of their child's development as a miracle.

2 This adds to the firstborn child's tendency to be very critical of himself or herself, sometimes bordering on perfectionism. These children may also believe that their way is the only way, causing them to have difficult relationships with peers.

3 By the time a second child arrives, the firstborn is used to being the leader and in charge; a sibling messes up his or her neatly controlled world. A firstborn child can take criticism very hard. One solution: Admitting your own mistakes will help this child relax.

(Note: Only children are likely to have some of the same characteristics as a firstborn child.)

Middle Children

4 Much is talked about the middle child. By the time a middle child comes along (this can include not only the second child, but the third, fourth, etc.), another child already has established himself or herself as the leader. A middle child may have a difficult time getting mom or

dad's undivided attention; middle children must negotiate a place for themselves.

5   To stand out, the middle child may develop a different temperament or personality than the other siblings. This may make him more of a discipline problem. One way to connect with middle children is to encourage communication because they may not be as likely to talk about their feelings as their siblings are. Also, make time alone for you and your middle child.

Youngest Child

6   The youngest child comes into a house where there is as least one other sibling. If there is only one other older sibling, the youngest child may develop some of the characteristics of a middle child.

7   The youngest child may be more outgoing than his siblings because he has to learn to get along with peers more readily. Parents may shape the youngest child's personality because they may not desire to let their youngest child grow up—they don't want to let go of having a "baby" in the house. Therefore, they may cater too much to this child or have a tendency to be too permissive. If this is so, this child may expect everyone else to serve his needs.*

■ Vocabulary

Read the following questions about some of the vocabulary words that appear in the previous selection. Before you look up the word, try to use the context of the passage to figure out the meaning. Then circle the letter of the correct answer for each question.

1. The author uses the word *tendency* in paragraph two. What does *tendency* mean?

   a. to move away from

   b. lengthy, longer than expected

   c. a proneness toward a particular thought or action

   d. to show comfort in a time of need

2. Paragraph two includes the word *peers*. How does the author want you to interpret the word?

   a. to peek through

   b. common enemies

   c. sheer

   d. one belonging to the same societal group

6

* Doreen Nagle, "Birth Order Can Impact Temperament," *Chicago Sun Times*, July 8, 2010, EASY 5. Print.

3. "Middle children must *negotiate* a place for themselves." What does the author mean when she uses the word *negotiate*? (paragraph 4)

   a. manage

   b. negligent

   c. underestimate

   d. overestimate

4. Paragraph seven uses the word *permissive* to describe the way parents act towards their youngest child. What does the word *permissive* mean?

   a. controlling

   b. smothering

   c. tolerant

   d. obsessive

5. The last paragraph includes the word *dote*. What does it mean to *dote*?

   a. to ignore, not pay attention to

   b. show compulsive behavior

   c. savvy

   d. to be lavish or excessive in one's fondness

■ Reading Skills

Respond to each of the following questions by circling the letter of the correct answer or by writing your answer on the blank provided.

1. "These children may also believe that their way is the only way, causing them to have difficult relationships with peers." The author has used which pattern of organization?

   a. list

   b. sequence

   c. cause/effect

   d. definition

2. The second section about middle children uses which pattern of organization?

   a. list

   b. sequence

   c. cause/effect

   d. definition

3. What is the implied main idea of the section titled "Firstborn"?

   a. New parents have an effect on firstborn children.

   b. Most firstborn children become world leaders.

   c. Firstborn children are stubborn.

   d. Being firstborn is better than being the middle child.

4. "Therefore, they may cater too much to this child or have a tendency to be too permissive." The author is using the word *therefore* as what type of transition word?

   a. list

   b. sequence

   c. cause/effect

   d. definition

5. What is the implied main idea of the section titled "Youngest Child"?

   a. The youngest child enjoys being the "baby."

   b. Parents and siblings have a great effect on the youngest child.

   c. Youngest children often end up in trouble.

   d. Youngest children try to emulate their peers.

Practicing the Active Reading Strategy

■ After You Read

Now that you have read the selection, answer the following questions, using the active reading strategies that you learned in Chapter 1.

1. Identify and write down the point and purpose of this reading selection.

2. Did you circle or highlight any words that are unfamiliar to you? Can you figure out the meaning from the context of the passage? If not, then look up each word in a dictionary and find the definition that best describes the word as it is used in the selection. You may want to write the definition in the margin next to the word in the passage for future reference.

3. Predict any possible questions that may be used on a test about the content of this selection.

■ Questions for Discussion and Writing

Respond to each of the following questions based on your reading of the selection.

1. Based on your own birth order, do you think the author is accurate in her description of birth order traits? Give specific examples.

   _____

   _____

   _____

2. Based on what you have read, if you had a choice, what would be your preferred birth order? Would you like to be firstborn, middle child, or youngest?

_____

_____

_____

_____

3. Compare and contrast what it is like to be a firstborn versus a youngest child.

_____

_____

_____

_____

Vocabulary Strategy: The Example Context Clue

You've learned that a *context clue* is a word, phrase, or sentence that helps you understand the meaning of an unfamiliar word you encounter as you read. In Chapter 4, you practiced recognizing the definition/restatement context clue. In Chapter 5, you learned about the explanation context clue. The **example** is a third type of context clue that can give you a sense of a particular word's definition. In this type, *an example somewhere near a word provides an illustration that allows you to draw a conclusion about the word's meaning.* For example, read the following sentence, which comes from one of the paragraphs in this chapter:

Finally, the bill includes a *watermark*. When the [$20] bill is held up to the light, there appears to the right side of the portrait of Andrew Jackson a faint image that is similar to the portrait. It's part of the paper itself, and it can be seen from both sides.

What does the word *watermark* mean in this paragraph? You get clues in the next two sentences, which give the example of a $20 bill. Phrases like "a faint image" and "it's part of the paper itself" help you conclude that a watermark is a design impressed upon paper.

Vocabulary Exercise

The following sentences all come from paragraphs in Chapters 3, 4, and 6. In each one, underline the example context clue that helps you understand the meaning of the boldfaced, italicized word. Then, on the blank provided, write a definition for the italicized word.

1. For example, a common *hygiene* rule might be "Brush your teeth every morning."

   _____

2. Even if the babies are not born prematurely, they are more likely to suffer from *afflictions,* such as heart problems or genetic disorders, that can affect their lifelong health.

   _____

3. Girls play *theatrical* games, such as playacting roles as members of a pretend family, that don't feature hierarchy or winners.

   _____

4. And the National Aquarium in Baltimore includes a *simulation* of an Australian river canyon, complete with waterfall.

   _____

5. A *nutraceutical* (a combination of the words *nutrition* and *pharmaceutical*) is either a pill or another *pharmaceutical* that has nutritional value, or a food that has had its nutritional value enhanced by drugs.

   _____

6. Many Americans believe in the *supernatural.* . . . A recent Gallup poll revealed that 69 percent of people believe in angels, half of them believe they have their own guardian angels, and 48 percent believe that there are aliens in outer space.

   _____

7. Another orangutan at a Seattle zoo came up with a *ploy,* too, by pretending to drop or lose a piece of fruit and then asking for a replaement while actually hiding it.

   _____

8. The second rule for becoming rich is to avoid *frivolous* temptations. For example, don't drive expensive luxury cars; instead, buy medium-priced cars.

   _____

6

Chapter 6 Review

Write the correct word or words in the blanks in the following statements.

1. A _____ is a consistent, predictable form or method for putting something together.

2. Patterns help readers find _____ and understand their relationships.

3. Five broad patterns for organizing details include _____, _____, _____, _____, and _____.

4. _____ often include clues to a paragraph's pattern of arrangement.

5. A _____ is a number of things that follow each other in succession. Lists in paragraphs may be examples, reasons, types, or other points.

6. _____ paragraphs, which include time order and processes, arrange details chronologically.

7. _____ paragraphs explain how supporting details are related to each other.

8. _____ paragraphs examine two or more subjects' similarities, differences, or both.

9. The _____ pattern includes a term's meaning plus one or more examples as illustration.

10. Paragraphs often use a combination of _____ to organize supporting details.

11. The two benefits to taking notes are _____ _____ and _____.

12. An *example* context clue provides an _____ that allows you to draw a conclusion about the word's meaning.

Inferences

Goals for Chapter 7

- ■ Define the term *inference.*
- ■ Explain how inferences are made.
- ■ State three reasons for asking readers to make inferences.
- ■ Use guidelines to make accurate inferences from reading selections.
- ■ Explain and apply the steps of the REAP strategy.

Reading selections don't always state everything you should know about a subject. Instead, you're expected to figure out information that's not actually in the text by drawing inferences, or conclusions. To see how well you already do this, take the pretest below.

Pretest

Read the following sentences and then respond to each question that follows by circling the correct answer.

1. I threw the stick, and he fetched it.

   What can you infer about the "he" in the sentence?

   a. He is my son.   c. He is a tree.

   b. He is a dog.   d. He is a squirrel.

2. Frank pulled the car over and asked the driver for his license.

   What can you infer about Frank from this sentence?

   a. Frank is a car thief.   c. Frank is a police officer.

   b. Frank needs a ride home.   d. Frank's car has broken down.

3. Women who gain too much weight during pregnancy have big babies, putting their children at risk of becoming heavy later on, a new study says.*

   What can you infer about weight gain in pregnant women?

   a. It is dangerous for the women.

   b. It may have lifelong negative effects on the baby.

   c. Weight gain is not important during pregnancy.

   d. Older mothers gain more weight.

4. John was a bright fellow who had been in college for seven years without graduating. During a class discussion, he related an experience that he said was typical of him: He had been studying for a midterm test in history when a friend called and asked for help with a test in biology, a course John had already passed. John set aside his own studies and spent the evening tutoring his friend. The next day John failed his history exam.†

---

* The Associated Press. *The Arizona Daily Star,* August 5, 2010, Nation & World A13. Print.

† From Skip Downing, *On Course,* 4th ed. (Boston: Houghton Mifflin Co., 2005), 112.

What can you infer about John from this passage?

a. John cares about his friends more than he cares about his grades.

b. John knows a lot about history.

c. John is a C student.

d. John finds studying boring.

5. In Phoenix, about two-thirds of the incoming ninth graders read at least a year below grade level. And the statistics from other cities are similar. That reading lag, experts say, is largely why almost every big-city school district has at least twice as many ninth graders as twelfth graders.*

What can you infer from this passage?

a. Small-town school districts are better than big-city districts at teaching kids how to read.

b. Overcrowded schools are to blame for kids' problems with learning how to read.

c. Many teenagers with reading problems drop out of school and don't graduate.

d. Twelfth grade is much more difficult than ninth grade.

Inferences

Writers do not write down everything they want you to understand about a topic, but they expect you to figure out this information anyway. How? They know you make inferences while you read. An **inference** *is a conclusion you draw that's based upon the stated information.* You made one type of inference when you learned how to determine implied main ideas in Chapter 4. When you consider a group of related supporting details and draw a conclusion about the point they suggest, you're inferring that main idea. But you make many more kinds of smaller inferences, too, as you read. For example, read the following paragraph.

A mother thought her three-year-old child was playing too quietly, so she went into the living room to check on the youngster. The child was not in the room, and the front door was wide open. Their dog

---

* Adapted from Tamar Lewin, "In Cities, a Battle to Improve Teenage Literacy," *New York Times*, April 14, 2004, http://www.nytimes.com/2004/04/14/education/14read.html.

was gone, too. She panicked and called the police. When they arrived, they began searching the neighborhood. One of the searchers saw a dog barking and running into and out of a wooded area beside the road. He followed the excited dog and found the three-year-old, crying and trembling, hiding behind a tree.

Did you conclude that the child left home and got lost but was rescued when the family dog revealed his or her whereabouts? If you did, you made quite a few inferences to reach that conclusion. For instance, the passage never says that the child was at home, so how do you know that? You figure that out because the child, the child's mother, and the dog are all there, and the child is in the living room. Therefore, you conclude that they're all in the house where they live. How did you—and the mother—know the child had wandered off? You get three clues: the child is gone, the door is open, and the mother panics. You add these three pieces of information together to make your conclusion. How do you know that the dog helps rescuers find the child? The animal tries to attract their attention by barking and running back and forth, and the child is found where the dog is exhibiting these behaviors. You put those clues together to figure out that the dog was "telling" rescuers where they could find the child. Therefore, even though the passage does not tell you exactly what happened, you still understand because of your ability to make inferences. To **infer** means *"to read between the lines."* You see more than what is actually there because you bring your own knowledge, experiences, and observations to your reading, allowing you to fill in the gaps. For instance, you've noticed before that a burning building sends black smoke into the sky, and you know that fire trucks rush to a fire with their sirens on. Therefore, when you see smoke and hear sirens, you conclude that something is on fire. You apply these same experiences and observations as you read.

Here is another example that illustrates how you use your previous knowledge to make inferences:

> Some people ask me if I worry about my girlfriend's getting off work late at night. I don't, though, because she has her black belt in karate.

These two sentences ask you to make a couple of inferences. The first sentence assumes that you know why people would worry; it asks you to access your memory of news stories, observations, or your own personal experiences that have taught you that a woman alone at night can be vulnerable to an attack. Then, the second sentence assumes you know that someone who possesses a black belt in karate is a practiced fighter who can defend herself against attackers. Even though these two pieces of information are never stated, you easily infer the meaning of these sentences because you use your previous knowledge to understand.

Exercise **7.1**

Read the following comic strips and look at the following photographs and then write a check mark next to each statement that expresses an accurate inference.

Calvin and Hobbes

by Bill Watterson

1. _____ Calvin doesn't like to take baths.

   _____ Calvin spends a lot of time on the roof.

   _____ Calvin's mother is having a good time.

   _____ Calvin lives in a very expensive house.

MOTHER GOOSE & GRIMM

BY MIKE PETERS

EXCUSE ME, MISS, BUT I THINK THIS MEAT IS **GOOD**.

2. _____ The restaurant's chef does not know how to cook steaks.

   _____ The buzzard likes its meat bad or rotting.

   _____ The waitress hears many complaints about the food.

   _____ The prices at this restaurant are very high.

7

3. _____ These two boys live in Denver.

_____ These two boys fight a lot.

_____ The boys are brothers.

_____ The younger boy attends a private school.

4. _____ These three people are students.

_____ The woman in the middle is the teacher, and the other people are her students.

_____ The students have just taken a test.

_____ The woman in the middle is angry at the other two people.

5. _____ The car is going too fast.

_____ The "Daddy" mentioned in the sign's message is a road construction worker.

_____ A child made the sign.

_____ It is rush hour on this highway.

Exercise **7.2**

Read the following paragraphs and then respond to the questions that follow by circling the letter of each correct answer.

1. YMCAs were founded in part to provide an alternative to the expensive, private city athletic club. Today, many Ys still run a wide variety of fitness programs, and provide lodging and dining to both long- and short-term guests.*

The author wants you to infer that

a. rich people do not work out at the Y.

b. people who are not wealthy still want to be fit.

---

* Kaye (Kye-Sung) Chon and Thomas A. Maier, *Welcome to Hospitality: An Introduction,* 3rd ed. (Clifton Park: Delmar, 2010), 349. Print.

7

   c. poor people sleep at the YMCA.

   d. only adults can use the YMCA.

2. Fresh from graduate school, Assistant Professor Popson was midway through his first semester of college teaching when his depression started. Long gone was the excitement and promise of the first day of class. Now, only about two-thirds of his students were attending, and some of them were barely holding on.*

   The author wants you to infer that

   a. Assistant Professor Popson is a poor teacher.

   b. Assistant Professor Popson does not care about his students.

   c. Assistant Professor Popson is inexperienced at teaching.

   d. Assistant Professor Popson will quit teaching soon.

3. Automotive service centers used to be fairly small operations. Usually there was a person who owned and managed the business while performing repairs and customer service at the same time.†

   The author wants you to infer that

   a. small automotive service centers no longer exist.

   b. small automotive service centers are efficient.

   c. automotive service centers today are much larger operations.

   d. automotive service centers today are not efficient.

4. Some guys in my neighborhood still sport their college's name on their car window. And they're in their 60s.‡

   The author wants you to infer that

   a. the men to whom he or she is referring are too old to be displaying their college's name on their car windows.

   b. the men to whom he or she is referring own cars.

   c. the men to whom he or she is referring have gray hair.

   d. the men to whom he or she is referring went to his college.

---

* Downing, Skip. *On Course: Strategies for Creating Success in College and in Life.* 6th ed. Boston: Wadsworth, 2011. Print. p. 64.

† Clifton E. Owen, *Today's Technician: Basic Automotive Service and Systems,* 4th ed. (Clifton Park: Delmar, 2011), CM25. Print.

‡ From Craig Wilson, "Picking a Future Alma Mater Is Anything but Academic," *USA Today,* July 25, 2001, 1D.

5. The more active you become in taking control of your reading process, the less likely you will be to lapse into passive reading habits. As an active reader, you are *doing something* throughout the process.*

The author wants you to infer that

a. passive readers always fail their classes.

b. active readers always take good notes.

c. active readers are aware of the activities they need to perform to read well.

d. passive readers fall asleep when they read.

Writers rely on readers' ability to make inferences for three reasons. First of all, passages that spelled out every detail would be boring and tedious to read. Second, they would be unnecessarily long. And finally, they would deprive readers of the pleasure they experience in figuring out some things for themselves.

Guidelines for Making Accurate Inferences

How can you make sure you're drawing the right conclusions from information in a text? Follow these guidelines:

■ **Focus only on the details and information provided, and don't "read in" anything that's not there.** It's surprisingly easy to take just a little bit of information and jump to unfounded conclusions. For example, think back to the earlier example about the three-year-old who wandered away from home. Would you say that the child's mother was careless in allowing the child to get away? Many people would; they would say that she should have been watching her child more carefully. Can you really make that assumption, though? Could there have been someone else in the house who may have been responsible for looking after the child? The passage did not say that anyone else was in the house, but it also didn't say that the mother and child were home alone. We read that into the story. Because we know that the mother is often the primary caretaker in a household, we also assume that it's her fault when something happens to the child. Now, without looking back at the passage, answer this question: Who rescued the child? Did you answer "a police officer"? Why? Because the mother called the police, who came and searched the neighborhood. But the person who found the child was actually referred to simply as a "searcher."

7

* Carol Kanar, *The Confident Student,* 7th ed. (Boston: Wadsworth, 2011), 164. Print.

That person could have been a neighbor rather than a police officer. We don't get enough information to be able to answer that question, so we should not leap to inaccurate conclusions.

■ **Don't ignore any details.** The details provide the important clues. For instance, in the earlier example, was the missing three-year-old child enjoying his or her time out of the house? Of course not. The paragraph says the child was "crying and trembling," two details that indicate the child's fear.

■ **Make sure nothing contradicts your conclusion.** Try not to overlook one or more details that may conflict with any preliminary conclusion you make about a passage. For example, read the following:

> Years ago a professor overheard me talking with other engineers about the engineering dropouts who then go into business. "Don't laugh," he said. "In five years, one of them will be your boss."*

In this passage, you can infer that the writer is an engineer because he's talking with "other engineers." Next, you're supposed to infer how these engineers feel about engineering dropouts. Are they sympathetic? Are they sad for the people who can't make it through the engineering program? If you answer yes to either of those questions, you are overlooking one important detail: the professor tells them not to "laugh." If you miss that detail, you won't accurately conclude that the engineers are making fun of those who failed.

■ **Don't let stereotypes and/or prejudices color your interpretation.** When you think back to that story about the missing three-year-old and try to picture the child in your mind, do you picture a boy or a girl? The passage never identifies the child's gender, but many readers think of the child as male. Why? Because we rely upon the stereotype that little boys are, in general, more adventurous and more disobedient. Therefore, a boy would be more likely to wander off and get lost. However, we should resist making that inference if there is no information in the passage that supports it, and we recognize that some of our assumptions are based on generalizations that may be incorrect.

Exercise **7.3**

Read the following passages and then circle the letter of the correct answer for each of the questions that follow.

Online consumer spending reached $74 billion in 2002. An important figure in terms of Internet shopping is that men are responsible for 49 percent of the purchases, a significantly larger percentage than those who shop in the

---

* Adapted from Steven Parish, "'Show and Style' vs. Experience," *USA Today*, July 30, 2001, 11A.

brick-and–mortar operations. This give the off-site retailers reason to use the Internet as a means of attracting men who would not be likely to visit their stores.*

1. What can you infer from the information in the first sentence?

    a. People are spending a great deal of money shopping online.

    b. People are spending less money shopping in brick-and-mortar stores.

    c. People are too lazy to go out of the house to shop.

    d. People can find items online that they cannot find in stores.

2. Based on the details in this paragraph, which of the following inferences is most accurate?

    a. Women shop for men.

    b. Men prefer to shop online.

    c. Men have less time to shop than women.

    d. Men have more money to shop than women.

3. The reader can infer that

    a. retailers do not care about men's shopping habits.

    b. retailers will use the Internet to attract male shoppers.

    c. retailers will close their men's stores.

    d. retailers who do not use the Internet will go out of business.

African American and Hispanic students were more likely than White students to fear for their safety regardless of location, either at school or away from school. As grade level increased, students' fear of an attack at school or on the way to and from school decreased. School location, however, was found to be related to students' fear of attack. Students who attended urban schools were more likely than students enrolled in suburban and rural schools to fear being attacked at school or on the way to and from school.[†]

4. What can you infer is that the least safe schools are

    a. in urban areas.

    b. in the suburbs.

    c. in rural areas.

---

* Ellen Diamond, *Fashion Retailing: A Multi-Channel Approach,* 2nd ed. (Upper Saddle River: Pearson Education, Inc., 2006), 30. Print.

[†] Robert Regoli, *Delinquency in Society: The Essentials,* Sudbury: Jones and Barlett Publishers, 2011, 285. Print.

5. What can you infer from the fact that African American and Hispanic students are more fearful of their safety than White students?

   a. White students cause the attacks.

   b. Urban schools do not have as many While students.

   c. African American and Hispanic students are more likely to be attacked.

   d. Urban schools have little security.

6. The reader can infer that

   a. rural students are never attacked.

   b. younger students are more likely to be attacked.

   c. older students are not as fearful of an attack because they can fight back.

   d. suburban schools are always safe.

Firefighters respond to emergency calls of all types. Although their primary responsibility is to fight fires, they are more often called on to assist with other kinds of emergencies, such as medical calls and vehicle accidents. As a public service, firefighters often visit schools, day-care centers, and senior centers to teach fire safety. Firefighters' schedules vary, but the typical shift is 24 hours on duty, followed by 48 hours off. Of course, firefighters cannot just leave the scene of an emergency and go home when their appointed shift ends.*

7. What can you infer from the use of the contrast transition "although" in sentence 2?

   a. Firefighters rarely fight fires.

   b. Firefighters spend more time with non-fire emergencies.

   c. Firefighters need more training.

   d. Fires are put out by people other than firefighters.

8. What can you infer about the type of training that firefighters need?

   a. Their training is not enough for the various jobs they must do.

   b. Their training is only for fighting fires.

   c. Their training must cover many different types of emergency services.

   d. Their training stops when they graduate.

---

* Jason B. Loyd, *Fundamentals of Fire and Emergency Services* (Upper Saddle River: Pearson Education, Inc., 2010), 20. Print.

9. What can you infer about the work schedules for firefighters?

   a. Their schedules may be unpredictable.

   b. Their schedules allow for them to have a second job.

   c. Their schedules allow for them to be with their families more than other careers.

   d. Their schedules allow them to sleep late every day.

Apple might have remained a hobbyist machine, but (Steve) Jobs could inspire people with his drive and enthusiasm. In 1976 they (Steve Jobs and Steve Wozniak) secured nearly $300,000 in funding. In 1977, Apple released the Apple II, based on the Motorola 6502 processor, and made a profit by year's end, doubling production every few months. The Apple II was compact, reliable, and "talked up" in the industry. It was also adopted by many schools and became many students' first experience with computers—making a lasting impression. What really pushed it toward broad acceptance was the ease with which programmers could write applications for it.*

10. What can you infer about Steve Jobs from the paragraph?

    a. He was difficult to work with.

    b. He could see the possibilities for the computer in the future.

    c. He did not have any money to invest in his company.

    d. He did not like children.

11. What can you infer about why the Apple II was adopted by so many schools?

    a. They were inexpensive.

    b. There were no other computers available at the time.

    c. Steve Jobs was an excellent sales person.

    d. They were small and did not break down often.

12. What can you infer about the importance of the Apple II being the first experience for students with a computer?

    a. Students will want this brand at home.

    b. Students will never buy an Apple computer.

    c. Students could not afford the Apple computer.

    d. Students will become computer programmers.

---

* Greg Anderson, David Ferro, and Robert Hilton, *Connecting with Computer Science,* 2nd ed. (Boston: Course Technology, 2011), 23. Print.

Whenever we fail to get adequate sleep, we accumulate what researchers call a *sleep debit*. With each night of too little rest, our body's need for sleep grows until it becomes irresistible. The only solution to sleep debit is the obvious one: paying it back. College students who extended their nightly sleep time were more alert, more productive, and less likely to have accidents. And because sleepy people tend to be irritable and edgy, those who get more rest also tend to be happier, healthier, and easier to get along with.*

13. What can we infer about the effects of the need for sleep on college students?

 a. Students who do not have enough sleep fail their classes.

 b. Students who have enough sleep get more accomplished.

 c. Students who have enough sleep always go to classes.

 d. Students who do not have enough sleep have many friends.

14. What can we infer from the statement "…our body's need for sleep grows until it becomes irresistible"?

 a. People will eventually just fall asleep.

 b. People can control falling asleep.

 c. People can sleep whenever they wish.

 d. People don't need much sleep.

15. What can we infer about sleepy people?

 a. They are pleasant to be around.

 b. They make good employees.

 c. They should not drive.

 d. They need to exercise.

Exercise **7.4**

Read the following passages and then write a check mark next to each statement that expresses an accurate inference.

1. Upset that your husband forgot to call? Think telling him off will make you feel better? Not so, says psychologist Brad Bushman, PhD, whose research shows that venting anger actually ends up making people unhappy. Why? We often say things we later regret, studies show. A better idea, according to Bushman, is reading a good book, watching a funny TV

---

* Dianne Hales, *An Invitation to Wellness: Making Healthy Choices* (Belmont: Thomson Higher Education, 2007), 142. Print.

show, or listening to a favorite CD. You'll soon calm down enough to deal more productively with the situation by having a calm discussion with whoever made you angry.*

_____ 1. Women vent their anger more than men do.

_____ 2. Venting anger often involves hurtful verbal criticism.

_____ 3. Venting anger can damage the relationship between two people, leading to more unhappiness.

_____ 4. Women have a right to feel angry when their husbands forget them.

_____ 5. A primary goal of the media is to help people better manage their anger.

2. Medical experts have warned for years that anorexia and bulimia can be deadly, but a growing number of teens are celebrating their eating disorders on the Web and sharing their tips and strategies for losing weight and exercising. It's a trend that worries and disturbs eating-disorder experts. "I love the feeling I get when I can feel my bones sticking out. I love feeling empty, like a hollow gourd.[1] I love knowing I went the whole day without eating." So says a posting on one website promoting eating disorders as a lifestyle.[†]

_____ 1. Teens don't take eating disorders as seriously as medical experts do.

_____ 2. Medical experts think that teens are stupid.

_____ 3. Medical experts are disturbed by how teens are dealing with eating disorders.

_____ 4. Teens think that medical experts don't know what they are talking about.

_____ 5. Teens with eating disorders don't care about other people.

3. It's 6:35 in the morning, and Cheryl Nevins, thirty-four, is dressed for work in a silky black maternity blouse and skirt. Ryan, two and a half, and Brendan, eleven months, are sobbing because Reilly, the beefy family

1. **gourd:** hollowed-out shell of certain fruits

---

* Adapted from Barbara Hustedt Crook, "Feel Happier Just by Doing These Six Simple Things," *Woman's World*, July 10, 2001, 21.

† Adapted from Nanci Hellmich, "Super-thin, Super-troubling," *USA Today*, July 25, 2001, 7D.

dog, knocked Ryan over. In a blur of calm, purposeful activity, Nevins, who is eight months pregnant, shoves the dog out into the backyard, changes Ryan's diaper on the family-room rug, heats farina[1] in the microwave, and feeds Brendan cereal and sliced bananas while crooning "Open, Shut Them" to encourage the baby to chew. Her husband, Joe, normally out the door by 5:30 A.M. for his job as a finance manager at Kraft Foods, makes a rare appearance in the morning muddle. "I do want to go outside with you," he tells Ryan, who is clinging to his leg, "but Daddy has to work every day except Saturdays and Sundays. That stinks."*

_____ 1. Cheryl Nevins has nice maternity clothing.

_____ 2. Cheryl Nevins has very busy mornings before she leaves for work.

_____ 3. Cheryl Nevins's husband is not around to help much in the morning.

_____ 4. Cheryl Nevins is regretting having another child.

_____ 5. Cheryl Nevins serves her children convenience foods when she can.

4. At the University of California, Davis, of the 196 plagiarism cases referred to the disciplinary office last year, a majority did not involve students ignorant of the need to credit the writing of others. Many times, said Donald J. Dudley, who oversees the discipline office on the campus of 32,000, it was students who intentionally copied—knowing it was wrong—who were "unwilling to engage the writing process." "Writing is difficult, and doing it well takes time and practice," he said.[†]

_____ 1. College students today work hard.

_____ 2. College students today know when they are cheating.

_____ 3. College students today are lazy.

_____ 4. College students today do not know how to write papers.

_____ 5. College students today do not know how to credit sources of information.

---

1. **farina:** cooked cereal

---

* Adapted from "The Case for Staying Home," by Claudia Wallis, *Time*, March 22, 2004, 51.

† Trip Gabriel, "Plagiarism Lines Blur for Students in Digital Age," *nytimes.com*, August 2, 2010, .../02cheat. html, p. 4. Web. http://www.nytimes.com/2010/08/02/education/02cheat.html?scp=1&sq=Plagiarism%20 Lines%20Blue%20for%20Students%20in%20Digital%20Age&st=cse

5. Resisting slavery seemed second nature to Harriet Tubman. Born a slave on a Maryland plantation in 1820, she quickly developed a fiery spirit and was not shy about protesting bad treatment. One such incident so angered the plantation overseer that he hit her over the head with a lead weight, inflicting a permanent brain injury that would cause her to suddenly lose consciousness several times a day for the rest of her life. To overcome this disability, she worked on building herself up physically, becoming an uncommonly strong woman. It was said that she could single-handedly haul a boat fully loaded with stones, a feat[1] deemed impossible for all but the strongest men.*

_____ 1. Harriet Tubman was an African American.

_____ 2. Harriet Tubman is now dead.

_____ 3. Harriet Tubman stood up for herself.

_____ 4. Men were frightened of Harriet Tubman.

_____ 5. Harriet Tubman freed herself from slavery.

Exercise 7.5

Read the following Aesop fable. This fable is written in the style of a parable, or story, written to make a point. Respond to each of the questions that follow by circling the letter of the correct answer.

The tortoise and the hare argued over which was the swifter. So, as a result, they agreed on a fixed period of time and a place and parted company. Now the hare, trusting in his natural speed, didn't hurry to set out. He lay down at the side of the road and fell asleep. But the tortoise, well aware of his slowness, didn't stop running, and, overtaking the sleeping hare, he arrived first and won the contest.[†]

1. What can you infer about the hare from this selection?

   a. He assumed that he could beat the tortoise.

   b. He was very tired.

   c. He had won many speed contests.

   d. He did not like the tortoise.

---

1. **feat:** an act of strength or courage

---

* From Carol Berkin et al., *Making America* (Boston: Houghton Mifflin Co., 2001), 276.

† Aesop fable from *The Complete Fables,* translated by Olivia and Robert Temple (New York: Penguin, 1998). Copyright © 1998 by Olivia and Robert Temple. Reprinted by permission of the authors.

7

2. What can you infer about the tortoise from this selection?

   a. The tortoise assumed that he could beat the hare without too much effort.

   b. The tortoise was aware of his slowness and worked hard to win the race.

   c. The tortoise wasn't as tired as the hare.

   d. There is nothing to infer about the tortoise from this selection.

3. What inference can you make about what the author is trying to convey in this selection?

   a. The author is warning against thinking too much of oneself.

   b. The author is saying that speed wins over intellect any day.

   c. The author is saying that hard work often triumphs over talent if the talents are not used effectively.

   d. The author isn't really saying anything worth mentioning.

Reading Strategy: REAP

REAP (Read-Encode-Annotate-Ponder) *is a strategy that guides you to respond to a text to improve your reading and thinking skills.* This method provides you with a system of four steps. When you follow these steps, you'll be training yourself to look deeper into the texts you read so you can more fully understand and evaluate them. As a result, your comprehension and critical thinking skills will improve.

STEP 1: Read. The first step involves *carefully reading the text* to understand the author's ideas and information.

STEP 2: Encode. Next, you *translate the text's message into your own words.* This step asks you to paraphrase the ideas or information to put it in language you understand.

STEP 3: Annotate. To **annotate** *means to write notes or comments about a text.* You can record these in the margins of the text, or in a notebook, or on separate sheets of paper. These notes can take the form of objective summaries or more subjective reactions to the ideas and information. For example, you could jot down your own feelings, opinions, or judgments.

STEP 4: Ponder. Finally, you continue to *reflect on what you have read and the notes you have written.* In this stage, you also read or discuss other people's responses to the same text in order to more fully explore its content. This sharing can take place formally in classroom settings or informally outside of the classroom.

Here is a sample passage annotated according to the REAP method:

Street Art

It's been called trash, scratching (by the ancient Greeks), and a crime (in today's society). Although many people see graffiti as a sign of gang activity or plain old defacement,[1] this very American grass-roots[2] art form blossomed in New York in the late 1960s, when inner-city kids just wanted to get noticed. Now a new book shows there's more to crafting graffiti than just spraying your name on a wall in black Rust-Oleum.

Most people are critical of graffiti. It seems like property destruction to me, but a new book claims that graffiti was more than just spray paint on walls.

The work of one such artist is chronicled in *Dondi White Style Master General: The Life of Graffiti Artist Dondi White* (Regan Books). Dondi, aka Donald White—who died of AIDS in 1998 at age 37—was one of the first "taggers," who used spray paint to transform subway cars and tunnels into irreverent[3] art galleries. What easier audience to capture than thousands of commuting strap-hangers?[4]

New book celebrates art of Dondi White. "Taggers" spray-painted subway cars and tunnels.

"His work looked like it had been taped off or die-cut.[5] Dondi made it look easy when, in fact, his planning was meticulous[6] and exhaustive,"[7] says Andrew "Zephyr" Witten, a friend who co-wrote the book with the artist's brother, Michael.

Dondi's friends and family believe he was very talented.

7

1. **defacement:** spoiling the surface or appearance of something
2. **grassroots:** related to the people or society at a local level rather than at the political center
3. **irreverent:** disrespectful
4. **strap-hangers:** subway riders who stand and hang on to straps
5. **die-cut:** cut out by a machine
6. **meticulous:** extremely careful and precise
7. **exhaustive:** thorough

Yesterday's trash has become today's treasure. While billions of dollars are spent each year to remove graffiti from public property, the works of White and other early taggers sell for thousands in galleries. And "bombing"—creating graffiti in one spurt—is sporadic[1] now, Witten says.*

Graffiti is expensive art now. Question: what form does the graffiti take? How can you buy paintings that were on subway walls?

If you are an auditory learner, try this link. This podcast from Australia discusses how to be a better reader.

https://academicskills.anu.edu.au/sites/default/files/skillsoup_tip_13.mp3

If you like to study with a group, you may want to try the KWL strategy that is demonstrated in this link.

http://www.studygs.net/texred3.htm

Now practice the REAP strategy on one of the following reading selections.

Reading Selections

Practicing the Active Reading Strategy

■ Before and While You Read

You can use active reading strategies before, while, and after you read a selection. The following are some suggestions for active reading strategies that you can employ before you read and as you are reading.

1. Skim the selection for any unfamiliar words. Circle or highlight any words you do not know.

2. As you read, underline, highlight, or circle important words or phrases.

3. Write down any questions about the selection if you are confused by the information presented.

4. Jot notes in the margin to help you understand the material.

---

1. **sporadic:** occurring irregularly

---

* Reading strategy adapted from "Street Art" by Robin Reid, as first appeared in *USA Weekend*, November 23–25, 2001, 17. Reprinted with permission of the author.

BIOGRAPHY:
Gullah

The first generation of slaves created a pidgin[1] so they could understand overseers and fellow slaves. Their children—second generation African Americans—had no use for their parents' mother tongues and they knew more English than their parents had. They transformed the pidgin into a creole.[2] Almost all slave creoles died out after emancipation. African Americans began to move around during Reconstruction and found their localized creoles useless.

1 On the "sea islands" off the coast of South Carolina and Georgia, Gullah, sometimes called Geechee, a creole language, survives to this day. It is still the language of home, church, and social occasions for thousands of people. At last count, between 5,000 and 8,000 mostly elderly sea islanders spoke only Gullah.

2 Because Gullah is not a written language, its history is something of a mystery. Even the origin of the name is disputed. The most obvious explanation is that Gullah is a corruption of Angola, which makes sense. During the final years of the legal African slave trade, 1803–1807, sea island planters imported 24,000 Africans, 60 percent of them from Angola (including present-day Congo). However, there is some evidence that the word "Gullah" was in use by 1750. Some linguists think it derives from Gola, a tribe that lived on the border of modern Liberia and Sierra Leone. Sea island planters favored Africans from that region because they were skilled rice growers. Similarities shared by Gullah and a creole still spoken in Sierra Leone, Krio, are so striking that Gullah may have first emerged not on the sea islands but in Africa.

3 Gullah's sounds are soft and spoken rapidly, not drawled. More than 90 percent of its vocabulary is English, but pronunciation differs so radically from American English pronunciation that visitors to the sea islands cannot understand more than the shortest, simplest statements. Spelled out phonetically, however, Gullah is easily deciphered. The first sentence of the Lord's Prayer in Gullah:

> Ow'urr Farruh, hu aht in Heh'um, hallowed be dy name, dy kingdom come, dy wil be done on ut as it done in heh'um.

4 How did Gullah thrive when other slave creoles died out? Cultural continuity is part of the reason. Before 1800, when the Angolans began to arrive, most sea island slaves' African roots were in a rather limited area of Sierra Leone. The isolation of the sea islands prevented the Gullahs from mixing with mainland slaves, reinforcing their sense of cohesion. Their creole was

---

1. **pidgin:** a simplified language that was consciously invented by different peoples in close contact who did not understand each other.

2. **creole:** When people elaborate on a pidgin so that it serves as their language, in which they can speak about a broad range of subjects

quite adequate for all their communications. Whites were few on the islands. Work was supervised by black slave drivers and even, at the top, black plantation managers. When the Civil War began, there were more than 33,000 blacks in the Beaufort district of South Carolina, and 6,700 whites. When Union troops occupied the islands early in the war, virtually every white southerner had fled. By 1870, 90 percent of St. Helena Island's population was black.

5   Because of their isolation, the Gullahs were generally more self-sufficient than most mainland slaves. When the Union army put up confiscated sea island plantations for sale, an astonishing number of Gullahs had enough money to buy farms albeit in small parcels. By 1870, seven of ten Gullah families owned their homes and farms.

6   African religious practices survived after the Gullahs became Methodists or Baptists in the early nineteenth century. White missionaries were frustrated to distraction when islanders explained that while a dead person's "soul" went to live with God in heaven, his "spirit" or ghost continued to roam the islands, sometimes helping descendants, sometimes doing them mischief. Only a century later was it learned that Gullah spirits had West African origins. The word *voodoo* entered the American language through the Gullahs, although, on the sea islands, it simply meant magic with none of the sinister connotations of West Indian voodoo as sensationalized in movies.

7   African folk tales survived longer and closer to the originals on the sea islands. Joel Chandler Harris, the white journalist who collected the B'rer Rabbit and other slave stories (now known to have African origins) found the sea islands his most productive hunting grounds. In 1925, DuBose Heyward wrote a play, *Porgy*, better known as the opera based on it, *Porgy and Bess*. It was set among Gullahs who, after the Civil War, moved to Charleston.*

■ Vocabulary

Read the following questions about some of the vocabulary words that appear in the previous selection. Before you look up the word, try to use the context of the passage to figure out the meaning. Then circle the letter of the correct answer for each question.

1. As used in paragraph 2, what does the word *corruption* mean?

   a. to saturate

   b. separation

   c. a departure from the original or from what is pure

   d. violation of ethical boundaries

---

* From CONLIN. The American Past, 9E. © 2010 Wadsworth, a part of Cengage Learning, Inc. Reproduced by permission. www.cengage.com/permissions

2. "Some *linguists* think it derived from Gola..." What does the word *linguist* mean? (paragraph 2)

   a. a specialist who studies human speech

   b. someone who teaches at a college

   c. a historian who studies slavery

   d. some who studies the history of languages

3. Paragraph 3 describes how Gullah managed to *thrive*. What does the word *thrive* mean?

   a. remain a secret   c. slacking

   b. grow vigorously   d. determined to finish

4. The author uses the word *cohesion* in paragraph 4. What does the word mean?

   a. same origin   c. hardship, hurt, and anger

   b. connection   d. isolation

5. "...an astonishing number of Gullahs had enough money to buy farms *albeit* in small parcel." What does the word *albeit* mean? (paragraph 5)

   a. since   c. purchased with assistance

   b. even though   d. needing to rent

■ Reading Skills

Respond to each of the following questions by circling the letter of the correct answer or by writing your answer on the blank provided.

1. The topic of paragraph 2 is

   a. sea island plantations   c. slaves from Sierra Leone

   b. origins of Gullah   d. the Krio tribe

2. What is the topic sentence of paragraph 3?

   a. sentence 1   c. sentence 3

   b. sentence 2   d. non stated

3. This reading selection refers several times to the isolation of the islands where Gullah developed. What can you infer about why these islands are so isolated?

   a. The islands are too far off the coast to be reached easily.

   b. The islands were privately owned and trespassing was not allowed.

   c. The plantation managers had large guard dogs to discourage people from visiting.

   d. The islands were swampy and filled with mosquitoes.

7

4. "Because Gullah is not a written language, its history is something of a mystery." What can you infer about this statement?

   a. Only written languages can be traced to their origins.

   b. Gullah is too confusing to ever be traced to its origins.

   c. The true origins of Gullah will never be known.

   d. Linguists' theories about the origins of Gullah must be based on spoken language similarities.

5. What is the major pattern of organization used in this reading selection?

   a. list

   b. sequence

   c. cause/effect

   d. comparison/contrast

Practicing the Active Reading Strategy

■ After You Read

Now that you have read the selection, answer the following questions, using the active reading strategies that you learned in Chapter 1.

1. Identify and write down the point and purpose of this reading selection.

2. Did you circle or highlight any words that are unfamiliar to you? Can you figure out the meaning from the context of the passage? If not, then look up each word in a dictionary and find the definition that best describes the word as it is used in the selection. You may want to write the definition in the margin next to the word in the passage for future reference.

3. Predict any possible questions that may be used on a test about the content of this selection.

■ Questions for Discussion and Writing

Respond to each of the following questions based on your reading of the selection.

1. Would you like to live on an isolated island? Explain your answer.

_____

_____

2. Do you think that the Gullah language and culture would have survived if there had been more white people on the islands? Explain your answer.

_____

_____

3. Is it important to study and preserve these unusual languages and cultures? Explain your answer.

_____

_____

Practicing the Active Reading Strategy

■ Before and While You Read

You can use active reading strategies before, while, and after you read a selection. The following are some suggestions for active reading strategies that you can employ before you read and as you are reading.

1. Skim the selection for any unfamiliar words. Circle or highlight any words you do not know.

2. As you read, underline, highlight, or circle important words or phrases.

3. Write down any questions about the selection if you are confused by the information presented.

4. Jot notes in the margin to help you understand the material.

TEXTBOOK READING: SPORTS MEDICINE
Disordered Eating: Extreme Weight Control

Have you ever participated in a sport where your weight was an issue? How did you control your weight? There can be serious health issues for young people who practice extreme measures to maintain a certain weight for athletic purposes.

1   Disordered eating patterns are extreme expressions of food and weight issues experienced by many individuals, particularly girls and women. They include anorexia nervosa, bulimia nervosa, and binge eating. These disorders are very dangerous behaviors that result in health problems.

2   Participants in sports that emphasize appearance and a lean body are at higher risk for developing disordered eating behavior. Many female athletes who engage

in harmful methods of weight control suffer from amenorrhea and bone loss. Amenorrhea is the abnormal suppression or absence of menstruation.

3   According to a 2007 Harvard University study, 25 percent of all the athletes with disordered eating behavior are male. The term now associated with this condition is manorexia. The symptoms of anorexia and bulimia are similar for men and women, but the underlying cause can be quite different. A common issue for men is having been overweight as a child and teased about it.

4   One particular issue with male disordered eating concerns the sport of wrestling, which has several different weight classifications. These classifications require the athlete to make the weight limit or forfeit the match. This encourages extreme weight- loss measures aimed at losing a few pounds as quickly as possible. These athletes often wear rubber suits while exercising, chew gum and spit excess saliva into a cup, fast, and drink no fluids. These methods of losing weight are unhealthy, and sometimes deadly. It is imperative that coaches and parents monitor these athletes carefully so that they do not "make weight" at the risk of their health.

5   In 1992, the American College of Sports Medicine termed a collection of symptoms diagnosed in female athletes the "female athlete triad." The triad consists of disordered eating, amenorrhea, and osteoporosis (bone loss). The triad is especially prevalent in sports that emphasize the aesthetic[1] of leanness, such as gymnastics, figure skating, diving, and dance. It is also seen in sports such as swimming and running, where leanness is thought to yield a competitive edge.

6   Because the triad may result in irreversible bone loss and death, early detection is important. Some signs and symptoms include eating alone, trips to the bathroom during or after meals, use of laxatives, fatigue, anemia, depression, and eroded tooth enamel from frequent vomiting. Treatment of the female athlete triad involves education, nutrition, determining contributing factors, and care from a medical specialist trained in disordered eating. The rate of eating disorders among non-athletes is believed to be between 3 and 8 percent, and among female athletes anywhere from 15 to 62 percent.*

---

1. **aesthetic:** beauty or good taste

---

* Robert C. France, *Introduction to Sports Medicine and Athletic Training,* 2nd ed. (Clifton Park: Delmar, 2011), 144–45. Print.

■ Vocabulary

Read the following questions about some of the vocabulary words that appear in the previous selection. Before you look up the word, try to use the context of the passage to figure out the meaning. Then circle the letter of the correct answer for each question.

1. *Suppression* in paragraph 2 means _____.

   a. secrets

   b. stoppage

   c. highlights

   d. encouragement

2. If a wrestler must *forfeit* a match, what must he do? (paragraph 4)

   a. lose

   b. win

   c. do over

   d. tie

3. Something that is *imperative* is _____. (paragraph 4)

   a. lost

   b. deadly

   c. extremely important

   d. not important

4. Eating disorders are *prevalent* in certain sports. What does *prevalent* mean? (paragraph 5)

   a. rare

   b. normal

   c. not present

   d. widespread

5. Paragraph 6 identifies *anemia* as a sign or symptom to watch for in female athletes. What is *anemia*?

   a. lack of energy

   b. need to be hospitalized

   c. need mental help

   d. are overweight

■ Reading Skills

Respond to each of the following questions by circling the letter of the correct answer or by writing your answer on the blank provided.

1. The topic sentence in paragraph 1 indicates that the pattern of organization for this paragraph will be _____.

   a. list

   b. definition

   c. cause/effect

   d. contrast

2. Paragraphs 2 and 3 each contain definition context clues. What two terms are defined?

a. _____

b. _____

3. From the information in the reading selection, what can be inferred about disordered eating among male athletes?

a. Football players do not have weight issues.

b. Male athletes were teased as young boys.

c. Male athletes were overweight as young boys.

d. Wrestlers are at risk for eating disorders.

4. What can be inferred about female athletes from the information in paragraph 5?

a. All female athletes suffer from eating disorders.

b. Female athletes care more than male athletes about their body image.

c. Certain female athletes are more likely to suffer from health issues.

d. Females should not participate in sports.

5. What can be inferred from the last two sentences of paragraph 6?

_____

_____

Practicing the Active Reading Strategy

■ After You Read

Now that you have read the selection, answer the following questions, using the active reading strategies that you learned in Chapter 1.

1. Identify and write down the point and purpose of this reading selection.

2. Did you circle or highlight any words that are unfamiliar to you? Can you figure out the meaning from the context of the passage? If not, then look up each word in a dictionary and find the definition that best describes the word as it is used in the selection. You may want to write the definition in the margin next to the word in the passage for future reference.

3. Predict any possible questions that may be used on a test about the content of this selection.

■ Questions for Discussion and Writing

Respond to each of the following questions based on your reading of the selection.

1. In what sport are males most at risk for eating disorders? _____
   List two sports where women are most at risk from eating disorders.

   _____

2. Have you ever participated in a sport where you had to maintain your weight? If so, what was your experience?

   _____

3. What can or should be done to help young athletes prevent these kinds of health problems?

   _____

Practicing the Active Reading Strategy

■ Before and While You Read

You can use active reading strategies before, while, and after you read a selection. The following are some suggestions for active reading strategies that you can employ before you read and as you are reading.

1. Skim the selection for any unfamiliar words. Circle or highlight any words you do not know.
2. As you read, underline, highlight, or circle important words or phrases.
3. Write down any questions about the selection if you are confused by the information presented.
4. Jot notes in the margin to help you understand the material.

7

WEBSITE READING: SOCIOLOGY
Americans with Accents Judged Less Credible than Native Speakers

by Elizabeth Weise

Do you think you speak with an accent? Do you know people who speak with an accent that is different than yours? Do you have trouble understanding them? Do you take them less seriously if you cannot understand them?

1   For the 24.5 million Americans who told the Census Bureau in 2007 that they spoke English less than "very well," it may not be their imagination that people don't take what they say quite as seriously as they do native English speakers.

2   Researchers in Chicago have shown that people with a noticeable accent are considered less credible than those with no accent. The stronger the accent, the less credible the speaker. The researchers asked Americans to listen to native and non-native speakers of English making simple statements such as "A giraffe can go without water longer than a camel can," and then judge how truthful they were. To guard against simple prejudice, the listeners were told the information came from a prepared script and wasn't based on the speaker's own knowledge. Even so, on a scale where 10 was most truthful, native English speakers got a score of 7.5, people with mild accents a score of 6.95, and people with heavy accents a score of 6.84.

3   "The accent makes it harder for people to understand what the non-native speaker is saying," Boaz Keysar, a professor of psychology at the University of Chicago said in a statement. "They misattribute the difficulty of understanding the speech to the truthfulness of the statements." While research has clearly shown accent affects how a person is perceived, how much having an accent affected a person's credibility hadn't been known, he said. Even when the participants were told that the test was to determine whether accents influence how truthful people sound, the effect didn't go away. In that case, speakers with mild accents were considered as truthful as native speakers but those with heavy accents were judged less truthful.*

■ Vocabulary

Read the following questions about some of the vocabulary words that appear in the previous selection. Before you look up the word, try to use the context of the passage to figure out the meaning. Then circle the letter of the correct answer for each question.

1. The word *native,* as it is used in paragraph 1, means _____.

   a. from birth

   b. adopted

   c. Indian tribes of the Southwest

   d. poor

2. In paragraph 2, what does *credible* mean?

   a. understandable

   b. believable

   c. wealthy

   d. interesting

---

* Weise, Elizabeth. "Study: Americans with accents judged less credible than native speakers." www.content .usatoday.com/communities/.../1 20 July 2010. Web. USA TODAY. July 20, 2010. Reprinted with permission.

3. *Prejudice,* as used in paragraph 2, means _____.

    a. doubt   c. opinions formed beforehand

    b. knowledge   d. ignorance

4. If someone *misattributes* information, what have they done? (paragraph 3)

    a. wrongly credit   c. cannot hear

    b. cannot understand   d. cannot read

5. *Perceived* in paragraph 3 is contrasted to credibility. What does *perceived* mean?

    a. believed   c. ignored

    b. understood   d. hated

■ Reading Skills

Respond to each of the following questions by circling the letter of the correct answer or by writing your answer on the blank provided.

1. What is the contrast transition in paragraph 2? _____

2. What sentence in paragraph 2 contains the topic sentence?

    _____

    _____

3. Which sentence in paragraph 2 contains the best information to support

    the main idea? _____

    _____

    _____

4. What did the researchers infer from their data about the believability of

    people with accents? _____

    _____

Practicing the Active Reading Strategy

■ After You Read

Now that you have read the selection, answer the following questions, using the active reading strategies that you learned in Chapter 1.

7

1. Identify and write down the point and purpose of this reading selection.

2. Did you circle or highlight any words that are unfamiliar to you? Can you figure out the meaning from the context of the passage? If not, then look up each word in a dictionary and find the definition that best describes the word as it is used in the selection. You may want to write the definition in the margin next to the word in the passage for future reference.

3. Predict any possible questions that may be used on a test about the content of this selection.

■ Questions for Discussion and Writing

Respond to each of the following questions based on your reading of the selection.

1. What did you learn about prejudice toward people with accents from this reading selection?

_____

_____

2. How do you behave toward people you cannot understand due to their accents?

_____

_____

3. Do you think that people who have heavy accents are believable? Why or why not?

_____

_____

Vocabulary Strategy: Formal vs. Informal Language

When you read, you should be able to distinguish between formal and informal language. **Formal language** *is usually serious, businesslike, and often sophisticated.* This is the type of language that is most prevalent in scholarly, academic, and business writing. Most textbooks, college assignments, and business reports, for example, are written using formal language. **Informal language** *is closer to that of conversation.* It is more casual, often including colloquial (everyday) words, slang terms, idioms (expressions like "She's trying to butter me up"), abbreviations, and even humor.

The level of formality in a reading selection helps the reader know how the author feels about his or her subject. A passage or document written in a formal style communicates the author's belief that the subject is important and significant. A more informal style can suggest that the author is more lighthearted about the topic.

To understand the difference between formal and informal language, first take a look at an informal statement from one of the examples in this chapter:

> There are **guys** in my neighborhood who still **sport** their college's name on their **car** window.

The boldfaced, italicized words are colloquial and casual. Notice, though, how the substitution of different words increases the sentence's formality:

> There are **gentlemen** in my neighborhood who still **affix** their college's name to their **vehicle** window.

Vocabulary Exercise

Use the italicized words in each of the following sentences to decide whether the language is formal or informal. Then, on the blank after each sentence, write *FORMAL* or *INFORMAL*.

1. He'll give you a new *'do* at 3 A.M. _____

2. One such *incident* so *angered* the plantation overseer that he hit her over the head with a lead weight, *inflicting* a permanent brain injury that would cause her to suddenly *lose consciousness* several times a day for the rest of her life. _____

3. *Mess up* one word and *you're history.* _____

4. [The middle class] has what is called a *conceptual orientation*, using their *mental capacities* to solve problems, and their jobs often involve the *manipulation of symbols* rather than objects. _____

5. *Barney-haters* may have fresh *ammo.* _____

6. *Nerds* are supposed to be friendless *bookworms* who *suck up* to authority figures. Furthermore, we're *sissies.* _____

7

Chapter 7 Review

Fill in each of the blanks in the following statements by writing the correct answer.

1. An _____ is a conclusion you draw that's based upon the stated information.

2. _____ use their knowledge, experiences, and observations to help them make inferences.

3. Writers ask readers to make inferences to keep their writing _____, and fun for the reader.

4. To make accurate inferences, readers should avoid _____ information that's not in a text. On the other hand, they should not ignore any details provided.

5. To make accurate inferences, readers should make sure nothing _____ a conclusion, and they should avoid letting stereotypes or _____ affect their conclusions.

6. When writing a paper for a history class, college students should use _____ language.

7. Slang is an example of _____ language.

8. Identify and explain each step of the REAP learning strategy:

   R _____

   _____

   E _____

   A _____

   _____

   P _____

Reading Visual Aids

Goals for Chapter 8

■ Define the term *visual aid*.

■ Summarize the reasons authors incorporate visual aids into texts.

■ Describe three general steps to follow to interpret a visual aid.

■ Define the term *table* and identify its purpose and parts.

■ Define the term *organizational chart* and identify its purpose and parts.

■ Define the term *flow chart* and identify its purpose and parts.

■ Define the term *pie chart* and identify its purpose and parts.

■ Define the term *line graph* and identify its purpose and parts.

■ Define the term *bar graph* and identify its purpose and parts.

■ Define the term *diagram* and identify its purpose and parts.

■ Define the term *map* and identify its purpose and parts.

■ Write a reading journal entry.

As you read, you will often encounter visual aids such as graphs, tables, and diagrams. Learning how to read and interpret these visuals will improve your overall comprehension of a text. To discover what you already know about visuals, complete the following pretest.

Pretest

A. Look at the following visual and then answer the questions that follow by writing your responses on the blanks provided.

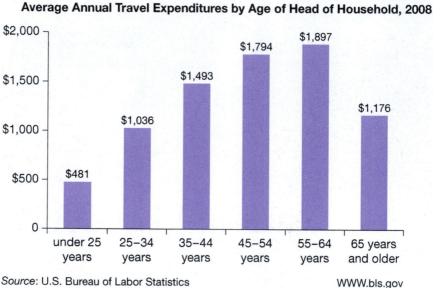

Average Annual Travel Expenditures by Age of Head of Household, 2008

Source: U.S. Bureau of Labor Statistics   WWW.bls.gov

Figure 8.1 Average annual travel expenditures by age of head of household, 2008

Source: http://www.bls.gov/spotlight/2010/travel/

1. What does this visual describe? _____

_____

2. Which group spent the most money on travel in 2008? How much did they spend? _____

3. How much money did people under 25 years old spend on travel in 2008?

_____

4. What seems to be the trend in the first five groups?

_____

5. Why do you think there might be a drop in travel spending for people 65 years and older? _____
_____

B. Study the following pie chart and answer the questions that follow by writing your responses on the blanks provided.

What Portion of Annual Household Expenditures is Spent on Travel?
Average annual travel-related expenditures, 2008

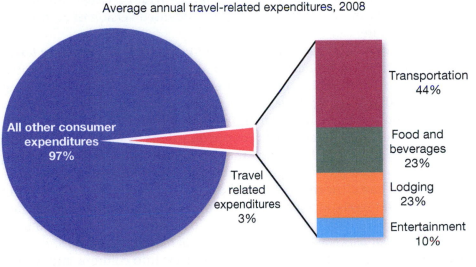

Source: U.S. Bureau of Labor Statistics   WWW.bls.gov

Figure 8.2 **What portion of annual household expenditures is spent on travel?**

Source: http://www.bls.gov/spotlight/2010/travel/

6. What percentage of a household budget is spent on travel? _____

7. How many categories is the travel expenditure split into? _____

8. Which travel category takes the most money? _____

9. What percentage of the travel expenditure is spent on lodging? _____

10. What travel category has the least travel money spent on it?

_____

Visual aids, which are also known as **graphics**, *are types of illustrations that represent data or information in a visual form.* Visual aids include tables, charts, different types of graphs, diagrams, and maps. You will often encounter all of these kinds of visuals when you read, especially when the purpose of a reading selection is to inform or explain. Publications such as textbooks, magazines, journals, and instruction manuals will often include visuals to aid, or help, the reader in understanding the information. Many job-related documents will also contain visual aids.

Texts include visual aids for many reasons. For one thing, *they can summarize a lot of information or complex information in a relatively small space.* Think about a flow chart, for instance. A flow chart provides a visual summary of the steps in a process. It allows you to see a condensed version of even a complicated procedure.

Another reason for visual aids is their ability to clarify and reinforce textual explanations. In most publications, visual aids do not substitute for written presentation of information. Instead, they provide another way of "seeing" what the words are saying. A diagram in an instruction manual is one example. When you are assembling something like a grill or a child's swing set, it's helpful to check your understanding of the directions by looking at a diagram that labels the parts and shows how they fit together. You use both the written explanation and the visual aid to figure out what you need to do.

Visual aids also allow readers to quickly see the important data or facts. For instance, a graph reveals, at a glance, trends over time. An organizational chart allows readers to quickly grasp the chain of command within a company.

Finally, visual aids provide a way for readers to find a particular detail quickly and easily. A table, for example, that organizes facts into columns and rows allows a reader to easily locate one specific piece of information he or she needs.

General Tips for Reading Visual Aids

The following tips will help you improve your comprehension of reading selections that include visuals:

■ **Don't skip a visual aid.** Passive readers ignore visual aids because they don't want to take the time to read them. Skipping visual aids, however, robs you of chances to improve and/or reinforce your understanding of the information in the text. Authors invest the time and effort necessary to create a visual because they believe a visual representation is particularly important. Therefore, get in the habit of reading over each visual as well as the text.

■ **Look at a visual aid when the text directs you to do so.** As you read, you'll come across references to visual aids. Resist the urge to "save them for later." Instead, when a sentence mentions a visual, as in "See Figure 2," or "Table 1 presents the results" and tells you where to find it (below, to the left, on page 163, etc.), find the visual and read it before going any further. Remember, most visuals reinforce information in a text. The writer's explanation will often state the conclusion you should draw from the visual, and the visual provides more insight into the textual explanation. Therefore, you'll get more out of both of them when you read a passage and corresponding visual together.

■ **Follow a three-step procedure for interpreting the information in a visual aid:**

1. **First, read the title, the caption, and the source line.** The title and caption, or brief description, will usually identify the visual aid's subject and main point. (Not all visuals will have a caption, however. So when a caption is available be sure to read the explanatory information.) They will help you understand what you're seeing. The source line, which identifies where the information comes from, will help you decide whether the information is accurate and trustworthy.

2. **Next, study the information represented in the visual and try to state the relationships you see in your own words.** For example, you might say, "This graph shows that sales of sport utility vehicles have been growing since 1985," or "This table shows that teachers in the Midwest earn higher salaries than teachers in the rest of the country."

3. **Finally, check your understanding of the relationship against its corresponding explanation in the text.** Locate where the visual is mentioned and verify that the conclusion you drew is accurate.

The remainder of this chapter will cover the most common types of visual aids and provide you with more specific tips for improving your understanding of each kind.

Common Types of Visuals

8

As you read, you'll most often encounter tables, charts, graphs, diagrams, and maps.

Tables

A **table** *is a visual aid that organizes information or data in rows and columns.* A table might list types, categories, figures, statistics, steps in a process, or other kinds of information. Its purpose is to summarize many related details in a concise format so that readers can read them easily and find specific facts quickly.

Tables contain the following parts:

- **Title.** The title states the visual aid's subject.

- **Column headings.** These labels identify the type of information you'll find in the vertical lists.

- **Source line.** The source line identifies who collected or compiled the information in the table.

These parts are labeled in the table below.

Table 8.1 **Number of Juvenile Arrests in 2006 — 2.2 Million**

The 2.2 million arrests of Juveniles in 2006 was 24% fewer than the number of arrests in 1997

Most Serious Offence	2006 Estimated Number of Juvenile Arrests	Percent of Total Juvenile Arrests		Percent Change		
		Female	Under Age 15	1997 — 2006	2002 — 2006	2005 — 2006
Total	2,219,600	29%	29%	–24%	–3%	1%
Violent Crime Index	**100,700**	**17**	**29**	**–20**	**8**	**4**
Murdur and nonnegligent manslaughter	1,310	5	8	–42	18	3
Forcible rape	3,610	2	36	–31	–20	–10
Robbery	35,040	9	23	–16	34	19
Aggravated assault	60,770	23	32	–21	–1	–2
Property Crime Index	**404,700**	**32**	**33**	**–44**	**–17**	**–5**
Burglary	83,900	11	32	–37	–6	5
Larceny-theft	278,100	41	34	–45	–19	–8

Data source: Crime in the United States 2006. Washington, DC: Federal Bureau of Investigation, 2007, tables 29, 32, 34, 36, 38, and 40. From Karen M. Hess, *Juvenile Justice,* 5th ed. (Belmont: Wadsworth, 2010), 168.

To understand the information in a table, first read the title, which will identify the kind of information the table includes. Next, familiarize yourself with the column and row headings. They will identify the kind of details included. Then, form an understanding of the relationships first by moving your eyes down each column to see how details compare and then across each row to see how those details are related. Finally, try to state in your own words the overall point revealed by the table's lists.

In the table on page 310, the title states that this visual aid will focus on the number of juvenile arrests in 2006. The most serious offenses are listed in the first column, which contains the row headings. These crimes are then broken up into subcategories so a reader can find both totals for types of crimes as well as more specific listings. The second column gives the estimated number of arrests for 2006 for each crime. The third and forth columns are subcategories of the percent of total juvenile arrests. Because there is no column for male arrests or for juveniles over the age of 15, those numbers would make up the difference from the percentage given for females and juveniles under the age of 15. The last columns in the table show the arrests made in a decade, a five-year period at the end of the decade, and a one-year period at the very end. A negative percentage would indicate that arrests had decreased from the previous time period.

Exercise **8.1**

Study the following table and then answer the questions that follow by writing your responses on the blanks provided.

Table 8.2 **Average January Low Temperatures (°F) for some of the Coldest Cities in the United States**

City	Average January Low Temperature (F°)
Fairbanks, AK	−19.0°
Tower, MN*	−13.6°
Int'l Falls, MN	−8.4°
Gumlson, CO	−6.1°
Grand Forks, ND	−4.3°
Bemldji, MN	−4.3°
Alamosa, CO	−3.7°
Williston, ND	−3.3°
Fargo, ND	−2.3°
St. Cloud, MN	−1.2°
Duluth, MN	−1.2°
Bismarck, ND	−0.6°
Carlbou, ME	−0.3°
Aberdeen, SD	0.6°
Minneapolis, MN**	4.3°

*Coldest inhabited place in lower 48 states.
**Coldest major metro area in the United States.
Source: From Ahrens/Samson. *Extreme Weather and Climate,* 1E. © 2011 Brooks/Cole, a part of Cengage Learning, Inc. Reproduced by permission. www.cengage.com/permissions.

1. How many cities are listed in the table for comparison? _____

_____

2. In which two cities does the average January low not drop below zero?

_____

_____

3. What is the coldest inhabited place in the lower 48 states? _____

_____

4. Which state has the most cities in this table? _____

_____

5. Where is the coldest major metropolitan area in the United States?

_____

Charts

Charts can be many different types. Three of the more common are organizational charts, flow charts, and pie charts. Each kind presents a different kind of relationship.

An **organizational chart** *is one that shows the chain of command in a company or organization.* It uses rectangles and lines to show the managerial relationships among the individuals within a group. Its purpose is to represent the lines of authority and responsibility in the organization.

An organizational chart contains the following parts:

■ **Title.** The title usually identifies the organization or the part of an organization being described.

■ **Boxes.** Each box, or rectangle, represents one entity within the organization. That entity might be an individual or a group of individuals, such as a department. Each box will be labeled with a name, a job title, or a department name. These boxes are arranged in a hierarchy, or ranking: the person or group with the most authority and responsibility is at the top of the chart. Each subsequent row of boxes represents the next layer of authority, a group of people or groups who are equal in rank and who all report to the individual(s) in the layer above.

■ **Lines.** The lines connect boxes to show managerial relationships. They indicate who reports to whom. The source line, if applicable, identifies who collected or compiled the information in the chart.

These parts are labeled in the following organizational chart:

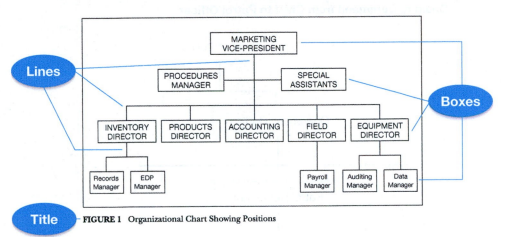

FIGURE 1 Organizational Chart Showing Positions

Figure 8.3 **Organization Chart Showing Positions**

Source: From *The Business Writer's Handbook,* 5th edition, by Charles Brusaw, Walter Oliu, and Gerald Alred. Copyright © 1997 by Bedford/St. Martin's. Used with permission of the publisher.

To understand an organizational chart, begin at the top. Read the label in the box at the top and then follow the lines to see which individuals and groups are related to each other.

The portion of the organizational chart on this page shows a company structure that places the marketing vice president at the top of the hierarchy. That individual has the most authority and responsibility. The staff positions listed beneath the vice president advise him and report to him, but they do not supervise the different directors who make up the next layer of authority. Those directors report to the vice president. The branching lines that descend from each box in the chart indicate the number and titles of individuals who are managed by that person.

Exercise **8.2**

Study the organizational chart and then answer the questions that follow by writing your responses on the blanks provided.

Chain of Command from Chief to Patrol Officer

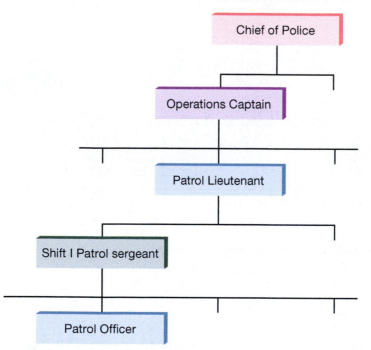

Figure 8.4 **Chain of Command from Chief to Patrol Officer**

Source: From Anderson/Ferro. *Connecting with Computer Science,* 2E. © 2011 South-Western, a part of Cengage Learning, Inc. Reproduced by permission. www.cengage.com/permissions.

1. What is the title of the person in charge of the police department?

   _____

2. To whom does the patrol officer report? _____

3. To whom does the operations captain give orders? _____

4. Why might there be lines on this organizational chart that do not have titles attached to them? _____

A **flow chart** *is a visual aid composed of boxes, circles, or other shapes along with lines or arrows.* The purpose of a flow chart is to represent the sequence of steps or stages in a process.

The parts of a flow chart are:

■ **Title.** The title identifies the process or procedure summarized in the chart.

■ **Boxes or other shapes.** Each box contains one step in the process. The boxes are arranged either top to bottom or left to right.

■ **Lines or arrows.** Lines or arrows show the sequence of steps.

■ **Source line.** The source line, if applicable, identifies who collected or compiled the information in the chart.

These parts are labeled in the following flow chart:

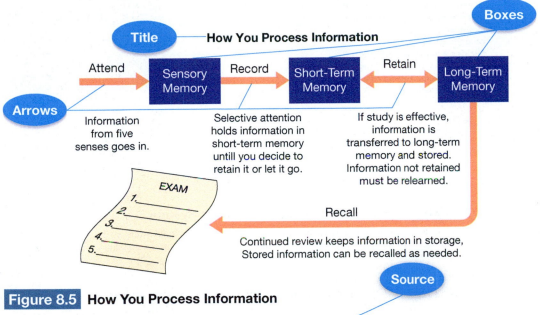

Figure 8.5 **How You Process Information**

Source: From Kanar. *The Confident Student*, 7E. © 2011 Wadsworth, a part of Cengage Learning, Inc. Reproduced by permission. www.cengage.com/permissions.

To interpret a flow chart, read the chart's title so you'll know what process is being summarized. Next, begin with the box at the top, if the chart is organized vertically, or the box at the far left, if the chart is organized horizontally. Read each step in order, following the lines and arrows to understand their sequence.

As the title indicates, the simple flow chart on this page summarizes how you process information. The process begins with attending to information. The arrow indicates that the information goes in to sensory memory first. The second arrow shows that the information is then recorded in short-term memory. From there the information, if learned, goes into long-term memory. If the information is not learned, then it must be relearned. The final arrow shows that information from long-term memory can then be recalled for an important exam.

Exercise 8.3

Study the flow chart below and then write your answers to the questions that follow by writing your responses on the blanks provided.

Three Functions of the Nervous System

The nervous system's three main functions are to receive information (input), integrate that information with past experiences (processing), and guide actions (output). When the alarm clock goes off, this person's nervous system, like yours, gets the message, recognizes what it means, decides what to do, and then takes action, by getting out of bed or perhaps hitting the snooze button.

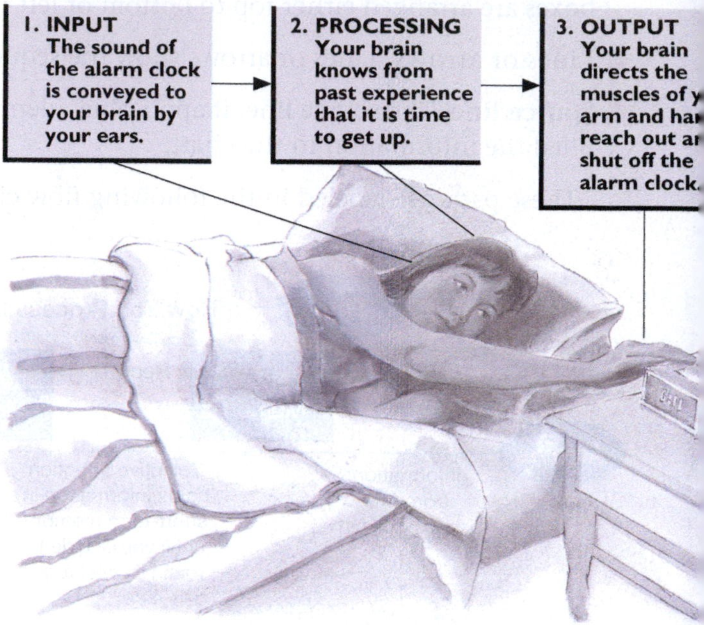

I. INPUT
The sound of the alarm clock is conveyed to your brain by your ears.

2. PROCESSING
Your brain knows from past experience that it is time to get up.

3. OUTPUT
Your brain directs the muscles of y[...] arm and ha[...] reach out a[...] shut off the alarm clock.

Figure 8.6 **Three Functions of the Nervous System**

Source: From Bernstein/Penner/Clarke-Stewart/Roy. *Psychology,* 6E. © 2003 Wadsworth, a part of Cengage Learning, Inc. Reproduced by permission. www.cengage.com/permissions.

1. What are the three major functions of the nervous system?

   _____

2. What example is used to illustrate the three functions of the nervous system on the flow chart? _____

3. As illustrated on the flow chart, what happens during the "input" stage? _____

4. According to the chart, what happens during step 2, or during the "processing" part illustrated on the flow chart? _____

   _____

5. During what stage illustrated on the flow chart does your "brain direct the muscles of your arm and hand to reach out and shut off the alarm clock"? _____

A third kind of chart is called a **pie chart.** This visual aid *is a circle that is divided into wedges or slices, like the pieces of a pie.* The purpose of a pie chart is to show the composition of something; it indicates the amounts of each part that make up the whole. Each part is identified with a percentage or other quantity that indicates its size in relation to all of the other parts. One common use of pie charts is to represent financial information such as budgets or expenditures.

Pie charts contain the following parts:

■ **Title.** The title identifies the whole entity that is being divided into parts.

■ **Lines.** The lines radiate from the center of the circle, dividing the pie in pieces that represent the amount of each part. These pieces are different sizes because they are designed to be proportional to the whole.

■ **Labels for names of parts.** Each piece is labeled to identify one part and its quantity in relation to the whole.

■ **Source line.** The source line identifies who collected or compiled the information.

These parts are labeled in the following pie chart:

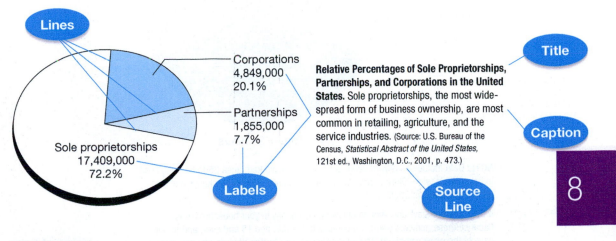

Figure 8.7 **Relative Percentages of Sole Propietorships, Partnerships, and Corporations in the United States**

To read a pie chart, first look at its title so you'll know the whole entity that is being divided. Then, read each label and amount. Try to summarize in your own words the relationships you see and notice the biggest part, the smallest part, and parts that are about equal.

The pie chart on page 317 shows the numbers and percentages of three forms of business ownership. The largest piece of the pie represents sole proprietorships, which account for about 72 percent of all businesses. Corporations are the next biggest group, and partnerships are the smallest. The percentages all add up to 100 percent to represent the whole. The caption provides more information by naming some examples of specific sole proprietorship businesses.

Exercise 8.4

Study the pie chart below and then write your answers to the following questions by writing your responses on the blanks provided.

Time Use on an Average Work Day for Employed Persons Ages 25 to 54 with Children

Total = 24 hours

NOTE: Data include employed persons on days they worked, ages 25 to 54, who lived in households with children under 18. Data include non-holiday weekdays and are annual averages for 2009.

If this "average day" does not sound like a typical day in your household, it is because these numbers are for all persons in the U.S. age 15 and over, and for all days of the week combined. The information can be further analyzed by age, sex, employment status, day of the week, or presence and age of household children.

Source: Bureau of Labor Statistics

Figure 8.8 **Time use on an average work day for employed persons ages 25 to 54 with children**

Source: http://www.bls.gov/tus/charts/home.htm

1. At what activities do people spend the least amount of time?

_____

2. At what two activities do people spend the greatest amount of time?

_____

3. How much time per day on average do people spend on leisure and sports activities? _____

4. This chart contains information about people with children. How much time on average per day is spend caring for others? _____

5. According to the caption, into what smaller categories might this information be subdivided? _____

_____

Graphs

A **graph** *is a visual aid composed of lines or bars that correspond to numbers or facts arranged along a vertical axis, or side, and a horizontal axis.* The purpose of a graph is to show changes or differences in amounts, quantities, or characteristics. Two types of graphs are the line graph and the bar graph. Each one presents information differently.

A **line graph** *is composed of points plotted within a vertical axis and a horizontal axis and then connected with lines.* Line graphs typically reveal changes or trends in numerical data over time. They demonstrate how two factors interact with each other. The horizontal axis is labeled with increments of time, such as years or minutes. The vertical axis is labeled with quantities. For each point in time, a dot on the graph indicates the corresponding quantity. Then, these dots are all connected to show upward and downward movement.

Line graphs contain the following parts:

■ **Title.** The title points out the type of numbers being examined. It corresponds to the label of the vertical axis.

■ **Vertical axis.** This line, which runs up and down, is divided into regular increments of numbers that correspond to the type of data being tracked. This axis is labeled to identify the type of data.

■ **Horizontal axis.** This line, which runs from left to right, is divided into segments of time. It, too, is labeled to identify the kind of time factor being used.

8

■ **Points.** Numerical data are plotted at the points where numbers and time factors intersect on the grid. These points may be labeled with specific amounts.

■ **Lines.** Points are connected with lines to show trends.

■ **Source line.** The source line identifies who collected or compiled the information in the graph.

These parts are labeled on the following line graph:

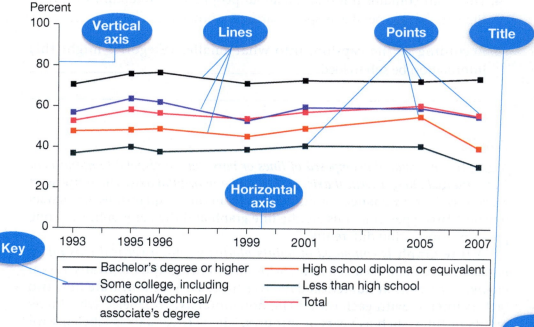

Figure 8.9 **Indicator ed1: percentage of children ages 3–5 who were read to every day in the last week by a family member by mother's education, selected years 1993–2007**

Source: U.S. Department of Education, National Center for Education Statistics, National Household Education Surveys Program.

To read a line graph, begin with the title. Read it carefully to understand the numerical value on which the graph focuses. Then, read the labels on the vertical and horizontal axes to understand what two factors are interacting. Finally, examine the line that connects the points and try to state in your own words the trends being revealed by the numbers. Do the numbers increase, decrease, or both? When? How much overall change has occurred during the time span indicated on the horizontal axis?

As the title indicates, the line graph on page 320 contrasts the educational level of mothers who have small children for whom a family member reads to each day. The vertical axis shows the percentage of children who are read to by a family member every day. The horizontal axis is divided into years to show the trends of reading to small children. There are five lines on the graph. Four of the lines indicate the educational level of the mother in the household and one line shows the total average of children who are read to each day. The points for all lines from 1996 to 1999 show a change with the top three levels dropping and the bottom level rising. There is another change from 2005 to 2007 with a drop in all but the top level of education.

Exercise **8.5**

Study the line graph below and then answer the questions that follow by writing your responses on the blanks provided.

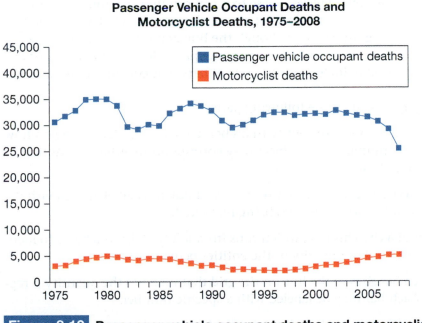

Passenger Vehicle Occupant Deaths and Motorcyclist Deaths, 1975–2008

■ Passenger vehicle occupant deaths
■ Motorcyclist deaths

Figure 8.10 **Passenger vehicle occupant deaths and motorcyclist deaths, 1975–2008**

Source: http://www.iihs.org/research/fatality_facts_2008/motorcycles.html. Used by permission of the Insurance Institute for Highway Safety.

1. Since the late 1990s, have motorcycle deaths increased or decreased?

   _____

2. What has been the trend in passenger vehicle occupant deaths since 2000?

   _____

3. Approximately how many people died as a result of a motorcycle accident in 2005? _____

4. Are you more likely to die as a result of a motorcycle accident or as a passenger in a vehicle? Why do you think there is such a difference in these numbers? _____

   _____

5. In what year was the number of motorcycle deaths the lowest?

   _____

A second kind of graph is a *bar graph*. **Bar graphs** *indicate quantities of something with bars or rectangles.* These bars can run upward from the horizontal axis or sideways from the vertical axis of the graph. Each bar is labeled to show what is being measured. Although the line graph includes a time factor, the bar graph may not; it focuses on varying quantities of some factor or factors, although it may include several sets of bars that correspond to different time periods.

A bar graph includes the following parts:

■ **Title.** The title reveals the entity that's being measured. Depending on how the graph is arranged, this subject may correspond to either the vertical or the horizontal axis.

■ **Vertical axis.** This line, which runs up and down, is labeled with either a kind of quantity or the entities being measured.

■ **Horizontal axis.** This line, which runs from left to right, is labeled to identify either a kind of quantity or the entities being measured.

■ **Bars.** Each bar rises to the line on the grid that matches the quantity it represents. Each bar may be labeled with a specific number.

■ **Key.** If entities are broken down into subgroups, the graph may include bars of different colors to represent each group. In that case, a key, or explanation of what each color signifies, may accompany the graph.

■ **Source line.** The source line identifies who collected or compiled the information in the bar graph.

These parts are labeled on the bar graph below:

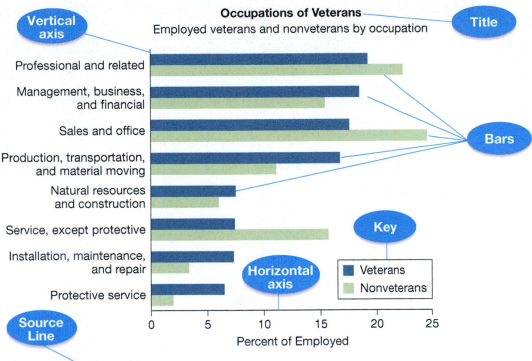

Source: U.S. Bureau of Labor Statistics

Figure 8.11 **Occupations of Veterans**

Source: http://www.bls.gov/spotlight/2010/veterans/

To interpret the information in a bar graph, read the title first to find out what is being measured. Next, read the labels of the vertical and horizontal axes to understand how the graph is arranged and what type of quantity is being used. Finally, examine each bar and try to state, in your own words, the relationship among them. Which entity is largest? Smallest? Are there large discrepancies between two or more of the entities?

The bar graph above shows the differences in various occupations of veterans and nonveterans. Among the notable relationships indicated by the bars are the following:

■ In 2009, veterans were more likely than nonveterans to work in production, transportation, and material moving occupations; installation, maintenance, and repair occupations; and protective service occupations.

■ Most veterans are men, and men are more likely than women to be employed in these occupations.

■ Nonveterans were more likely than veterans to work in service occupations, excluding protective service, and in sales and office occupations.

Exercise **8.6**

Study the bar graph below and then answer the questions that follow by writing your responses on the blanks provided.

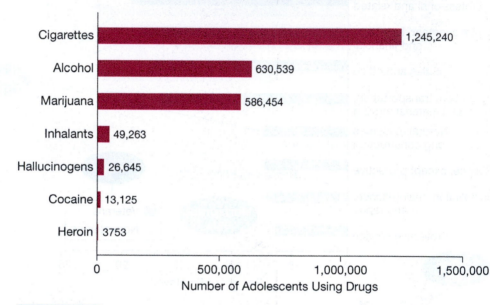

Daily Prevalence of Adolescent Substance Use

Cigarettes	1,245,240
Alcohol	630,539
Marijuana	586,454
Inhalants	49,263
Hallucinogens	26,645
Cocaine	13,125
Heroin	3753

Number of Adolescents Using Drugs

Figure 8.12 **Daily Prevalence of Adolescent Substance Use**

Source: Adapted from OAS report, *A Day in the Life of American Adolescents: Substance Use Facts* (Rockville, MD: Office of Applied Studies, Substance Abuse and Mental Health Services Administration, 2007).

From Rober M. Regoli, John D. Hewitt, and Matt DeLisi, *Delinquency in Society: The Essentials* (Sudbury: Jones and Bartlett Publishers, 2011), 319.

1. Which substance is most abused? _____

2. Which substance is least abused by adolescents? _____

3. How many adolescents abuse inhalants and hallucinogens? _____

4. Why do you think so few adolescents abuse heroin? _____

_____

Diagrams

A **diagram** *is a visual aid that includes a pictorial illustration, usually in the form of a drawing created by hand or by computer.* The purpose of diagrams is to clarify and condense written information through images, so they are very common in instruction manuals and textbooks. They often illustrate processes or sequences of information.

8

A diagram typically contains these parts:

■ **Title.** The title identifies the subject of the drawing.

■ **A picture or series of pictures.** Diagrams communicate information through images. These images are usually line drawings, but may be photographs as well.

■ **Labels.** Parts or areas of the images will often be labeled to identify what they are.

■ **Key.** A diagram that contains special symbols, colors, or shading will usually include a key to explain what these features represent.

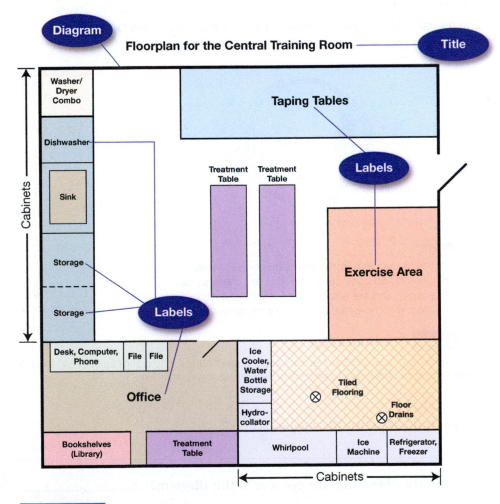

Figure 8.13 **Floorplan for the central training room**

Source: From France. *Introduction to Sports Medicine and Athletic Training (Book Only)*, 2E. © 2011 Delmar Learning, a part of Cengage Learning, Inc. Reproduced by permission. www.cengage.com/permissions.

Reading a diagram begins with understanding the subject and main point identified in the title. Then, you can examine the labeled parts of the diagram to understand how they illustrate that point. Also, make sure you review the key, if applicable, to help you draw accurate conclusions.

The example diagram illustrates the floor plan for a central training room for a sports facility. It includes a line drawing (a picture) of the various parts of the facility, along with labels to identify each part. Because this diagram contains no special symbols, colors, or shading there is no need for a key.

Exercise 8.7

Study the diagram below and then write your answers to the questions that follow by writing your responses on the blanks provided.

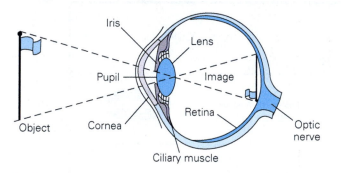

The Human Eye

The lens of the human eye forms an image on the retina, which contains rod and cone cells. The rods are more sensitive than the cones and are responsible for light and dark "twilight" vision; the cones are responsible for color vision.

Figure 8.14 **The Human Eye**

Source: From Shipman. *Introduction to Physical Sciences*, Revised Edition, 12E. © 2009 Brooks/Cole, a part of Cengage Learning, Inc. Reproduced by permission. www.cengage.com/permissions.

1. What is the topic of this diagram? _____

_____

2. What is the object that the eye sees in this diagram? _____

_____

3. According to the text accompanying the diagram, which are more sensitive, rods or cones? _____

_____

4. Which parts of the eye are responsible for color vision? _____

_____

5. What part of the eye, according to the graph, is at the back of the eye?

_____

Maps

A **map** *is a visual depiction of an area and its physical characteristics*. Maps illustrate spatial relationships; they show sizes and borders and distances from one place to another. They can also be used to make comparisons. For instance, a U.S. map may color in the states that apply the death penalty in red and color those that don't blue.

Here are the parts of a map:

- **Title.** The title identifies either the area itself or the relationships among different areas.

- **A diagram of the area.** A map includes a proportionate drawing that represents the geographical features and spatial relationships.

- **Key.** Many maps incorporate symbols, so the key explains what these symbols mean.

- **Labels.** Maps will usually label parts or features that help the reader understand the overall point stated in the title.

- **Source line.** The source line identifies who collected or compiled the information shown in the map.

8

The map below labels all of these parts:

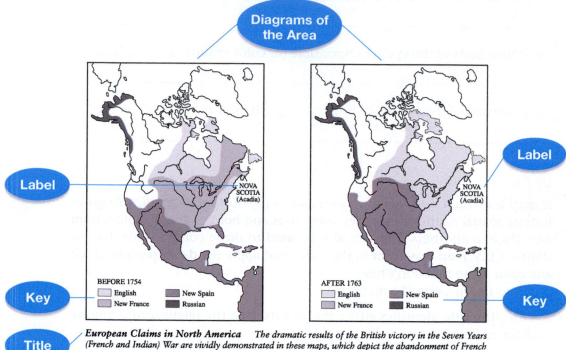

Figure 8.15 European claims in North America

Source: From Norton. *A People and a Nation*, 7E. © 2005 Wadsworth, a part of Cengage Learning, Inc. Reproduced by permission. www.cengage.com/permissions.

To interpret a map, read the title first to understand the idea or information on which you should focus. Then, familiarize yourself with symbols in the key (including the scale that indicates distance, if applicable) and read the labels that name different areas. If the map is illustrating a comparison, try to state in your own words a conclusion based on that comparison.

The visual aid on this page is composed of two maps that illustrate several different sets of relationships. In the first map, as the key indicates, the English claims in North America before 1754 were roughly equal to those of the French and Spanish. Notice how the continent is shaded with different shadings that correspond to the four different nations. These shadings show the relationship of the areas to each other. The second map, which represents these same countries' claims after 1763, reveals a much different distribution. France (represented by a light shading) has been virtually eliminated, and the English and Spanish have overtaken France's former areas. Taken together, the two different maps show the significant changes that occurred in less than ten years in North America.

Exercise **8.8**

Study the map below and then write your answers to the questions that follow by writing your responses on the blanks provided.

Percent of People Aged 15 Years and Older Who Engaged in Sports or Exercise Activities on an Average Day, by Region, 2003–06

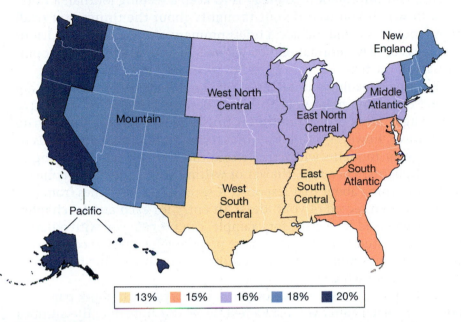

Figure 8.16 **Percent of people aged 15 years and older who engaged in sports or exercise activities on an average day, by region, 2003–06**

Source: American Time Use Survey | Chart Data http://www.bls.gov/spotlight/2008/sports/.

1. In what region of the country do people engage in sports or exercise most frequently? _____

2. What percent of people in Atlanta might engage in sports or exercise?

   _____

3. What two regions of the country have 18% of people participating in sports or exercise? _____

4. What two regions of the country exercise the least?

   _____

8

Reading Strategy: Keeping a Reading Journal

In Chapter 1 of this book, you learned that active readers are those who interact with the text by thinking about what they read. Active researchers also consciously try to connect the text's information to their own experiences and beliefs. One useful strategy for understanding and absorbing new information you read is to keep a reading journal, a notebook in which you record your thoughts about the things you read. These thoughts could include a brief summary of the selection, a list of new ideas or new information you learned, or your reactions to or opinions about the text.

Keeping a reading journal offers two important benefits. First of all, the act of writing helps your thoughts become clearer. You may have some vague ideas or reactions after finishing a text. When you write them down, however, you'll find that trying to find the right words to express your thoughts will actually result in a better understanding of those thoughts. Therefore, the act of writing your response becomes a tool for learning about that response. A second benefit comes from creating a written record of your ideas. An entry for each article, chapter, or essay you read for a class, for example, can provide you with a handy reference for study. Later, when you're preparing for a test or completing an assignment, simply reread your entries to refresh your memory about the content of each text.

To keep a reading journal, obtain a notebook with blank pages inside. Immediately after you read a text, write down its title, the author's name, and the date you read it or finished reading it. Then, let your purpose for reading the text determine the type of response you compose. If you'll be expected to discuss the content of the selection in class or to write about its topic for an assignment, you may want to record several or all of the following:

■ A brief summary of the text

■ Your reaction (your feelings or your own opinions about the subject)

■ Your judgment of the selection's merit or accuracy

■ A comparison of this work with other works you've read

■ Your experiences or observations that either support or refute the text's ideas and conclusions

■ Your questions about the text

If you are reading for your own pleasure or to expand your general knowledge about a particular topic, you might want to focus on just one or two of the items in the list above. No matter what your purpose, though, plan to put forth the little bit of extra effort it takes to better understand what you've read.

Choose one of the reading selections in the next section and then write a reading journal entry that includes at least three of the items in the bulleted list above.

http://www.lifehack.org/articles/productivity/back-to-school-keep-an-academic-reading-journal.html

The web link above is an article that discusses why it is important for college students to keep different kinds of reading journals.

Reading Selections

Practicing the Active Reading Strategy

■ Before and While You Read

You can use active reading strategies before, while, and after you read a selection. The following are some suggestions for active reading strategies that you can employ before you read and as you are reading.

1. Skim the selection for any unfamiliar words. Circle or highlight any words you do not know.

2. As you read, underline, highlight, or circle important words or phrases.

3. Write down any questions about the selection if you are confused by the information presented.

4. Jot notes in the margin to help you understand the material.

8

BIOGRAPHY
Ichiro Suzuki: International Baseball Star

Quiet, popular, hardworking, Ichiro Suzuki was the first Japanese baseball player to play for the major leagues in the United States, opening the way for other talented Asian baseball players.

1   Ichiro Suzuki has millions of dedicated fans in his native Japan, with his image appearing in daily newspapers and smiling from billboards, coffee mugs, and T-shirts. There is even a museum dedicated to him. Known to his adoring public simply as "Ichiro," Ichiro Suzuki is more than just a baseball player; he is a national institution. Considered by many to be the greatest hitter in Japanese baseball history, Ichiro dominated the game in his homeland for nearly nine years until he was snapped up in 2001 to play professional baseball for the American League's Seattle Mariners. As a result, he became the first Japanese position player (meaning a nonpitcher) to be signed by a U.S. team. Since then the fleet-footed, left-handed outfielder has broken dozens of records and has garnered an enormous American following. In 2004, Ichiro had his hottest streak ever, finishing the year by breaking a record that had stood untouched for eighty-four years: scoring the most hits in a single season. He is called a "hitting machine" by sportswriters. This is no exaggeration, because according to Leigh Montville of *Sports Illustrated*, "Any pitch, any time, any place, any situation—you throw it, Ichiro will hit it."

2   Ichiro Suzuki was born on October 22, 1973, in Kasugai, Japan. Ichiro's father, Nobuyuki, was determined that Ichiro, who he thought had a natural talent for baseball, would play the sport, and play it well. The elder Suzuki made it clear from the beginning that his son was special. In fact, the name Ichiro means "first boy," even though he was actually the second boy born to the family. From the time he was three years old, Ichiro was practicing in his backyard with a tiny bat and ball, and by elementary school, Nobuyuki, who was a former high school ballplayer himself, was putting his son through batting drills for up to four hours per day.

3   In high school Ichiro already displayed a dedication to the game that he would become known for as an adult. It was a tradition at Nagoya Electric High School that freshman players were responsible for washing the uniforms of the seniors, so to make sure he had plenty of time for practice Ichiro would get up at 3:00 AM to do laundry. The young batter also maintained a rigorous class schedule and excelled academically. By his senior year Ichiro was a familiar face at Japan's National High School Baseball Tournament, known as

8

Koshien. Upon graduation from high school in 1991, he was drafted to play professional ball for the Pacific League's BlueWave, a team owned by the Japanese leasing company Orix.

4   Ichiro's prowess in the batting box quickly helped make him the most well-known and celebrated person in Japan, but it was his style that catapulted him to mythic proportions. With a lean, teenager-like physique, spiky hair, and a penchant for wearing sunglasses and his baseball cap backwards, the five-foot-nine Ichiro was not the typical, conservative Japanese player. He especially appealed to younger fans, who viewed him as something of a rock star. Ichiro soon became a one-man industry, with his own line of sports apparel, including colorful Nike Air Max sneakers that were snatched up by the millions.

5   Another suggested reason for Ichiro's popularity was his notoriety for being tight-lipped in interviews. "He is a man of few words, so he doesn't talk so much," noted Michael Knisley of *Sporting News.* "And the more mysterious he acts, the more mystique he has." According to Jeff Pearlman of *Sports Illustrated,* the reason for Ichiro's reserve was more practical: If he thinks he has not contributed to a game he feels there is simply nothing to say. The fashionably dressed hitter may have been aloof with the press, but he obviously enjoyed playing to, and sometimes with, the crowd. In fact, during game lulls Ichiro was known to play catch with fans sitting in the right-field stands.

6   Although he was a star in Japan, Ichiro had been setting his sights on American baseball since the spring of 1999, when he spent two weeks in spring training with the Seattle Mariners. In 2000 he announced to Orix that once his full nine years playing pro ball in Japan was up, which it would be in 2001, he was going to consider offers from other teams, including those from the United States. Aware that Ichiro's departure was unavoidable, and faced with business losses, Orix decided to "post" Ichiro, meaning they put Ichiro on the auction block. The Mariners beat out other hopeful franchises, and on November 9, 2000, offered Orix more than $13 million for a thirty-day window to negotiate with Ichiro. On November 18, the powerhouse hitter signed a three-year deal with Seattle worth a reported $15 to $20 million. He became the first Japanese position player to sign with a U.S. baseball team.*

8

* From Gale. *Encyclopedia of World Biography,* 2E. © 2004 Gale, a part of Cengage Learning, Inc. Reproduced by permission. www.cengage.com/permissions.

Table 8.3 Ichiro Suzuki: Career Hitting Stats

CAREER STATS | SPLITS | GAME BY GAME LOG | HITTING CHART | POSTSEASON & ALL-STAR

Hitting Stats:

Next Stats >>

SEASON	TEAM	G	AB	R	H	2B	3B	HR	RBI	TB	BB	SO	SB	CS	OBP	SLG	AVG
2001	Seattle Mariners	157	692	127	242	34	8	8	69	316	30	53	56	14	.381	.457	.350
2002	Seattle Mariners	157	647	111	208	27	8	8	51	275	68	62	31	15	.388	.425	.321
2003	Seattle Mariners	159	679	111	212	29	8	13	62	296	36	69	34	8	.352	.436	.312
2004	Seattle Mariners	161	704	101	262	24	5	8	60	320	49	63	36	11	.414	.455	.372
2005	Seattle Mariners	162	679	111	206	21	12	15	68	296	48	66	33	8	.350	.436	.303
2006	Seattle Mariners	161	695	110	224	20	9	9	49	289	49	71	45	2	.370	.416	.322
2007	Seattle Mariners	161	678	111	238	22	7	6	68	292	49	77	37	8	.396	.431	.351
2008	Seattle Mariners	162	686	103	213	20	7	6	42	265	51	65	43	4	.361	.386	.310
2009	Seattle Mariners	146	639	88	225	31	4	11	46	297	32	71	26	9	.386	.465	.352
2010	Seattle Mariners	133	552	59	171	24	3	5	34	216	41	73	35	7	.360	.391	.310
Career Totals		1559	6651	1032	2201	252	71	89	549	2862	453	670	376	86	.376	.430	.331

Source: http://mlb.mlb.com/team/player.jsp?player_id=400085

■ Vocabulary

Read the following questions about some of the vocabulary words that appear in the previous selection. Before you look up the word, try to use the context of the passage to figure out the meaning. Then circle the letter of the correct answer for each question.

1. Paragraph 1 includes the word *native*. What does the word mean?

   a. foreign

   b. living

   c. belonging to a particular place by birth

   d. origin of bananas

2. "The young batter also maintained a *rigorous* class schedule." What does the word *rigorous* mean? (paragraph 3)

   a. weak

   b. harsh, severe

   c. undeveloped

   d. worthless

3. The author uses the word *physique* in paragraph 4. What does the word mean?

   a. superb condition

   b. heavy lifting

   c. extreme exercise

   d. form or structure of a person's body

4. Paragraph 5 includes the word *aloof*. What does the word mean?

   a. energetic

   b. to behave in an alarming manner

   c. removed or distant either physically or emotionally

   d. unable to walk

5. "During game *lulls* Ichiro was known to play catch with fans sitting in the right-field stands." What does the word *lulls* mean? (paragraph 5)

   a. sing along

   b. pause

   c. constant play

   d. tomfoolery

8

■ Reading Skills

Respond to each of the following questions by circling the letter of the correct answer or by writing your answer on the blank provided.

1. Based on the information in paragraph 2, which of the following statements best expresses an inference you could make?

   a. It did not matter to Ichiro's father if Ichiro played baseball.

   b. All Japanese fathers want their sons to play baseball.

   c. Ichiro had to play baseball because that is what his father wanted.

   d. Ichiro's brother was the one who was a gifted baseball player.

2. Which paragraph begins with a contrast transition word?

   a. paragraph 1

   b. paragraph 6

   c. paragraph 2

   d. paragraph 4

3. According to the statistics table, in what year did Ichiro Suzuki have the highest batting average (AVG)?

   a. 2001

   b. 2004

   c. 2005

   d. 2008

4. Based on the information in paragraph 5, which of the following statements best expresses an inference you could make about Ichiro Suzuki?

   a. Ichiro feels that he is above everyone else.

   b. Ichiro cannot be bothered.

   c. Ichiro is a quiet guy who likes his fans, but keeps to himself.

   d. Ichiro doesn't like the press.

5. According to the statistics table, in what year did Ichiro Suzuki have the most runs batted in (RBI)?

   a. 2001

   b. 2002

   c. 2003

   d. 2004

Practicing the Active Reading Strategy

■ After You Read

Now that you have read the selection, answer the following questions, using the active reading strategies that you learned in Chapter 1.

1. Identify and write down the point and purpose of this reading selection.

2. Did you circle or highlight any words that are unfamiliar to you? Can you figure out the meaning from the context of the passage? If not, then look up each word in a dictionary and find the definition that best describes the word as it is used in the selection. You may want to write the definition in the margin next to the word in the passage for future reference.

3. Predict any possible questions that may be used on a test about the content of this selection.

■ Questions for Discussion and Writing

Respond to each of the following questions based on your reading of the selection.

1. Do you believe that Ichiro would have become a famous Major League Baseball player if his father did not encourage him when he was young? Explain your answer.

_____

_____

_____

2. Do you think that Ichiro deserves the money that he receives from the Seattle Mariners? Use the statistics table to help you with your answer.

_____

_____

_____

3. Based on Ichiro's statistics, do you think he will play well in the future? Give examples to support your answer.

_____

_____

_____

8

Practicing the Active Reading Strategy

■ Before and While You Read

You can use active reading strategies before, while, and after you read a selection. The following are some suggestions for active reading strategies that you can employ before you read and as you are reading.

1. Skim the selection for any unfamiliar words. Circle or highlight any words you do not know.

2. As you read, underline, highlight, or circle important words or phrases.

3. Write down any questions about the selection if you are confused by the information presented.

4. Jot notes in the margin to help you understand the material.

TEXTBOOK READING: COMPUTER SCIENCE
Passwords

How many passwords do you have? Are they safe? Do you know how to create a password that will keep your information protected? Internet security is of great concern today. The following reading selection will help you understand how to create a more secure password.

1   Easily guessed passwords are a serious problem for system security. Common and simple passwords that can be guessed include a carriage return (that is, pressing Enter), a person's name, an account name, a birth date, a family member's birth date or name, or even the word "password" possibly repeated and spelled frontward or backward. Do you use anything like that? Then you are vulnerable.

2   Better passwords are longer and more obscure. Short passwords allow crackers[1] to simply run through all possible combinations of letters and numbers. Take an extreme example. Using only capital letters, how many possibilities are there in a single-character password? Twenty-six. Expand that to an eight-character password, however, and there are more than 200 million possible combinations (see Table 8.4).

---

1. **crackers:** people who can easily break a code

Table 8.4 **Password protection using combinations of the letters A through Z**

Number of Characters (A through Z)	Possible Combinations	Human Avg. Time to Discovery (max time/2) — Tries per Second: 1	Computer Avg. Time to Discovery (max time/2) — Tries per Second: 1 million
1	26	13 seconds	.000013 seconds
2	26 × 26 = 676	6 minutes	.000338 seconds
8	26 raised to 8 = 208,827,064,576	6640 years	58 hours
10	26 raised to 10 = 1.4 × 10 raised to 14	4.5 million years	4.5 years

3   A good password should be long (at least eight characters), have no real words in it, and include as many different characters as possible. Maybe a password such as "io\ pw83 mcx?$" would be a good choice. Unfortunately, passwords this complicated are often written down and taped up in plain view, which negates the purpose of having a password. One mnemonic[1] for remembering a password is to come up with an easily remembered phrase and use its acronym as a password. Say you take the last sentence of the opening for the original Star Trek: "To boldly go where no man has gone before." You get "TBGW0MHGB" (replacing the "no" with a zero just to confuse things a bit). Not a bad password. Of course, if you have Star Trek posters on your walls, wear Spock ears, and wander around spouting off about "the prime directive" all the time, a proficient social engineer might still figure it out.

1.   **mnemonic:** a device to aid memory

8

4   Although people can make significant changes to protect themselves and their companies, corporate cultures can include many subtle and dangerous security weaknesses. Proficient crackers become aware of corporate cultures and find these weaknesses.

5   Many major institutions also confuse what's essentially public identification information (but often perceived as private because it's less readily accessible), such as a Social Security number or birth date, with a password. What identification questions were you asked the last time you called your credit card company? Name, birth date, last four digits of your Social Security number, possibly? This practice confuses identification (who the person is) with authentication (proof that the person is who he or she claims to be). Because of the problems with passwords, many secure locations are moving to a combination of three authentication techniques:

- Something you know—such as a password

- Something you have—such as an ID badge

- Something you are (often called *biometrics*)—such as a fingerprint, retinal scan, or DNA sample*

■ Vocabulary

Read the following questions about some of the vocabulary words that appear in the previous selection. Before you look up the word, try to use the context of the passage to figure out the meaning. Then circle the letter of the correct answer for each question.

1. If something becomes *obscure,* what has happened to it? (paragraph 2)

   a. obvious   c. light

   b. not easily understood   d. open

2. *Negates* in paragraph 3 means _____.

   a. proves   c. makes invalid

   b. warns   d. allows

3. An *acronym* is a _____. (paragraph 3)

   a. a word formed from the first letters of a name or sentence

   b. a word formed from nonsense words

   c. a word formed from numbers

   d. a word formed from a person's name

* From Anderson/Ferro. *Connecting with Computer Science,* 2E. © 2011 South-Western, a part of Cengage Learning, Inc. Reproduced by permission. www.cengage.com/permissions.

4. If someone is *proficient,* what are they? (paragraph 4)

    a. poor   c. clumsy

    b. skillful   d. tall

5. To be *perceived* means _____. (paragraph 5)

    a. unrecognized   c. questioned

    b. forgotten   d. thought of

■ Reading Skills

Respond to each of the following questions by circling the letter of the correct answer or by writing your answer on the blank provided.

1. Write the topic sentence for paragraph 1.

   _____

2. In paragraph 3, which sentence is the topic sentence?

    a. sentence 1   c. sentence 5

    b. sentence 3   d. sentence 8

3. Paragraph 4 starts with what kind of transition?

    a. list   c. time order

    b. definition   d. contrast

4. According to the information found on Table 8.4, how long would it take a human to crack a password with eight characters in two tries?

   _____

5. According to the information found on Table 8.4, how long would it take a computer to crack a password with ten characters in two tries?

   _____

Practicing the Active Reading Strategy

■ After You Read

Now that you have read the selection, answer the following questions, using the active reading strategies that you learned in Chapter 1.

1. Identify and write down the point and purpose of this reading selection.

2. Did you circle or highlight any words that are unfamiliar to you? Can you figure out the meaning from the context of the passage? If not,

8

then look up each word in a dictionary and find the definition that best describes the word as it is used in the selection. You may want to write the definition in the margin next to the word in the passage for future reference.

3. Predict any possible questions that may be used on a test about the content of this selection.

■ Questions for Discussion and Writing

Respond to each of the following questions based on your reading of the selection.

1. What are two examples of simple passwords that people might use?

_____

_____

_____

2. What are three things a good password should include?

_____

_____

3. How good are your passwords? What can you do to improve them?

_____

_____

_____

Practicing the Active Reading Strategy

■ Before and While You Read

You can use active reading strategies before, while, and after you read a selection. The following are some suggestions for active reading strategies that you can employ before you read and as you are reading.

1. Skim the selection for any unfamiliar words. Circle or highlight any words you do not know.

2. As you read, underline, highlight, or circle important words or phrases.

3. Write down any questions about the selection if you are confused by the information presented.

4. Jot notes in the margin to help you understand the material.

TEXTBOOK READING: WEATHER AND CLIMATE
Tornadoes!!

Have you ever witnessed a tornado or seen its destruction in person? These weather events can be terrifying. Do you know where and when you are most likely to experience a tornado?

1   The frequency of tornadic activity shows a seasonal shift. For example, during the winter, tornadoes are most likely to form over the southern Gulf states when the polar-front jet is above this region, and the contrast between warm and cold air masses is greatest. In spring, humid Gulf air surges northward; contrasting air masses and the jet stream also move northward and tornadoes become more prevalent from the southern Atlantic states westward into the southern Great Plains. In summer, the contrast between air masses lessens, and the jet stream is normally near the Canadian border; hence, tornado activity tends to be concentrated from the northern plains eastward to New York State.

2   In the following bar chart we can see that about 70 percent of all tornadoes in the United States develop from March to July. The month of May normally has the greatest number of tornadoes (the average is about six per day), whereas the most violent tornadoes seem to occur in April when vertical wind shear tends to be present as well as when horizontal and vertical temperature and moisture contrasts are greatest. Although tornadoes have occurred at all times of the day and night, they are most frequent in the late afternoon (between 4:00 P.M. and 6:00 P.M.), when the surface air is most unstable; they are least frequent in the early morning before sunrise, when the atmosphere is most stable.

3   Although large, destructive tornadoes are most common in the Central Plains, they can develop anywhere if conditions are right. For example, a series of at least 36 tornadoes, more typical of those that form over the plains, marched through North and South Carolina on March 28, 1984, claiming fifty-nine lives and causing hundreds of millions of dollars in damage. One tornado was enormous, with a diameter of at least 2.5 miles (4 km) and winds that exceeded 230 miles/ hour. No place is totally immune to a tornado's destructive force. On March 1, 1983, a rare tornado cut a 3-mile swath of destruction through downtown Los Angeles, California, damaging more than 100 homes and businesses, and injuring thirty-three people.

4   Tornadoes are also rare in Utah, with only about two per year being reported. However, during August, 1999, a tornado rampaged through downtown Salt Lake City. While only on the ground for about 5 miles, the tornado damaged more than 120 homes, injured a dozen people, produced a fatality, and caused over $50 million in damage.*

---

* Donald C. Ahrens and Perry Samson, *Extreme Weather and Climate,* 1st ed. (Belmont: Brooks/Cole, 2011), 337–38. Print.

8

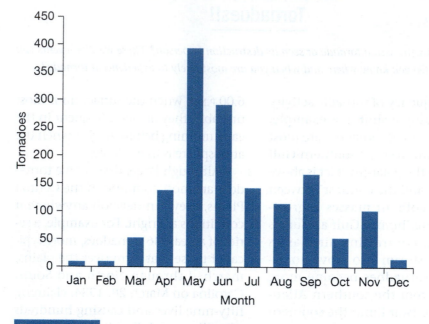

Figure 8.17   **Average tornado frequency by month of year 2003—2005**

Source: http://lwf.ncdc.noaa.gov/oa/climate/severeweather/tornadoes.html.

Special note: Spring of 2011 saw a record breaking number of tornado outbreaks that have changed the deadliest month to April. The single month record prior to 2011 was May of 2003 with 542 tornadoes. As of June 6, 2011, the preliminary record count for April of 2011 was 875 tornadoes. On May 22, 2011, the eighth worst tornado in U.S. history hit Joplin, Missouri. The last tornado to make the top 16 list was in Flint, Michigan in 1953.

■ Vocabulary

Read the following questions about some of the vocabulary words that appear in the previous selection. Before you look up the word, try to use the context of the passage to figure out the meaning. Then circle the letter of the correct answer for each question.

1. In paragraph 1 the author writes about the "polar-front *jet.*" What kind of a *jet* is he referring to?

   a. a fast airplane   c. a deep black color

   b. a squirting stream of water   d. a high-altitude, fast-moving airstream

2. If something becomes more *prevalent*, what is happening to it? (paragraph 1)

   a. happening more frequently   c. happening more strongly

   b. happening less frequently   d. happening more weakly

3. What does the author mean by "vertical wind *shear*" in paragraph 2?

   a. to cut hair   c. a sudden change of wind direction

   b. to be very steep   d. to be very thin

4. *Immune* as it is used in paragraph 3 means _____.

   a. protected   c. open

   b. in the path   d. too large

5. What is a *swath,* as used in paragraph 3?

   a. a short distance   c. a pool of water

   b. a long, broad strip   d. corn rows

■ Reading Skills

Respond to each of the following questions by circling the letter of the correct answer or by writing your answer on the blank provided.

1. What is the pattern of organization in paragraph 1?

   a. list   c. definition

   b. time order   d. contrast

2. Write the two contrast transitions from paragraph 2 here.

   _____

3. Which sentence in paragraph 3 contains the main idea for that paragraph?

   a. sentence 1   b. sentence 3

   c. sentence 4   d. sentence 5

8

4. According to the accompanying bar chart, what three months had the least tornado activity between 2003 and 2005?

_____

5. According to the accompanying bar chart, approximately how many tornadoes occurred on average in the month of September between 2003 and 2005?

a. 150   b. 200

c. 160   d. 100

Practicing the Active Reading Strategy

■ After You Read

Now that you have read the selection, answer the following questions, using the active reading strategies that you learned in Chapter 1.

1. Identify and write down the point and purpose of this reading selection.

2. Did you circle or highlight any words that are unfamiliar to you? Can you figure out the meaning from the context of the passage? If not, then look up each word in a dictionary and find the definition that best describes the word as it is used in the selection. You may want to write the definition in the margin next to the word in the passage for future reference.

3. Predict any possible questions that may be used on a test about the content of this selection.

■ Questions for Discussion and Writing

Respond to each of the following questions based on your reading of the selection.

1. Where do most tornadoes occur in the spring? In the summer?

_____

_____

2. Why are tornadoes more likely to occur in the late afternoon?

_____

3. Do you know what actions to take if a tornado is coming? What are those actions?

_____

_____

8

Vocabulary Strategy: The Contrast Context Clue

In Chapters 4, 5, and 6, you learned about the three different types of context clues: definition/restatement, explanation, and example. One last type of context clue is **contrast.** *In this type of clue, nearby words, phrases, or sentences may give the opposite meaning of the unfamiliar word,* allowing you to conclude what it means by noticing this contrast. For example, read this next passage, which comes from one of the paragraphs in Chapter 4.

> When Sir Edmund Hillary and Tenzing Norgay planted the first flag atop Mount Everest on May 29, 1953, they surveyed an utterly ***pristine*** place. Nearly fifty years later, dozens of teams line up to take their crack at the sacred Nepalese monolith. Scores of guides jockey to get high-paying clients to the top. Trash on the roof of the world has become so bad that climbers mount expeditions specifically to clean up after past expeditions.

If you're wondering what *pristine* means, you can look at the next three sentences, which include a contrast clue. The word is contrasted with "dozens of teams," "scores of guides," and "trash." Therefore, it must mean the opposite: "pure and unspoiled by civilization."

Vocabulary Exercise

The following examples all come from paragraphs in Chapters 2, 3, and 4. In each one, use the explanation context clue to help you determine the meaning of the boldfaced, italicized word and then write a definition for this word on the blank provided.

1. People used to stop their lives to pay close attention when astronauts went into space, but now, the Space Shuttle goes up and comes back with little *fanfare.* _____

2. Different people have different types of living styles. You can look right on our block for perfect illustrations of this. For example, the Hammonds' house down the block is a *ramshackle* affair. . . . By contrast, just next door, the Rubellas' house is a model of upkeep. _____

8

3. Authoritarian parents tend to be strict, ***punitive,*** and unsympathetic. They value obedience from children and try to shape their children's behavior to meet a set standard and to curb the children's wills. They do not encourage independence. They are detached and seldom praise their youngsters. In contrast, permissive parents give their children complete freedom and *lax* discipline._____

4. Authoritarian parents tend to be strict, punitive, and unsympathetic. They value obedience from children and try to shape their children's behavior to meet a set standard and to curb the children's wills. They do not encourage independence. They are detached and seldom praise their youngsters. In contrast, permissive parents give their children complete freedom and *lax* discipline._____

5. As I looked back and evaluated my own college training, I saw that the training and experience I had had in public speaking had been of more practical value to me in business—and in life—than everything else I had studied in college all put together. Why? Because it had wiped out my ***timidity*** and lack of self-confidence and given me the courage and assurance to deal with people._____

8

Chapter 8 Review

Write the correct answer in each of the blanks in the following statements.

1. _____ are types of illustrations that represent data or information in a visual form.

2. Visual aids _____ information in a small space; clarify and rein reinforce _____ allow readers to see important _____ easily, and provide a way for readers to find a particular _____ quickly.

3. To interpret the information in a visual aid, first read the <u>title</u>, caption, and _____. Next, try to state in your own words the relationships you see. Finally, check your understanding of those relationships by reviewing the corresponding explanation in the _____

4. A _____ is a visual aid that organizes information or data in rows and columns. It summarizes related details so readers can find them quickly and easily.

5. An _____ is a hierarchy of boxes and lines that are connected to show lines of authority and responsibility in an organization.

6. A _____ represents the sequence of steps in a process.

7. A _____ is a circle divided into wedges that indicate the amounts of each part that make up a whole.

8. A _____ plots points on a grid and then connects them to show changes or trends in numerical data over time.

9. A _____ identifies quantities of something.

10. A _____ is a pictorial illustration, usually in the form of a drawing created by hand or by computer.

11. A _____ is a visual depiction of an area and its physical characteristics. It illustrates spatial relationships and/or makes comparisons.

12. The first benefit of keeping a reading journal is _____

_____

13. The second benefit of keeping a reading journal is

_____.

14. A _____ context clue will give the *opposite* information about an unfamiliar word.

INDEX